LIVING IN
INDIGENOUS
SOVEREIGNTY

LIVING IN INDIGENOUS SOVEREIGNTY

Elizabeth Carlson-Manathara

with Gladys Rowe

FERNWOOD PUBLISHING
HALIFAX & WINNIPEG

Editing: Lisa Frenette
Cover design: Tania Craan
Printed and bound in Canada

Published by Fernwood Publishing
32 Oceanvista Lane, Black Point, Nova Scotia, B0J 1B0
and 748 Broadway Avenue, Winnipeg, Manitoba, R3G 0X3
www.fernwoodpublishing.ca

Fernwood Publishing Company Limited gratefully acknowledges the financial support of the Government of Canada, the Canada Council for the Arts, the Manitoba Department of Culture, Heritage and Tourism under the Manitoba Publishers Marketing Assistance Program and the Province of Manitoba, through the Book Publishing Tax Credit, for our publishing program. We are pleased to work in partnership with the Province of Nova Scotia to develop and promote our creative industries for the benefit of all Nova Scotians.

Library and Archives Canada Cataloguing in Publication

Title: Living in Indigenous sovereignty / written by
Elizabeth Carlson-Manathara and Gladys Rowe.
Names: Carlson-Manathara, Elizabeth, author. | Rowe, Gladys, author.
Description: Includes bibliographical references and index.
Identifiers: Canadiana (print) 20210152273 | Canadiana
(ebook) 20210152338 | ISBN 9781773632384
(softcover) | ISBN 9781773632636 (EPUB) | ISBN
9781773632643 (Kindle) | ISBN 9781773634517 (PDF)
Subjects: LCSH: Indigenous peoples—Canada. | LCSH:
Canada—Race relations. | LCSH: Canada—Ethnic
relations. | LCSH: Decolonization.
Classification: LCC E78.C2 C37 2021 | DDC 305.897/071—dc23

CONTENTS

*For those who have gone before, including
Byron Matwewinin, Troy Fontaine, and
Dr. Nicholas Cooper-Lewter,
who contributed to my journey in immeasurable ways, and who I miss dearly.*

*For the future generations — including our
twenty-three nieces and nephews:
Dwayne, Sammy, Travis, Michelle, Rosemary, Kiniw,
Jesse, Dylana, Thomas, Maria, Roseanne, Willis,
Wabun, Leif, Bryn, Annemary, Jaedyn, Soren,
Joseph, Susanne, Lars, Kaleb, and Emmanuel.*

FOREWORD

Aimée Craft, Leona Star, and Dawnis Kennedy

As we write this, the world feels like it is burning around us. From the destruction of property and physical violence by non-Indigenous fishermen toward Mi'kmaw lobster fishermen in Mi'kma'ki (literally burning buildings to the ground), to the racist and violent death suffered by Atikamekw mother Joyce Echaquan in a Joliette, Québec, hospital, to the continued forcible removal of Indigenous people who occupy their territories and protect their lands and waters against industrial commodification and environmental degradation in the form of pipelines (Unist'ot'en), land development (Six Nations of the Grand River), fracking (Camp Morning Star at Hollow Water First Nation), hydroelectric dams (Tataskweyak Cree Nation and the Jenpeg Dam), forestry (Grassy Narrows Blockade) ... and the list goes on ...

The individual and systemic racism faced by Indigenous people in Canada is alarming. And it does not appear to be getting better, even in an era of reconciliation and the "real systemic change" called for by the Truth and Reconciliation Commission of Canada (TRC). We repeatedly hear the call for radical change in Indigenous relations in Canada echoed; from almost a decade ago by the Idle No More movement to more recently, when Indigenous people in Canada were marching in the streets for Tina Fontaine, Colten Boushie, and Cindy Gladue. Hearts continue to break with recent events. Dreams of nation-to-nation politics in Canada continue to fade.

At the heart of this is the denial of basic human rights, the violations of sacred treaty relationships and the disregard for constitutionally protected rights, all marked by institutionally accepted violence. This is an assault on the stated values of Canada as an international human rights defender. Outrage has been met with inaction, which in turn, sparks further indignation. Who amongst Canadians is prepared to sacrifice to protect human rights to the point of being arrested, criminalized, or ostracized for their stances against the violence done to the land and the people?

This book takes up one of the most challenging questions that Canadian society faces today: how to navigate the ongoing relationship between Indigenous people and settler Canada, and particularly the role of non-Indigenous settlers in redefining that relationship. There is no singular answer to this question and while the challenge remains daunting, this book beautifully weaves theory and scholarship with first-person narrative to provide an embodied response towards Indigenous sovereignty.

Too often the burden of decolonization is taken up by Indigenous people, or in effect placed on Indigenous people's shoulders. Turning the gaze not away from, but rather in support of Indigenous Peoples, this book engages with what it is to be a settler-ally in all forms and based on the lived experience of a variety of non-Indigenous people. This book provides a range of illustrations of the multiple paths that orient toward Indigenous sovereignty and tackles directly "what Indigenous people have asked of us."

The purpose of this book is to critically engage with how to not only think differently but to also *be* and *do* things differently. Elizabeth (Liz) Carlson-Manathara's work is immensely valuable; her research and depth of scholarship, blended with her ability to ask difficult questions while listening honestly and gently engaging is exactly the type of approach required to get to the heart of the matter. All three of us have met Liz through her participation in ceremonies and other community activities and we have first-hand exposure to her kindness, reciprocity, and attentiveness to being a good relative. These same qualities are reflected in the substance and form of this book, including the shared authorship of chapters, the attention to narrative and authenticity, and the assurance that relationships remained good and that people were listened to throughout the research and publication process.

In this time of an international pandemic many of us are contemplating how we continue to advance reconciliation, to develop and maintain mutually respectful relationships (TRC 2015), and to create the space to reset the relationships. One key element of this redefinition is proposed as a return: a return to awareness that Indigenous Lands have their own stories, relationships, responsibilities, and laws, all of which have been practised by Indigenous people since time immemorial. For Liz and her collaborators, the focus has narrowed to understanding what "land back" could and should look like.

Each of us is called upon regularly to answer these questions: what is it going to take to reach into spaces of reconciliation? How can non-Indigenous or settler-allies do more or do better? We're grateful to this book as a resource for them to be able to begin or further their journeys into their support of Indigenous Peoples and sovereignties.

ACKNOWLEDGEMENTS

Boozhoo Nindinawemaaganidog. Thank you for your help with this, and with everything.

I acknowledge the Anishinaabe, Muskeko-Ininiwak, Dakota, Nakota, and Red River Métis peoples as the sovereign peoples of the Treaty 1 lands where I lived and when the dissertation on which this book is based was written. I acknowledge the Anishinaabe people of the Robinson-Huron Treaty of 1850, where this book was completed. This work has taken me into a deeper understanding of what it means to live in your sovereignty. I acknowledge the hundreds of years of fierce and loving resistance and resurgence of the Indigenous Peoples of these lands. I am grateful to have been connected with amazing and vibrant activist communities in Winnipeg and in Sudbury, and I wish to acknowledge the kindness, care, rage, beauty, and struggle of these communities, as well as the contributions they have made to this work.

I am so grateful for the pipe carriers, water drum carrier, and singers who sent the research and book forward in a good way: Niizhosake (Sherry Copenace), Don Robinson, Daabaasanaquwat (Peter Atkinson), Belinda Vandenbroek, Chickadee Richard, Ed Azure, Christy and Maegan Salwan. Your work has made all the difference.

I acknowledge the fourteen white settler decolonial and anti-colonial activists who had the courage and the trust in me to share their beautiful and inspiring stories. Thank you John, Franklin, Monique, Rick, Adam, Victoria, Joy, Susanne, Paulette, Murray, Dave, Steve, Silvia, and Kathi for letting me into your lives and sometimes your homes. I have initiated some friendships — and deepened others — through this research journey and I count myself lucky to call you my friends. Much love and respect for all you have taught me.

This work would not have been possible, nor would it have taken its shape, without the generous, inspiring, and insightful contributions of

Indigenous scholars, activists, and Knowledge Keepers who informed the values and knowledge base of this study as well as countless decisions in the research process. Chi-miigwech, kinana'skomitina'wa'w, pidamayaye to the following treasured friends and teachers in particular. To Zoongigaabowitmiskoakikwe, who has helped me with many kind and loving prayers and ceremonies for over twenty years, and through many joys and challenges, including the journey of this book. To Lorraine (Whitecrow) Derman, who taught me early and patiently much of what knowledge of Anishinaabe Protocols, and what little of Anishinaabemowin, I have managed to learn. To Nii Gaani Aki Inini, who invited me to join his ceremonial community two decades ago, who has graciously taken the time to help me with many questions, and whose teachings have had an immense impact on my life and on this research. To Byron Matwewinin, of course, whose teachings and healing presence have profoundly impacted my life and undergirded much of this work. To Rosemary Christensen, whose scholarly guidance, support, stories, and belief in my work have meant so much. To Leona Star and Aimée Craft, who have been so kind and generous since we first met at Makoose Ka Win, and who shared defining insights at a number of critical stages of the research. To Chickadee Richard, who has sat with me for many hours in discussion about the research, offering guidance, and who provided spiritual leadership during the research feast. To Don Robinson, for his guidance regarding the research as well as his help with the research feast venue and particulars. To the pipe carriers who sent the research forward in a good way, and to Daabaasanaquwat for blessing us with the water drum ceremony. To Manito Mukwa, Louis Sorin, and Belinda Vandenbroek for your beautiful and supportive friendships and for your guidance during the research journey. To Dawnis Kennedy, whose humble and loving teachings were shared late in my process but contained threads that wove so much of this work together. To Niizhosake, Rose Roulette, and Pebaamibines for many things, including your help with words and conceptions of white people in Anishinaabemowin. Any mistakes or misinterpretations of your words are my own.

I am grateful to have been able to access literatures by such profound and sophisticated Indigenous scholars during my research process. Your clarity and generosity are gifts to us all. Thank you for leading the way: Leanne Simpson, Taiaiake Alfred, Aimée Craft, Michael Hart, Aaron Mills, Sakej Ward, Sylvia McAdam, Jeff Corntassel, Lynn Gehl, Eve Tuck,

Emma LaRocque, Arthur Manuel, Cindy Blackstock, Raven Sinclair, Waziyatawin, Michael Yellow Bird, Glen Coulthard, Niigaan Sinclair, Harold Johnson, Chelsea Vowel, Pam Palmater, Lee Maracle, Glen Coulthard, and so many others. A special thanks to Sakej Ward and Lynn Gehl for allowing me to quote your work extensively.

I am grateful to members and affiliates of the Decolonizing Network, Manitoba for your support, encouragement, and input into this work. You have no doubt influenced its usefulness for other settlers. Thanks to Kate Sjoberg, David Camfield, Lark Gamey, Leah Decter, Linda Goosen, Thor Aitkenhead, Joy Eidse, Chuck Wright, Monique Woroniak, Ashlyn Haglund, and others.

Thanks to the beautiful friends who have supported me in so many ways, including Carolyn Dyane who found many ways to support this work — sewing, serving, and feasting. Thanks to Christy and Maegan Salwan for drumming at the feast and to Jason Buousquet and Tanis Richard for your excellent help during the feast. Thanks to Tom Simms, Silvia Straka, Joy Eidse, and Lark Gamey for our conversations over those years. Thanks to Michael Posluns for your example, and to you and Marilyn Eisenstadt for your time. To Gladys Rowe for the Starbucks sessions and for your friendship, insights, collaboration, and encouragement. My doctoral studies have meant meeting classmates who have become friends.

Thanks to Carolyn Christie for your advocacy, and Lea Soliman for your excellent transcribing.

Although I am grateful to all of the scholars who have been my academic instructors over the years, there are a few whose words connected with me at deep levels, who particularly inspired my growth, and who have expressed their belief in me: Nicholas Cooper-Lewter, Curt Paulsen, and Michael Hart. To my doctoral committee members, who oversaw the research upon which this book was based and nudged me forward in my growth while respecting my process and perspectives. Tuula Heinonen, my advisor, has been kind, nurturing, supportive, encouraging, and respectful. Michael Hart has been a supportive mentor throughout my program, and his thinking has greatly inspired my work. Peter Kulchyski, himself a settler activist, has pushed me to deepen my understanding of critical theory, and has challenged my stances while communicating respect for my scholarship. Yvonne Pompana's suggestion of creating a film related to the study has led to many gifts and a meaningful way to make this work accessible.

The film project initiated as a result has meant the absolute pleasure of spending loads of time with some really great people who have become cherished friends. Thanks to Teddy Zegeye-Gebrehiwot and Gladys Rowe for being who you are and for filming the research interviews. Thanks to Teddy, Gladys, and Sarah Story for co-directing and co-producing *Stories of Decolonization: Land Dispossession and Settlement.* I look forward to our future antics.

Thanks to my parents and siblings for your love and support over the years despite our differences. Thanks to my adopted family though Byron Matwewinin for allowing me to be your white sheep. I am profoundly grateful to be the proud auntie to many. Thanks for keeping me close to what is important. You are the hope for our future.

I am grateful to Joseph Thomas Manathara for all kinds of support. Your love and humour have kept me grounded and you have been my home throughout this journey.

Candida Hadley, Lisa Frenette, and Fernwood have indeed been supportive, patient, encouraging, and flexible folks to work with during the publication process. I am grateful that you have allowed me the space to make choices that align with my values.

This work has truly been a community effort. Although I have tried here to recall all who contributed, my own limitations at this moment may mean I have left people out. If this is true of you, please forgive me and know that your contributions are appreciated.

ACKNOWLEDGEMENT OF FUNDERS

I acknowledge with gratitude the following funders and scholarships that have supported this book and its associated projects.

Doctoral Program Funding

Joseph-Armand Bombardiere Canada Graduate Scholarship-Doctoral, Social Sciences and Humanities Research Council of Canada.

Manitoba Graduate Scholarship, the Government of Manitoba.

Duff Roblin Fellowship/University of Manitoba Graduate Fellowship, University of Manitoba.

Enid Driben-Triller Memorial Scholarship in Social Work, Freda Driben, Faculty of Social Work, University of Manitoba.

Elizabeth Hill Scholarship, Faculty of Social Work, University of Manitoba.

Doctoral Research Funding

Manitoba Research Alliance Dissertation Researcher Stipend, through their Social Sciences and Humanities Research Council of Canada, through the Manitoba Research Alliance grant: Partnering for Change: Community-based solutions for Aboriginal and inner-city poverty.
Graduate Enhancement of Tri-council Stipend Award, University of Manitoba.

Research feast funding

Faculty of Social Work Endowment Fund, University of Manitoba.
Manitoba Research Alliance grant, through their Social Sciences and Humanities Research Council of Canada grant: Partnering for Change: Community-based solutions for Aboriginal and inner-city poverty.

Film Project Contributions and Funding

Social Sciences and Humanities Research Council of Canada Connection Grant.
Manitoba Research Alliance, through their Social Sciences and Humanities Research Council of Canada grant: Partnering for Change: Community-based solutions for Aboriginal and inner-city poverty.
Faculty of Social Work Endowment Fund, University of Manitoba.
Centre for Creative Writing and Oral Culture, University of Manitoba.
Inner City Social Work Program, University of Manitoba.

CONTRIBUTORS

A rather large community has contributed to this book and to the research upon which it is based. Truth be told, all should be listed as co-authors. Please know how grateful I am for your generosity. In this list, however, I include those who were authors and co-authors of chapters.

Aimée Craft is an associate professor at the Faculty of Common Law, University of Ottawa and an Indigenous (Anishinaabe-Métis) lawyer from Manitoba. Craft is an internationally recognized leader in the area of Indigenous laws, Treaties, and water. She prioritizes Indigenous-lead and interdisciplinary research, including visual arts and film, co-leads a series of major research grants on decolonizing water governance and works with many Indigenous nations and communities on Indigenous relationships with and responsibilities to nibi (water). She plays an active role in international collaborations relating to transformative memory in colonial contexts and relating to the reclamation of Indigenous birthing practices as expressions of territorial sovereignty.

Leona Star is a Cree woman from Thunderchild First Nation, Saskatchewan, within the Treaty 6 Territory. She works as the director of research for the First Nations Health and Social Secretariat of Manitoba (FNHSSM) and currently sits as a Manitoba representative and the chair of the First Nations Information Governance Committee (FNIGC). Leona is a strong advocate of First Nations self-determination in research grounded in the First Nations principles of ownership, control, access, and possession (OCAP). She has worked collaboratively locally, regionally, and nationally to ensure research and information is governed according to Protocols defined by First Nations and has contributed to many research projects as a principal applicant, principal knowledge user, co-applicant, decision maker, knowledge user, and collaborator. Most importantly, she is a helper for First Nations people, communities, and organizations when it comes to respectful relationships and self-determination in research and data sovereignty.

Minnawaanigogiizhigok is a second-degree Midewiwin (Way of the Heart) person and was raised as Ogijiidaakwe (Warrior woman/Woman of a Big Heart) by the Ogijiidaa Society and Elders of her home community Bagwaanishkoziibing (Roseau River Anishinaabe First Nation).

Also known as **Dawnis Kennedy**, Minnawaanigogiizhigok is a scholar of Western and Anishinaabe law and a community educator at the Manitoba Indigenous Cultural Education Centre. She is of both European and Ojibwe Anishinaabe lineage and is dedicated to reclaiming and revitalizing both traditions in her life and in her work. At the Centre she is able to work with people across age groups, sectors, and communities. She also works in her community through her participation in ceremony, non-profit organizations, and community groups. However, her primary commitment is learning to live a good life amidst continuing colonization.

Minnawaanigogiizhigok is dedicated to the pursuit of Minobimaadiziwin (Good Life). She seeks and creates opportunities to live life from her heart. She builds on the good choices her family, mentors, and friends made in their lives: their choices to work hard, raise their families, put down alcohol, help their relatives, support the people, and reconnect to Midewiwin — living the ways of life, languages, and traditions that our ancestors sent forward to us. In the footsteps of all her ancestors, Minnawaanigogiizhigok continues to learn and to grow, taking joy in this good life and doing what she can to support others who seek to do the same.

Gladys Rowe, she/her, is a Swampy Cree scholar and a member of Fox Lake Cree Nation in northern Manitoba, Canada. Gladys supports possibilities and transformations through her use of Indigenist research, arts-based and participatory methodologies, and Indigenous innovation and evaluation. Her doctoral research used storytelling and poetry as a mechanism to learn more about Indigenous birth workers and their experiences reclaiming traditional birthing practices. Gladys is passionate about fostering meaningful connection and deep understanding through the sharing of stories.

Grandmother **Sherry Copenace, Niizhosake, Saagimaakwe**, Atik n'dodem (Elk Clan), Midewewin, was born and raised on the community of Ojibways of Onigaming, which is located in northwestern Ontario and on the east side of Lake of the Woods. Sherry is firm in her ways of knowing and being Anishinaabe. Sherry speaks her original language — Ojibway — and has a great love for the land and waters. Since 2011, Sherry has led a renewal of Makoosekawin-Anishinaabe young women coming of age teachings and ceremonies. Sherry helps at Anishinaabe Teaching and Sacred Lodges. Sherry has her MSW degree and is associated with several institutions and organizations who continually engage her for her knowledge and lived experience.

Benais Quimiwin Ikwe — Thunder Rain Woman, or Chickadee Richard, is a member of the Sandy Bay First Nation, raised alongside the west side of Lake Manitoba. She is a mother of three biological children and two adopted sons, a Grandmother of seven children, and an aunt or grandmother to many in the Indigenous communities across Turtle Island. She has worked alongside many great grassroots leaders of the Indigenous communities in making safe places for our peoples. She is a proud Anishinaabekwe who has dedicated her life for the betterment of the life of our land, our water, and our Indigenous communities. She has been a believer and educator for change and for justice for many years, regionally and nationally, by creating awareness and sharing the strength and beauty of our Indigenous culture. She has worked with peoples who are open and willing to change the current ways that still harm our land, waters, and our people's ways of life.

Dr. Yvonne Pompana, associate professor in the Faculty of Social Work, University of Manitoba, is Dakota from Sioux Valley First Nation (Manitoba). She completed her PhD in Indigenous Studies from Trent University. Yvonne has twenty-eight years of experience working within the Inner-City Social Work Program (ICSWP), Faculty of Social Work. She has served in many capacities within the ICSWP and from 2015 to 2019, she served as the program's director. Yvonne's areas of academic specialization include colonization/decolonization, with particular emphasis on the devolution of social services to First Nations and the implications of this policy on First Nations in areas such as child welfare, criminal justice, and education. Yvonne also has an interest in issues related to First Nations women, Indigenous knowledges, research, and research methodologies. Yvonne is a co-founder and long-standing member of the Indigenous Helpers Society Incorporated and is co-founder of the Indigenous Caucus, Faculty of Social Work.

Elizabeth Carlson-Manathara's Swedish, Sámi, German, Scots-Irish, and English ancestors settled on lands of the Anishinaabe and Omaha Nations, which were unethically obtained by the U.S. government. Her scholarship is focused on the anti-colonial and decolonial work of settlers, anti-colonial social work practice and research methodologies, and anti-colonial public education through film. Liz is currently learning to live in Indigenous sovereignty as a Treaty relative of the Robinson-Huron Treaty of 1850 while working as an assistant professor in the School of Social Work at Laurentian University.

Monique Woroniak, a settler woman of Ukrainian and French heritage, was born and raised in Winnipeg on Treaty 1 Territory and the heart of the Métis Nation homeland, where she still lives.

Murray Angus spent thirty-five years as a researcher, policy analyst, media advisor, and educator for Inuit and other Indigenous organizations. He received the Order of Canada in 2015 "for his varied contributions to building awareness and respect for Canada's Native people and their traditions, and for the role he has played in empowering Inuit youth as co-founder of Nunavut Sivuniksavut."

Steve Heinrichs is a settler Christian from Winnipeg, Manitoba — Treaty 1 Territory and the homeland of the Métis Nation. The director of Indigenous-Settler Relations for Mennonite Church Canada, Steve is a student of activism who loves to march with his partner, Ann, and their children, Izzy, Aiden, and Abby. Steve has been blessed to edit a number of books on reconciliation and Indigenous justice, the latest being *Unsettling the Word: Biblical Experiments in Decolonization* (Orbis, 2019).

Franklin Jones is a pseudonym for a wonderful person whose story appears in this book.

Adam Joseph Barker is a white settler Canadian from the overlapping territories of the Haudenosaunee and Anishinaabe peoples, near what is currently called Hamilton, Ontario. He is an academic with specializations in the human geography of settler colonialism, Indigenous resurgence and decolonization, and analyses of social movements and social change. He largely works in collaboration with his partner, Emma Battell Lowman, and currently lives in the United Kingdom.

Susanne McCrea McGovern has been involved in land and water defence her entire adult life. She uses her media training and experience to work on Indigenous led campaigns across Turtle Island. She is the executive director and co-founder of the Boreal Action Project and former executive director and communications director of the Boreal Forest Network. Prior to that, she was director of the Manitoba Greenpeace office for ten years. Over the years, she's worked on many issues, including pulp and paper, toxics, uranium mining, nuclear testing, PVC plastics, mining, fracking, and pipeline campaigns. She co-produced and directed the documentary film series *Voices of the Land*, working with Garry Raven of Hollow Water. She is a writer, painter, and performance artist.

Joy Eidse is a cis-hetero woman of Dutch and English heritage, living in Winnipeg, Manitoba, on Treaty 1 Territory. Joy works as a counsellor in her private practice.

Dr. Kathi Avery Kinew, a creative and energetic person, has worked for five decades with and for First Nations and First Nations organizations. Her professional and academic experience has been dedicated to strengthening First Nations Treaty and inherent rights, protecting and strengthening settlement of land issues (and ending hegemonic use of "claims" terminology), and to better the quality of life of First Nations. She is a researcher specializing in participatory action research and Indigenous methodologies and has been a University of Manitoba sessional instructor in Native Studies since 1998.

Rick Wallace lives on a small fishing island in Atlantic Canada, where he does local community work, gardens, hikes, and hangs out. He's a former academic, researcher, international humanitarian worker, mediator, writer, and educator.

John Doe is a pseudonym for a wonderful person whose story appears in this book.

Silvia Straka (PhD), is an assistant professor, School of Social Work and Human Services, at Thompson Rivers University. Dr. Straka is a social change agent, educator, capacity builder, and researcher. Her research focuses on anti-oppressive perspectives on aging, with projects involving diverse older rural men, older women living with intimate partner violence, and Indigenous aging. Dr. Straka also has expertise in northern, rural, and remote social work practice. She highlights the importance of a participatory community development approach involving a wide range of stakeholders, with a special concern for under-represented and marginalized voices.

Dave Bleakney is a postal worker and labour activist. With the Canadian Union of Postal Workers and in the international labour movement, he advocates on issues such as climate change, Indigenous sovereignty and decolonization, and education for solidarity building. Dave has worked at the CUPW National Office for twenty-four years. He's currently second national vice-president, responsible for union education, the environment, and human rights, among other areas.

Victoria Freeman is an independent scholar, public historian, writer, scriptwriter, and educator. For more than thirty years, she has collaborated with Indigenous scholars, artists, community members, and organizations on community-based research, conferences, workshops, public education projects, and artistic creation. She has taught at York University and the University of Toronto. She is the author of *Distant Relations: How My Ancestors Colonized North America* and *A World Without Martha: A Memoir of Sisters, Disability, and Difference.*

CHAPTER 1

INTRODUCTIONS

Elizabeth Carlson-Manathara and Gladys Rowe

Canadian journalist, author, and activist Naomi Klein began her sold-out talk to a Winnipeg audience in April 2016 by acknowledging they were gathered on Treaty 1 Territory and challenging the audience with the words, "It is not enough for us to simply say that this is Indigenous Land. We need to *act* like it is Indigenous Land" (25:36–25:46). This is what we mean by *living in Indigenous sovereignty*. Elizabeth (Liz) first encountered similar phrases in the writings of white Australian scholars Fiona Nicoll (2004) and Michelle Carey (2008), who wrote of *being in Indigenous sovereignty* and *being in Aboriginal sovereignty*, respectively.

At an Anishinaabe water gathering, Dawnis Kennedy (personal communication, June 19, 2015) suggested a paradigm shift for non-Indigenous people. Rather than seeing themselves solely as main characters in their own stories, she suggested that they begin to think of themselves as characters in the stories of Indigenous Peoples, *living in Indigenous sovereignty*. This represents a powerful shift because as non-Indigenous people begin to see themselves this way, they can begin to sow the seeds of a different reality. The similarities in context between settler colonial states allow us to learn from Australian writings such as that of Nicoll (2000), who emphasizes that Indigenous sovereignty is reality and Indigenous stories are true, regardless of the failure of white Australians to respond appropriately to this reality and these truths. Only when Indigenous sovereignty is acknowledged rather than dismissed as impractical will relationships between Indigenous and non-Indigenous Australians, and indeed the project of Australian nationhood, begin to shift (Nicoll 2004).

In Canada, we argue, Nicoll's words also ring true. And yet we question Nicoll's contention that "the current terms of engagement between Indigenous and non-Indigenous peoples are determined by a non-Indigenous system of governance" (2000: 384). While we certainly agree that it is problematic that the Canadian state attempts to assert its own supposed sovereignty over Indigenous Peoples, and while we hope for and work toward the acknowledgement of Indigenous political and legal sovereignty, we wonder: Do good relations between Indigenous and non-Indigenous peoples rely exclusively on what the Canadian state does or does not do?

As Indigenous Peoples articulate practices of living their sovereignty, they often do this outside of a need for state recognition. For example, Glen Coulthard warns of the danger that contemporary forms of state legal and political recognition "which seek to 'reconcile' Indigenous assertions of nationhood with settler state sovereignty" (2014: 3) will ultimately reproduce colonialist state power. Rather than this political and legal recognition, Coulthard espouses the self-empowerment of Indigenous Peoples through individual and collective cultural practices. Leanne Simpson (2011) stresses that to re-establish the processes and frameworks of living as Indigenous Peoples there is no need for permission, ripe political climates, or funding. Rather, she writes, "we need our Elders, our language, and our lands, along with vision, intent, commitment, community, and ultimately action" (2011: 17). Nii Gaani Aki Inini (Dave Courchene) (2016b) emphasizes that Indigenous sovereignty and nationhood are derived from the land and from the Creator, based on spiritual and natural laws rather than settler governments and laws.

While simultaneously expecting more of the state and working towards a transformation of colonial relationships at multiple levels (decolonization), and while recognizing that the relationship between Indigenous and non-Indigenous peoples will no time soon be completely unmediated by the state or by its systems and institutions; we believe that *living in Indigenous sovereignty* sets an important frame for decolonial action. Indigenous sovereignty *just is*, regardless of Canada's opinion. Recognizing and living this can serve as an orienting framework for settler lives and relations. It represents that part of settlers that can choose how they relate with Indigenous Peoples and Indigenous Lands, the part that is not governed by the state. This reorientation of our lives and relationships is no small thing. Although Simpson's (2017) words describe the transformation of Indigenous Peoples when they engage deeply with Indigeneity and Indigenous intelligence systems, we believe they are also relevant for non-Indigenous people who engage deeply with Indigenous sovereignty. Simpson says that such engagement "changes the relationships that house our bodies and our thinking" (2017: 19), not only transforming our neuropathways, but also creating a different world. "We need to live a different present," Simpson writes, "so that present can fully marinate, influence, and create different futurities" (2017: 20). This is the potency of living in Indigenous sovereignty.

INTRODUCING OURSELVES

Liz's Story

In many ways, this work is motivated by my wish to gain a deeper and more embodied understanding of what living in Indigenous sovereignty could mean in my life. As I was engaging in the research that resulted in this book, I consulted with Dawnis Kennedy, and she shared the following words, which frame much of what my process with the research has been:

> It sounds like you're asking that question for yourself: *How do I live in Indigenous sovereignty?* And you look at the literature, but you're finding *these are the things that are important to me to learn how to do so that I can live in Indigenous sovereignty.* I see a process of going out, just like anybody else, *what do I want to know?* And then going and finding people, finding Elders, finding mentors. *What is it that I can pick up for my bundle, to be able to [live in Indigenous sovereignty]?* And then learning from everyone.… It's about finding all of the people who are able to help you fill your bundle to do what you want to do. For you, it's like *this is the life that I want to live. What do I need?* And then going through that process of picking all that up. (Kennedy, personal communication, April 9, 2016)

Having come to pursue decolonization in varying, often problematic, and generally increasing ways for almost twenty years, I have often thought of how useful and comforting it might have been to receive more explicit and nuanced guidance from other anti-colonial white settler occupiers in addition to what I was receiving from generous Indigenous and/or racially marginalized friends, relatives, and mentors who have informed my journey. Thus, this book is also motivated by my wish to gift it to other white settler occupiers who are seeking to initiate or deepen their own anti-colonial and/or decolonial work at a time when this work is needed. The period that elapsed during the research and writing of this book has seen a number of iterations of centuries-old Indigenous struggles on lands occupied by the Canadian state. These have included the Idle No More movement and the sustained resistance of the Wet'suwet'en Hereditary Chiefs and peoples to a proposed pipeline on their lands, both of which involved calls for settler participation. We have seen the Truth and Reconciliation Commission of Canada and the National Inquiry into Missing and Murdered Indigenous Women and Girls come to a close, issuing recommendations and calls to action. Increasing numbers of settlers are wondering what they can do to support Indigenous resurgence and resistance and to engage in reconciliation.

I come to this work from what are perhaps unlikely places. With Swedish, Sámi, German, Scots-Irish, and English ancestors who "settled" on the lands of the Anishinaabe Nation occupied by the state of Wisconsin, and the lands of the Omaha Nation occupied by the state of Nebraska, I grew up in the evangelical religious right. Surrounded by some very kind people and some powerful teachings, there was a time when this life held much meaning for me. Some of the religious teachings I received have strengthened my decolonial value framework. Nonetheless, I was also sensitive to the hypocrisy, oppression, and injustice around me; in certain instances, these left big marks on me. What I wouldn't become aware of until later was my socialization as a colonizer.

When I was sixteen, I began to study social work at a Baptist university. There I studied under the late Dr. Nicholas Cooper-Lewter, who taught about structural racism and became a mentor. As an African-American professor teaching social change, he received death threats from a conservative alumnus. Another mentor, a white sociology professor who taught liberation theology, was fired after an influential local pastor complained about his progressive views regarding Christian heterosexism. These occurrences enraged me. I knew in my core they were wrong. A few years later, I was employed as a school social worker at an Indigenous alternative school in Minneapolis. I knew little about the history of Indigenous Peoples or about the colonial dynamics operating in my own beliefs and actions. Despite my best intentions, I likely did more harm than good. While working at the school, I began to study Anishinaabemowin, attended weekly community language table gatherings, and became close friends with the school's language and culture teacher, Lorraine (Whitecrow) Derman. She coached me on the language and introduced me to Anishinaabe Protocols. When the school's students were invited to a ceremonial youth gathering and staff were needed to chaperone, Lorraine and I volunteered.

The sacred fire was to be kept during the entire gathering, and being a morning person, I volunteered to accompany a student in putting logs on the fire at 4 a.m. The lights I saw that morning, which the student did not, were something for which I had no explanation. I spoke with Knowledge Keeper Dave Courchene (Nii Gaani Aki Inini) from Sagkeeng First Nation, who had been leading the gathering; my feeling, along with his counsel, led me to experience what I had seen as a call. When, a year or so later, I developed pain in my joints — eventually diagnosed as rheumatoid arthritis — Lorraine suggested we make a trip to Sagkeeng First Nation to seek help from Dave. He explained that as the Earth is experiencing pain at her destruction by humans, many women are resonating this pain in their bodies. He invited us to stay for their ceremonies and asked questions on my behalf. He shared that I would heal faster by connecting with ceremonies, and I was invited to take part. Determined to defeat my disease and wanting to respect the call I had experienced, I began to travel multiple times each year to Sagkeeng. In these travels, I connected with Zoongigaabowitmiskoakikwe, who was a helper at the ceremonies and lived in Minneapolis. She would become a close friend and mentor, sharing teachings and spiritual guidance. I was influenced by a sentiment expressed by a number of Indigenous and non-Indigenous members of the ceremonial community led by Nii Gaani Aki Inini (Dave Courchene) that by attending Indigenous ceremonies, non-Indigenous people can learn the spiritual skills necessary to connect directly with their own ancestors and ancestral traditions.

In the late nineties, I began my MSW program in Minneapolis, focusing on anti-oppression, intergenerational and cultural trauma, and clinical social work. And I got tired of making the long trip to Manitoba multiple times a year. Thus, after I graduated, I found work as a school social worker in rural Manitoba. As I continued to attend ceremonies, I met Byron Matwewinin. He recognized me from his dreams and asked to adopt me as his sister. He explained to me the meaning of this ceremonial adoption, and he became an important and healing influence in my life. The exploration I had done during my master's studies persisted inside of me. When I was invited to write a piece for a North American Sámi journal, I was connected with Anno Nakai, who is Sámi. When I described to her the work I had engaged in during my master's program, she said,

"It sounds like you are talking about decolonization." And it made sense to me. Now I had a word for what I was doing.

I began my doctoral studies in 2007 at the University of Manitoba with this focus. The research study I engaged in, and dissertation I wrote (Carlson 2016) with the support and guidance of brilliant people, evolved to become much of this book. The timing was great. There was a solid and growing body of interdisciplinary literature by Indigenous scholars and activists (Adams 1999; Alfred 2005; Cardinal 1969; Manuel and Posluns 1974; Simpson 2008). Regan (2006: 35) had written, "We are still overly-focused on researching, analyzing, and interpreting Indigenous experience. What is missing is a corresponding research emphasis on our own experience as descendants of Settlers who colonized." I would become aware of her work, Freeman's (2000) *Distant Relations*, and the work of Adam J. Barker (2006). During my studies, I learned from the work of Indigenous social work scholars (Hart 2002, 2007; Blackstock 2009; Sinclair, Hart, and Bruyere 2009) and applied the anti-colonial and decolonial material I read to social work both academically and in practice as I continued to work as a counsellor and therapist.

Upon moving to Winnipeg shortly before the advent of Idle No More, I became more connected with local activist circles and Indigenous-led initiatives and events. Soon after, I had the good fortune of meeting Gladys Rowe. Gladys has become a treasured friend as we shared our academic and personal journeys over a number of years. She has been close to this project in a variety of capacities and has made significant contributions to the research and the book. In addition to the writings and poetry she has contributed, Gladys did significant reviewing of the book, sharing feedback and co-editing. Further, Gladys is one of the three filmmakers of our film project, *Stories of Decolonization*. We have been co-learners and co-educators through our work. Silvia Straka, in Chapter 16, and Victoria Freeman, in Chapter 18, note the importance of relationship and dialogue with Indigenous Peoples for settlers who engage with decolonial work, for a number of reasons. For one, these reciprocal and authentic relationships can help keep us accountable to Indigenous lives, futures, and perspectives. Further, according to Freeman's narrative, "personal friendship connection[s] … [hold] possibilities of creating a prototype for a new society." Some of the relationship work of living in Indigenous sovereignty connects deeply to personal friendships. Thus, it has been only natural that Gladys would be involved with the creation of this book.

Her observations and feedback have taught me much in my journey and in the work of this book.

Although I had been attending Indigenous gatherings and ceremonies since the late nineties, as I continued to listen to Indigenous Knowledge Keepers speak about their connections to the land, I knew I didn't really understand. There was a different quality to what they were saying. I wanted to understand more and felt responsible to learn how to connect with the land in a deeper way. There were a number of times when I asked the land to teach me. In November 2014, I had a dream that greatly impacted my emotional and spiritual understanding of my relationship with the land.

I dreamed of walking over an area of wooded land in which a house sat in a clearing. My attention was being guided toward a number of things. I was shown a few raspberry bushes on the periphery of where someone had come in with machinery and removed a section of land and the majority of the raspberry bushes, leaving a large hole in the earth. My attention was drawn to an individual raspberry, and I was told about the process by which the raspberry plant gathers energy over its growing season, the berries gathering vitality from the earth, the water, and the sun as they ripen. As the raspberries ripen and become red, this represents the fullness of months of gathering nourishment in order to create their ultimate gift to other beings — a beautiful, sweet, ripe, red raspberry. When picked, the ripe raspberry almost falls off of the bush in an effort to gift itself to others. In my dream, I understood the process and the gift as the plant's way — and land's way — of expressing its love and kindness. When I experienced this in my dream, I was overcome by the waves of love given by the land, which brought tears to my eyes and generated a realization of how greatly the land was honouring me by offering the berries. A feeling of immense gratitude and love for the land welled up in me in response to this gift. I realized in a new way just how insulting and violent it is that humans have opted to bring in machinery to gouge out a section of land and raspberry bushes in order to demand and take this gift on our own terms, how it was a slap in the face of the lovingness with which the land seeks to give. In my dream, my attention was then guided to a cluster of large boulders covered with mosses and lichens. It was communicated to me that those rocks are our relatives, and they are like us. The mosses are their skin. This love and connection I experienced from the land in this dream inspired in me a different motivation to find a way to change my exploitative relationship with her. In the past, my motivations had been fear (of the crises in store if we don't change) and justice (an ethic of doing the right thing). My new motivation was love. Not the abstract, vague love of the past, but a concrete, embodied, and powerful love.

Gladys' Story

My name is Gladys Rowe, and I am named after two of my grandmothers, Rita Lorene Hykaway and Gladys Moose. I am Swampy Cree of mixed ancestry and a member of Fox Lake Cree Nation in northern Manitoba. This is where my Cree family is from. My mixed ancestry includes Norwegian, Irish, and English ancestors. In my previous research and publications, I share my reflection on this journey to understand who I am as a Cree person (Rowe 2013, 2014). As an Indigenous researcher and as a member of many communities, I understand the centrality of location. Who I am, where I come from, the knowledge I have, the teachings I have been given, why the research is important to me — all of this *is* the point (Absolon 2011; Absolon and Willett 2005; Wilson 2008). The research is personal. Everything I write is personal. I am bound together within a nest of my experiences and all of my relations. It is these relations that guide my work, always. With this understanding I am accountable to the Knowledge Holders and communities with whom I collaborate and with whom I am in relationship.

My communities of relational accountability include Indigenous educators, scholars, and researchers. It also includes my geographic community, the many places I call home — from Fox Lake Cree Nation to Winnipeg, Edmonton to Seattle. My community is my circle of friends and family — those chosen and by birth. My community includes Indigenous people more broadly, as I work to contribute and share my work with the goal of making a change. My community also includes people who are engaged in decolonial journeys and are committed to understanding more about what these relations can look like and are stepping onto this path with myself and other Indigenous Peoples. As I reflect on my purpose in this world, I am committed wholeheartedly to actively transforming, at a fundamental level, dysfunctional relationships that the structures of colonialism have established and have maintained for hundreds of years.

One of the spaces where I spend my energy is in the university, where I work to build relationships with students and colleagues. This priority comes from the intention to educate and provide space to transform understandings of colonialism and Indigenous Peoples. When I began teaching in 2009, students in the faculty of social work came to my classes not having heard of residential schools. Since then I have seen some, but not enough, progress. As a collective society, the lessons that are being offered about what it means to be in relationship with one another are not being picked up quick enough or by as many people to reach a critical decolonial mass. In reimagining, redesigning, and reconciling post-secondary education I feel compelled to contribute to work that deepens a sense of relationship and responsibility felt towards decolonial possibilities. There is value in building relationships, educating potential allies, ensuring valued space for Indigenous knowledges, and fighting for a university that I would have loved to have entered as an undergraduate.

When I think about how transformation can take place, it connects to this work of living in Indigenous sovereignty — of being in relationship with one another and the land in ways that centre Indigenous knowledge systems, governance structures, and priorities. To support this transformation, it will take more than building awareness and offering education, hoping that people will then choose to do differently. I believe this transformation is complex and challenging because it is a fundamental paradigm shift. Some of my work with Liz has been with the purpose of illuminating guideposts and beacons for a transformed future where living in Indigenous sovereignty is a reality. Initially I came to know Liz as we supported each other in our academic journeys while Liz was working on her PhD and I was finishing my thesis for my master's of social work. We would sit for long hours in the corner of a Starbucks, writing, discussing, and ruminating about the purposes for each of our research and ultimately careers in social work.

As I was finishing my MSW, I was also applying to an interdisciplinary PhD program and drafting my accompanying dissertation proposal. I knew I wanted to incorporate arts-based methods and was contemplating film as a way to share the research stories. Concurrently, Liz was working with a colleague, Teddy Zegeye-Gebrehiwot to capture the dissertation interviews and conceptualize a documentary based upon her dissertation research. They were looking for partners who could be a part of their team. It was in this discussion in 2013 that our work began to intersect, which is more fully described in a previous publication (Carlson, Rowe, Story, and Zegeye-Gebrehiwot 2017).

My work with Liz is connected to the relational accountability that I spoke of earlier in this section. The choices I make about what to support, who to support, and how has meant that for the last seven years I have walked in support of Liz in her dissertation research. I travelled with her as a member of the film crew recording her dissertation interviews. I also reviewed the footage for the films that we have released and those on which we are currently working. We have engaged in many days of dialogue, writing, and editing in coffee shops and through computer screens — making sense of what has been shared and how it relates to the work to which I am committed. Currently, as we complete the second film in the series *Stories of Decolonization*, I reflect on my own understanding that has evolved based on the work with which Liz has invited me to engage. As I support Liz in bringing together and presenting what it means to live in Indigenous sovereignty, I know that I will continue to walk with her in order to be accountable to all of the relations that I carry.

INTRODUCING THE BOOK

In addition to being a personal quest for Liz to work toward a more embodied way of living in Indigenous sovereignty and a desire to gift the stories to other anti-colonial settler occupiers, as is illustrated below, this book responds to calls from Indigenous scholars. For Gladys, this book is about supporting people to engage deeply with the idea of relationship and to understand the responsibilities that come from being in relation. How we are in relationship with one another and the actions that can result from this work are a necessary mechanism for transformation.

Simpson (2008) states that in order for the Eighth Fire of peaceful co-existence to be lit, which was foreseen according to Anishinaabe prophecies, settler society must decolonize their ways and relationships with Indigenous nations and lands. In the context of Minnesota's dispossession of the Dakota peoples, Waziyatawin (2008) calls upon Wasicu [white] Minnesotans who have benefited from Dakota dispossession to learn the true history regarding Wasicu–Dakota relations, to help repair tremendous harms and injustice, to take part in land restoration and reparations, to help restore the integrity of the land and people, and to participate in decolonization as the creation of a new social order in which all peoples will be liberated. Harold Johnson (2007), who is Cree, calls upon the dominant culture to free our minds from tyranny; to cease assuming that our structures are natural, necessary, and superior; to end our domination; and to return to the original intention of Treaty and recognize that we are relatives in order to walk into the future in a good way. Manuel and Derrickson (2017) call on Canadians to walk with them in remaking Canada based upon principles of Indigenous sovereignty. They write, "I call on Canadian people because in all honesty, I do not see any reason to have hope in this [Canadian] government" (2017: 266). Answering these calls from Indigenous scholars is an important dimension of this book's accountability to Indigenous Peoples.

While much of the content of this book is heavily influenced by Indigenous scholars, activists, and Knowledge Holders, it also seeks to address the question: *what can we learn about living in Indigenous sovereignty from the lives, thoughts, and work of white settler occupiers who have engaged deeply in anti-colonial, decolonial, and/or solidarity work?* Here, *living in Indigenous sovereignty* is framed as living in an awareness that we are on Indigenous Lands containing their own stories, relationships, laws, Protocols, obligations, and opportunities, which have been understood and practised by Indigenous Peoples since time immemorial.

This book has a corresponding film project, *Stories of Decolonization*, which draws upon visual recordings of the dissertation research interviews of those whose stories appear in the following chapters, as well as many other film project interviews in order to provide basic and accessible understandings for Canadians regarding colonialism and decolonization in relation to lands occupied by the Canadian state. At this book's printing, the first film of the project was completed and is accessible on the film project website <www.storiesofdecolonization.org> and on YouTube, while the second of the four-film series is nearing completion. Five of the dissertation research interviewees appear in the first film and it is likely that many others will appear in the subsequent films of the project. Viewing the films as you read this book may render the stories more vivid.

As will be clear in the remainder of the book, the work of living in Indigenous sovereignty often involves navigating tensions and paradoxes that may operate in dynamic and complementary ways. These tensions do not always have easy or clear answers, but we illuminate them nonetheless as they are part of the struggle of settler peoples finding their own pathways into decolonial work. Certainly, the reader will find that the research participants whose stories appear in this book sometimes come to different conclusions and engage in differing ways.

Harvey writes,

> Naming and living the edges of paradox is the only way for those of us who are white to move into justice work with authenticity, competency and ground-under-our-feet. On the flip side, I'm convinced that failure to see, understand and wrestle (hard) with paradox is why many of us who are white and well-intentioned, justice-loving, and longing to be counted against racism stay stuck. (2013: para. 4)

Because of the way Euro-Canadians are taught by the dominant culture around them to think and behave in colonizing ways, and due to participation in European-based governmental, medical, legal, and educational systems operating on the Indigenous Lands occupied by Canada, Euro-Canadians currently cannot be other than colonizers. At the same time, we are more than colonizers. LaRocque writes,

> Inasmuch as we must seek to recognize the faces of both the colonizer and the colonized, we must at the same time acknowledge that we are human beings and, as such, are more than the sum total of our colonial parts. (2010: 13)

Kennedy (personal communication, April 9, 2016) says, "I know that the literature is complicated, the relationships are complicated, the history is complicated because of colonialism and the racialization and the positionality of that." Yet, she urged that we leave room "for that humanity in this whole understanding, for real people with hearts, and minds, and bodies, and spirits that know something." Anti-racism, settler decolonial scholarship, and activist teachings rightly emphasize the importance of listening to, taking direction from, and being accountable to Indigenous and racially marginalized peoples (Wilmot 2005; Gehl n.d.). This is sometimes interpreted and enacted in ways that would have Euro-Canadians behave as soldiers taking orders, or as robots leaving their hearts, minds, and skills outside of their work. Kennedy (personal communication, April 9, 2016) offers a counterpoint to this:

> You are a spirit too. You have a spirit too. And you have a purpose, and you came to this world for a purpose. You have work to do that's your own. And that's okay. And you don't need permission from other people for that. That's between you and the spirit.

Undertaking a journey of decolonization can lead settlers to question and re-examine the foundations of their lives and identities. Many struggle with self-judgment, guilt, and negative views of their communities and identities. Mills offers a point of balance to this dynamic: "The most radical thing anyone can do with respect to decolonization is to allow that he or she is a sacred person, has gifts others need and is worthy of receiving others' gifts, and is part of creation" (2016: para. 27). He explains that recognizing their role as settlers can lead some to step back in defeat rather than stepping up with creation and taking part in the practice of Anishinaabe law on Anishinaabe Territory.

Kennedy (personal communication, April 9, 2016) reveals another tension of the work when she states, "A lot of the colonial, anti-colonial literature isn't about love. It's just about responsibility." This is particularly true from the settler side of the equation, due in part to centuries of socialization into frameworks of unaccountability and to socialization that cuts off the mind from the heart and spirit (Ani 1994; Spretnak 1999). Euro-Canadian settlers indeed have a long tradition of ignoring the wishes and well-being of the Indigenous people of lands occupied by Canada in their decisions and actions and of neglecting to relate through their hearts and spirits. Feminist (e.g., Collins 2000; Nicoll 2000) and Indigenous scholars have sought to disrupt this disconnection. For example, Hart writes of Indigenous research values involving the "awareness and connection between logic of the mind and feelings of the heart" (2007: 132) and emphasizes deep listening in which one attends to "how his/her heart and sense of being is emotionally and spiritually moved" (2007: 132). In this book, we aim to correct the disconnection of settler decolonization literature from love and present a work that is about responsibility, accountability, reciprocity, spirit, *and* love in addition to a host of other things. It is our belief that this is a meaningful and balanced way to approach the work of living in Indigenous sovereignty. For Gladys, this work is held in her heart; it creates a space of relational possibility — where these stories demonstrate struggle, hope, and deeply vulnerable contemplation about the possibility of a new relationship. For Liz, this book is about *who* Euro-Canadians are — as colonizers, occupiers, invaders, settlers, spirit, and Creator's creation, and *where* we are — on Indigenous Lands and in Indigenous sovereignty, which means we will need to find more loving and accountable ways to be good relatives to Indigenous Peoples and lands.

CHAPTER 2

SETTLER COLONIALISM AND RESISTANCE

Elizabeth Carlson-Manathara

The first steps of a journey for settlers toward more loving and accountable ways to be good relatives to Indigenous Peoples and lands often involve gaining awareness of some of the current structures and dynamics of settler colonialism operating on Indigenous Lands occupied by the Canadian state, including an awareness of how we relate to these. This is a process of truth-seeking in which we begin to pull back some of our layers of denial and the other defences and mythologies that we carry (Tuck and Yang 2012; Regan 2010) in order to look squarely into the eyes of the colonial genocide that is Canada (Hubbard 2014; Ladner 2014; Logan 2014; MacDonald 2019; Maracle 2017; National Inquiry into Missing and Murdered Indigenous Women and Girls 2019; Palmater 2015; Woolford and Benvenuto 2016). As Sakej Ward says,

> We cannot build relationships on illusions. We cannot turn this blind eye to the real atrocities that have happened for 500 years in the Americas, and then say we can be friends.... Because what you're asking of us is for us to turn our back on our ancestors. You're asking us to forget about the genocide of a hundred million Indigenous people. You're asking us to forget about the stealing and abusing of our children. We can't do that.... So if we're going to talk about our relationship, we have to start acknowledging these things. These are the barriers right from the get-go; right from the very beginning. These become the barriers that ensure we're not going to have a good relationship. You have to acknowledge the history of colonialism. And when you do, that's when we can start from a good place. (2015: 22:25–23:45, used with permission)

How do we begin to break down and transform the narratives we have been taught from an early age that cause and maintain these unjust relations? How do we pursue knowledge of the truth about Canada and its genocidal settler colonial foundations and dynamics? How can we come to understand who we are in this? How do we find a new way forward to just relationships and a decolonial future? By examining Indigenous and non-Indigenous scholarship on these issues, this chapter explores foundational knowledge toward living in Indigenous sovereignty.

TERMINOLOGY AND COLONIAL LOCATION

Coming to understand who we are in relation to the settler colonial project of Canada necessitates a look at terminology around identities and around where we fit within the power structures of society. This, as LaRocque (2010: 6) points out, is a minefield due to a history of "stereotypes and legislative divisions, *real* cultural and historical differences." Terminology regarding both Indigenous and non-Indigenous peoples can be complex and problematic, given dynamic and changing landscapes of understanding and the shifting politics of anti-colonialism and decolonization. When I asked Knowledge Keeper Nii Gaani Aki Inini (Dave Courchene) for guidance around terminology, he emphasized the importance of these decisions, as our words can have a big impact with ripple effects (personal communication, September 4, 2013). With regards to First Peoples generally, the sovereign peoples of the lands currently occupied by the settler colonial states of Canada and the United States, I most often use the term *Indigenous Peoples*. I do this following Alfred and Corntassel, who claim this identity as one "constructed, shaped and lived in the politicized context of contemporary colonialism" (2005: 597), and prefer it to using terms imposed and designated by colonial governments, such as *Aboriginal*. They write, "the communities, clans, nations and tribes we call *Indigenous peoples* are just that: Indigenous to the lands they inhabit, in contrast to and contention with the colonial societies and states that have spread out from Europe and other centres of empire" (2005: 597). Vowel (2016) also favours the term *Indigenous Peoples* to refer to First Nations, Inuit, and Métis peoples living on lands occupied by Canada.

Here, I pause to acknowledge some of the controversy that surrounds identifying as Indigenous. In recent years there have been public discussions regarding the Indigenous identities, or lack of Indigenous identities of, for example, filmmaker Michelle Latimer, novelist Joseph Boyden, and U.S. senator Elizabeth Warren. In addition, the work of Darryl Leroux (2019) has challenged the Indigenous self-identification of French descendants, particularly in Canada, who have a distant or tenuously evidenced Indigenous ancestor. Kim TallBear (2013: 510) emphasizes that Indigenous communities' definitions of Indigeneity often include biological ancestry, but also connection to land: "biological, cultural, and political groupings constituted in dynamic, long-standing relationships with one another and with living landscapes that define their people-specific identities." It is a way of being that "facilitates survival and acknowledges the historical rupture of colonialism" (TallBear 2013: 514), resisting its continuing dispossession. She cautions against conceptualizations of Indigeneity that undermine collective self-determination and sovereignty. Indeed, one of the findings of Darryl Leroux's critique of "the shifting of otherwise white, French descendants in Canada (and the United States) into an Indigenous identity" (2019: 1) is that it is sometimes done in order to access Aboriginal land rights, which can then undermine the legitimate land rights of Indigenous communities. Leroux (2019) makes it clear that his critiques are not aimed at people whose families have been torn apart by colonial policies around child welfare, residential schools, and the Indian Act and who are subsequently beginning to reconnect with their Indigenous families and communities. Gosnell-Meyers, who is Nisga'a and Kwakwak'awakw, describes feeling both angered and heartbroken to learn that Michelle Latimer used an "unsubstantiated claimed Indigenous ancestry to advance her career" (2020: para.1). People who do this often benefit from both white privilege and from advantages of Indigenous positionality (such as occupying spaces or winning awards intended for Indigenous Peoples) without experiencing the impacts of colonialism or having connections to community (Gosnell-Meyers 2020). She urges people who do have newly found Indigenous ancestry to begin their journey by building relationships with family and community rather than taking these spaces.

When I am discussing specific First Peoples, in keeping with a focus on Indigenous sovereignty, I use their self-definitions such as Anishinaabe, Nehiyawak, or Dakota. Indeed, in forums where I have heard Indigenous Knowledge Holders or community members speak, some express a strong preference for the way they call themselves as distinct nations. Lee Maracle (2017) writes that the real name for people of her Nation is

Sto:Loh. She argues that using a collective name for the First Peoples of Turtle Island results in the racializing of what are separate nations with distinct cultures and languages. If it must be done, she suggests *Turtle Islanders* (tongue in cheek? or maybe not). It should be no surprise, given the diversity of Indigenous nations, and the diversity of people within each of these nations, that there is no term that all Indigenous Peoples agree upon (Vowel 2016). In light of this, Vowel (2016) suggests that we listen when Indigenous Peoples give us feedback regarding the terms we are using and respect the ways they would like to be called. I believe it is particularly important to pay attention to terminology used in local communities as we build relationships.

Various terms are being used in the literature to refer to non-Indigenous people, each with their political and descriptive ramifications, and none fully satisfactory when it comes to descriptive specificity, accuracy, and comfort (Lowman and Barker 2015; Vowel 2016). *Non-Indigenous* itself as an identifier may be understood to position Indigeneity as the reference point in keeping with locating oneself in Indigenous sovereignty, following the logic of Carey (2008) and her use of the term *non-Aboriginal* in the context of Australia. I also consider that the term *non-Indigenous* focuses on what we are not (Flowers 2015; Lowman and Barker 2015; Vowel 2016), which "says little about what we *are*" (Lowman and Barker 2015: 15). For Flowers (2015), *non-Indigenous* is often used as a neutral, comfortable, and depoliticized descriptor. Further, when the focus is Euro-Canadians, the term non-Indigenous lacks specificity, erasing non-Indigenous people of colour and centring whiteness. The term *Euro-Canadian*, however, in my mind is also problematically comfortable and depoliticized.

As was alluded to in the previous chapter, there is a growing body of literature that specifies Canadian colonialism as *settler colonialism* and non-Indigenous people in Canada as *settlers*. Scholars such as Alfred (2005), Alfred and Corntassel (2005), Flowers (2015), Lowman and Barker (2015), Regan (2010), and many more have used this terminology in referring to non-Indigenous people. Flowers (2015: 33) views *settler* as a "critical term that denaturalizes and politicizes the presence of non-Indigenous people on Indigenous lands, but can also disrupt the comfort of non-Indigenous people by bringing ongoing colonial power relations into their consciousness." However, she cautions that when *settler* is used as synonymous with *non-Indigenous*, it lacks "a critical understanding of its meaning and the relationships embedded within it, rendering it an empty signifier" (2015: 33). In this instance it reduces the focus onto the two identity categories of settler and Indigenous rather than attending to the full set practices, privileges, relationships, and responsibilities that the term *settler* encompasses (Flowers 2015). Lowman and Barker (2015) see *settler* as a relational and structural term that connects to history and to our daily choices and actions, to the benefits received from settler colonialism, and to the complicity and responsibility we have in the systems that cause violence against and dispossess Indigenous Peoples.

After initially finding terms like *settler* and *colonizer* to feel adversarial and angry as a Haudenosaunee woman, Koleszar-Green (2018) explored other terms she might use. Her examination takes into account both structural and individual attributes. In the end, she resolved to consider non-Indigenous people to belong to one of three categories: the *ignorant*, who are not aware of their privilege and are intolerant and damaging in relation to Onkwehonwe (Indigenous) Peoples; the *settlers*, who are starting to learn, but whose engagement is superficial; and the *guests*, who act as stewards and not owners of the land and who are in respectful and reciprocal engagement, supporting Onkwehonwe Nations and Treaties (Koleszar-Green 2018). Although the framework Koleszar-Green has articulated is useful and generous, my self-reflection has shown me that despite my efforts to engage respectfully and reciprocally with Indigenous Peoples and Treaties, I continue to be impacted by my socialization as a colonizer. Letting my guard down by conceptualizing myself as a guest might leave me vulnerable to unexamined colonizing ways of relating. While Indigenous Peoples with whom I am in relationship may think of me as either an ignorant, a settler, or a guest, it is important for me to remain vigilant about my socialization and my structural location as a person benefiting from colonialism.

Certainly, I have heard non-Indigenous people express discomfort with the term *settler*, wanting to distance themselves from "the beliefs and values of the early settlers" (Carey 2008: 11) and their position of benefiting from invasion. As Macoun and Strakosch (2013: 430) write, "settler colonialism is structural which means we are all still settlers in a colonial space and it can serve no interests but our own to erase this." I tend to agree with Macoun and Strakosch and the use of *settler* to describe myself and others who are complicit in and benefiting from settler colonialism. Although I am aware that some find it guilt-inducing, wrestling with and coming to terms with my positioning in relation to settler colonialism has been an important part of my journey. I suspect that many who find the term *settler* most offensive may not have fully faced and struggled with these realities at a deep level, and as Tuck and Yang (2012) demonstrate, may be clinging to ideas of their own innocence.

Sakej Ward (2015) finds the term *settler* to be problematic for very different reasons. From his perspective, *settler* is not too unsettling, but rather, it may not be unsettling enough: "the image of the frontiersman settler going out and carving a whole new life — builds a home, brings his family, has access to wide open expanses of free land … it leaves the Indigenous population out of the equation" (19:47–20:11, used with permission). He says,

> *Settler* does not speak to genocide. The term *settler* does not speak to ethnic cleansing. The term *settler* does not talk about the imposition of a reserve system as a way of controlling the Indigenous population so you can take the rest of the land. The word settler is historically and politically sterile. (20:12–20:38, used with permission)

Ward argues that the appropriate way, from his perspective as Mi'kmaw, to describe the status of *xwelítem* (the hungry or greedy ones, European settlers) on the land is that of an *occupier*. I find Ward's critique important, and to address it in my work, I also often use *settler occupier*.

A number of scholars emphasize that Indigenous Peoples have their own linguistic terms for settlers, which often describe their observations of settlers around the time of contact (Corntassel 2006; Flowers 2015; Vowel 2016). Learning these words, and the meanings and stories behind them, is a way to respect Indigenous sovereignty and to respect "'naming' as an Indigenist epistemological priority" (Carey 2008: 235). Some of these meanings are justifiably unflattering in light of the harm that settlers have perpetrated. Perhaps, akin to Koleszar-Green's (2018) idea of differentiating non-Indigenous people based on their individual attributes, as settlers engage in decolonial transformation, we will one day begin to be called something else. When I sat down with Knowledge Holder Daabaasanaquwat "Lowcloud" (Peter Atkinson) of Roseau River First Nation and asked for his thoughts on how to refer to settlers, he suggested using the term *non-Anishinaabe* (personal communication, September 8 and October 3, 2013). He uses the term *Anishinaabe*, coming out of the Creation Story he shares, to include all those who are Indigenous to this land. Daabaasanaquwat 'Lowcloud' directed me to share the Creation Story in the following way:

> When the Creator told his children that he made them a beautiful place to go, there were four spirits, four colours of his children. They were each lowered to what is today their homelands. The spirit of our [Anishinaabe] people did not want to leave the Creator, so he was the last to leave. When this spirit was finally lowered here, the Creator took four scoops of Mother Earth, four elements and created the physical being of Anishinaabe. The spirit and the physical being became Weynabooshoo, original man. Weynabooshoo and the fire keeper's daughter of the North married and had four sons, and each one went to the four directions. This is where all the different tribes came from. (Personal communication, December 7, 2013)

In this sense, non-Anishinaabe would refer to those who were not lowered onto Turtle Island, or people not Indigenous to these lands. This has important and relevant spiritual, philosophical, and political ramifications related to Indigenous sovereignty and land connection.

Another critique of the use of the term *settler* relates to its potential vagueness regarding who is in the category and who is outside of it. Are all non-Indigenous peoples settlers? Some scholarship reads this way. Sometimes when *settler* is used, whiteness seems to be assumed, but where does this leave Black people and people of colour? Vowel (2016: 16) uses *settler* as short for *settler colonial,* which in her case refers to "the non-Indigenous people living in Canada who form the European-descended sociopolitical majority." However, will we always know this when reading the term in her work? This is one reason I find it to be important to use the phrase *white settlers* when this is my specific meaning. I realize that there are those who find the language of whiteness problematic as it risks the implication that race is a biological reality, which it is not. I nonetheless believe the terms *white* and *whiteness* are important because they are indicators of the ongoing social relations of racial categorization and marginalization. Eliminating use of these terms seems a convenient way to obscure the white supremacy of Canadian society, while whiteness remains closely tied to settler colonialism in Canada and the U.S. (Lopez 2005: 6).

There are differing thoughts on the relationships of racially marginalized and/or recently arriving immigrants to the term *settler* and to settler colonialism (Amadahy and Lawrence 2009; Byrd 2011; Jafri 2012; Lawrence and Dua 2011; Patel 2010; Phung 2011; Sehdev 2011; Vowel 2016). This is an important area of scholarship that grapples with both the oppression of people of colour in relation to structures of white supremacy in Canada and the U.S. and the complicity of people of colour who may also participate in and benefit from colonization (Phung 2011). It also grapples with the role of Euro-descended recent immigrants who may not have a direct colonial history on these lands, but nonetheless may enter into structures of privilege and quickly benefit. They may or may not have undergone colonial socialization and may not perpetuate similar unconscious colonizing and racist actions as have many people of European descent whose families have been on these lands for generations. Chelsea Vowel writes,

> The term *settler* does not, and can never, refer to the descendants of Africans who were kidnapped and sold into chattel slavery. Black people, removed and cut off from their own indigenous lands — literally stripped of their humanity and redefined legally as property — could not be agents of settlement. (2016: 17)

But what of Black people who were not brought as slaves? Might some be positioned as settlers within the structure of settler colonialism while simultaneously being oppressed by white supremacy? Kyle Powys Whyte writes that despite the way (and time) that someone's ancestors arrived (in the U.S., according to his context),

> Having settler privilege means that some combination of one's economic security, U.S. citizenship, sense of relationship to the land, mental and physical health, cultural integrity, family values, career aspirations, and spiritual lives are not possible — literally! — without the territorial dispossession of Indigenous peoples. (2018: para. 2)

Whyte's statement would implicate most non-Indigenous people living on these lands. These questions of identity and relatedness are important as more and more Indigenous scholars and activists are observing and embodying solidarity and mutual support between Indigenous Peoples, Black people, and people of colour (e.g., Lawrence 2020; Newton, Sweeny, and Walker 2020; Simpson 2017).

As non-Indigenous people undertake our own journeys toward living in Indigenous sovereignty, I invite readers to consider their own histories and positionalities with regard to settler colonialism and to do so with courage. I invite readers to consider the terminology that might apply to their own situations reflexively. It is true that we exist in multiple matrices of privilege and oppression. It is also true that being oppressed in one area does not necessarily exempt one from experiencing colonial privilege and benefiting from Indigenous dispossession. I fear that many may wish to avoid terms like *settler* or *occupier* because of the discomfort they produce. I fear that this may relate to an unwillingness to look truthfully at their participation in settler colonial systems and at their responsibility for change, ultimately resulting in doing little or nothing to dismantle these systems. It may also prevent people from undertaking the painful yet necessary process of reckoning with themselves. In the narratives of white settlers that are presented in this book, a number of people shared in depth about their own internal and emotional processes. For example, in Chapter 10, Adam Barker describes the pain and discomfort he experienced in his journey, his efforts to find innocence and legitimacy, and his eventual acceptance of his complicity and commitment to the work. Over time, he found that "discomfort is an indicator that I'm going the right way." He says, "So I used it as my compass. I followed the discomfort." Victoria Freeman, whose narrative appears in Chapter 18, engaged in an intense exploration of her family's history and complicity in Canadian settler colonialism, during which she shifted her feeling of guilt into a sense of responsibility. In order to move forward, she had to face and grieve the horrible damage of colonialism.

In some ways, I suspect that the function of our word choices may be more important than the words themselves. What do our terminology choices prompt us to do? How do they help us move through our process? How do they impact our relationships with Indigenous Peoples? And how do they ultimately help bring us to live in Indigenous sovereignty in deeper ways?

I began this exploration of terms by noting Nii Gaani Aki Inini's (Dave Courchene's) counsel about the importance of terminology and its impacts, which was shared with me upon travelling to visit him in Sagkeeng First Nation. What I didn't mention was that my late adopted brother, Byron Matwewinin (Anishinaabe/Cree), accompanied me on this journey. I must have mentioned to Byron the questions I would ask of Nii Gaani Aki Inini (Dave Courchene) because a few weeks later Byron contacted me, letting me know he dreamed the answer to my questions about terminology for Euro-Canadians. The answer he shared was *Creator's Creation*. At that time I was not ready to take this seriously. I was approaching my work with a mindset that I needed to maintain a critical perspective and not let my ancestors off the hook in relation to our complicity with settler colonialism. But about six months later, when Byron made his journey into the spirit world, I was left to reflect more deeply on what he had shared. I do believe that engaging with pain, discomfort, guilt, and grief have been essential to more deeply processing my learnings and to preventing me from taking short cuts and moves to innocence as I grew. However, Byron's words, in addition to those of Emma LaRocque, (2010: 13) that we are "more than the sum total of our colonial parts"; those of Dawnis Kennedy (personal communication, April 9, 2016), that we are spirits who come to this world with a purpose and with our own work to do; and those of Aaron Mills (2016), who urges us to stand with Creation as sacred persons worthy of giving and receiving gifts, helped me to bring my learning and self-understanding into greater balance. While maintaining a critical perspective, I could also love and value my worthiness and purpose, as well as those of my ancestors.

As is clear from this discussion, there are no easy answers to questions of terminology. For the purposes of this work, I use various terms to refer to Euro-Canadian and non-Indigenous people depending on the context. When I am referring to non-Indigenous people generally, I often use the term *settler* for the political and structural reasons. Although this term is complicated for all of the reasons mentioned above, especially in relation to Black people and people of colour, it is a commonly used term. When I am referring to Euro-Canadian peoples, I use *white settler, colonizer,* or *white settler occupier* often in order to be specific and politically and historically accurate. This is indeed politicized work. When I am referring to specific Euro-Canadian peoples on a specific nation's lands, I am working toward using that nation's term for us if I know it, for the purpose of honouring Indigenous sovereignty. When my reference is within the context of the scholarship or knowledge shared by a particular person or persons, I use the terminology most often associated with their work.

COLONIALISM AND SETTLER COLONIALISM

As is reflective of colonial dynamics, much of the mainstream academic literature regarding historical and contemporary political and social realities in Canada is written from the colonizer's perspective, which, when it comes to issues around colonialism, is often shrouded in denial. But Indigenous documentation and theorizing of colonialism and its dispossession have been occurring for centuries (LaRocque 2010). In keeping with a focus on Indigenous sovereignty, it is critical to listen to what Indigenous Peoples are saying about colonialism and its impacts. Hart and Rowe refer to colonialism as:

> The evolving processes where we, as peoples of this land, face impositions — from genocide, to assimilation, to marginalization — of views, ideas, beliefs, values, and practices by other peoples at the cost of our lives, views, ideas, beliefs, values, practices, lands, and/or resources. It is when we, as peoples of this land, are stopped, hindered, cajoled, and/or manipulated from making and enacting decisions about our lives, individually and as a group, because of being a person of the peoples of this land. (2014: 35)

A specific assault was made on the connection between Aboriginal nations and the land due to the colonizers' desire to claim and legitimize their domination over Aboriginal land and resources (Hart 2002). King and Pasternak explain:

> The assertion of *discovery* and demand for surrender as the basis of Crown sovereignty is the overt form of colonization in Canada. This claim to discovery is enacted every day through ongoing forms of land alienation on the territories of Indigenous nations. Each of these enactments performs a denial of Indigenous authority over their lands and waters. (2019: 17)

This is especially important for settlers to understand, given the relationships of Indigenous Peoples to their lands, which will be further discussed in Chapter 8. As previously noted, this relationship is not something easily comprehended by settlers given our socialization to see land as property and commodity. Simpson (2017) emphasizes colonialism's daily attacks on her presence on the land as well as her freedom and well-being.

After the initial invasion and dispossession of land and theft of resources, LaRocque (2010) describes the demoralization and exile of Indigenous Peoples. She lists estimates of 415–418 million Indigenous lives lost in Canada and three quarters of the entire Indigenous population of America. However, she says, "invasion is only the beginning of the colonization process" (2010: 74). She writes,

> As the invasion deepens, the colonizer moves to protect and enhance his newly gained position of power. This is done in many ways ... from the colonizer's perspective, "peopleing" the "empty" spaces, renaming the "natives" and (their) landscape, building strategic points of entry and defence (i.e., forts), and occupying strategic roles as (re) educators, employers, and, gradually, as legislators. (LaRocque 2010: 74)

In other words, colonialism is a structure and not an event (Wolfe 1999). When colonizers came, they brought with them and built their own structures such as legal, medical, economic, political, and educational systems, which they imposed here. Further, they set into motion ways of relating to Indigenous Peoples and Lands that are exploitative and that persist into the present such that "the dispossession and the dying continues" (LaRocque 2010: 76). Land dispossession and destruction often continue through "megaprojects to extract or produce hydroelectricity, lumber, gas and oil, and uranium and other minerals" (LaRocque 2010: 76). Manuel and Derrickson paint a stark picture of just how immense this loss has been:

> It is the loss of our land that has been the precise cause of our impoverishment.... In Canada the overall percentage is even worse, with Indigenous peoples controlling only .2 per cent of the land and the settlers 99.8 per cent. (2015: 8)

LaRocque (2010) emphasizes that Indigenous Peoples continue to lose their lands and also their lives. One need not look further than *The Final Report of the National Inquiry into Missing and Murdered Indigenous Women and Girls* (2019) and news stories about Indigenous Peoples killed by police or in police custody (e.g., Porter 2020) to see evidence of this.

Colonialism is historical, colonialism is present, and colonialism is daily; not only for Indigenous Peoples, but also for settlers. Simpson (2013a: 53) writes, "Colonialism was and is a choice that Canadians make every day. It is a choice to maintain and uphold a system that is based on the hyperexploitation of the land and of Indigenous peoples." Colonialism is a specific form of imposition and domination in the context and forms described by LaRocque, Hart and Rowe, and Simpson. When defining colonialism, I believe it is important to attend to local contexts as well as historical, contemporary, structural, process-oriented, relational, personal, social, institutional, ideological, and material components. Thus, I see colonialism as a process whereby settlers have come to North America, taken Indigenous Land, set up their own systems and structures, perpetrated genocidal policies and practices, and murdered, dispossessed, and marginalized original Indigenous inhabitants. Colonialism is also responsible for the current structures that have resulted from this process, the reproduction of these structures, and the ideologies, relations, and everyday choices of everyday settlers that have supported and reproduced these structures.

Settler Colonialism

Colonialism takes two major forms: On the one hand, there is colonialism aimed at economic exploitation and the extraction of resources and wealth for the benefit of the colonizer, and on the other is colonization framed around settlement, the creation of new living space for the colonizer at the expense of the ways of life of the colonized (Young 2001). The latter, known as *settler colonialism*, defines the colonialism that has ravaged what are now called Canada and the United States. Tuck and Yang (2012: 5) argue that settler colonial nation-states require "total appropriation of Indigenous life and land, rather than the selective expropriation of profit-producing fragments … settlers come with the intention of making a new home on the land, a homemaking that insists on settler sovereignty over all things in their new domain." As a result of this objective, settler colonialism is intent on the destruction and erasure of Indigenous Peoples, communities, and claims to land. Indigenous legal scholar Pam Palmater argues that the aim of settler governments in assimilating and eliminating Indigenous Peoples is twofold: "1) to acquire Indigenous lands and resources; and 2) to reduce any financial obligations to Indigenous peoples that they acquired through treaties and other agreements" (2015: 2). Lowman and Barker (2015: 24) argue, "Settler colonialism is a way of thinking about power and migration that allows us to better understand the nature of contemporary Canadian society." In the case of settler colonialism, "the settler society becomes so deeply established that it is naturalized, normalized, unquestioned, and unchallenged" (Lowman and Barker 2015: 26).

Colonialism may sometimes be excused as mere migration — the movement of humans around the world. In fact, it is a Canadian mythology that Canada is a land of immigrants. Many Canadians have family narratives of immigrating to Canada with virtually nothing, working hard, and prospering. Monique Woroniak shares her family story of immigrating from the Ukraine in Chapter 4. Over time, she came to the realization that her family's success was due to more than hard work: they had benefited by receiving stolen land. Joy Eidse, in Chapter 9, tells a similar story of her Dutch immigrant grandparents who were able to become somewhat wealthy as a result of Indigenous dispossession. Steve Heinrichs, in Chapter 6, describes the *Mennonite myth* of his family's history; a story of the persecution of his ancestors who were hard-working and a blessing to others, while they didn't talk about who was already there when his ancestors arrived. But what is it to be an immigrant to another land? While many intend to — and succeed — in keeping aspects of their cultures of origin alive, people generally immigrate with the intention of also respecting and fitting into the laws already operating in their new home. This is not what happened with settler colonialism. Tuck and Yang make an important point when they write, "Settlers are not immigrants. Immigrants are beholden to the Indigenous laws and epistemologies of the lands they migrate to. Settlers become the law, supplanting Indigenous laws and epistemologies. Therefore, settler nations are not immigrant nations" (2012: 6–7).

As this discussion demonstrates, colonialism is often seen by settlers as a thing of the past, an event that has already happened and cannot be undone. But Indigenous scholars remind us that settler colonialism is not simply a historical incident but is also "present structure ... formed and maintained by a series of *processes* for the purpose of dispossessing, that create a scaffolding within which my relationship to the state is contained" (Simpson 2017: 45). The presence of current processes of settler colonialism offers an opportunity for current intervention — for anti-colonialism and decolonization.

ANTI-COLONIALISM AND DECOLONIZATION

As settlers come to a deeper understanding of the settler colonial present, including their roles and their families' roles, many are moved to act. As has been noted, providing guidance for those who wish to act is a primary purpose of this book. In the remainder of this chapter, I describe theoretical frameworks for such action as well as some historical perspective around anti-colonial and decolonial work. While some scholars make a strong distinction between anti-colonialism and decolonization, below I explain why I view these two concepts similarly.

Anti-Colonialism

At face value, *anti-colonialism* can be understood as an orientation and set of practices that resist, disrupt, and weaken colonialism. Some scholars note, however, that anti-colonialism has come to be conflated with social justice struggles more generally. For example, Tuck and Yang (2012) associate anti-colonialism with transnational struggles and anti-imperialism rather than with struggles against settler colonialism as I do. Further, Benally (2013) and Lowman and Barker (2015) describe anti-colonialism as associated with class struggle, anti-capitalism, and resisting heteropatriarchy. While I certainly believe that capitalism and heteropatriarchy are related to colonialism, these structures are not one and the same, and therefore resisting one cannot fully equate with resisting another. I believe that anti-colonialism can, and sometimes should, be conceptualized as resistance to local settler colonial processes and structures. Hart's (2009) definition is compelling. Citing Ashcroft, Griffiths, and Tiffin (2000: 29), he writes that anti-colonialism is "the political struggle of colonized peoples against the specific and existing ideology and practice of colonialism."

Some people critique the concept of anti-colonialism because it appears to focus on what one is against rather than what one is for; it sounds more connected to resisting than to building an alternative to colonialism. For Hart (personal communication, January 14, 2016), however, Indigenous resurgence is the centre of anti-colonialism, pushing outwards from this centre and reclaiming space that had been occupied by settler colonialism. For L.R. Simpson (2004), anti-colonialism involves the recovery of traditional knowledge as a strategy that resists the replacement of Indigenous ways and knowledges with Western ways and knowledges, processes that are endemic in colonialism. Anti-colonial strategies "foster the political mobilization to stop the colonial attack on Indigenous Knowledge and Indigenous Peoples" and "require ... Indigenous control over Indigenous national territories, [and] the protection of Indigenous lands from environmental destruction" (2004: 381). From these definitions, it is clear that anti-colonialism has dimensions of both resistance and resurgence.

Decolonization

Just as some scholars view anti-colonialism as focused on resisting structures of oppression that are not synonymous with colonialism, Tuck and Yang (2012) point out that decolonization has also been conflated with other social justice struggles. They write, "Decolonization is not a metonym for social justice ... [and] is not a generic term for struggle against oppressive conditions and outcomes." (2012: 21). Specifically, decolonization "requires the repatriation of Indigenous land and life" (2012: 21). Waziyatawin and Yellow Bird (2012: 3) emphasize that "decolonization is the meaningful and active resistance to the forces of colonialism that perpetuate the subjugation and/or exploitation of our [Indigenous people's] minds, bodies, and lands." For Lowman and Barker (2015: 111) decolonization is "an intensely political and transformative process with the goal of regenerating Indigenous nationhood and place-relationships while dismantling structures of settler colonialism that oppose or seek to eliminate Indigenous peoples from the land." In some cases, scholars and activists tend to view decolonization through a very personal lens. For example, Dine' activist Klee Benally (2013) sees decolonization as a personal and collective process of Indigenous communities that includes relearning traditional languages, reconnecting with traditional food systems, learning one's prayers and cultural practices, and simply reconnecting with who one is. When people speak of decolonization without addressing Indigenous sovereignty and rights, without regard to unsettling and de-occupying the land, they avoid engaging with settler colonialism (Tuck and Yang 2012). Decolonization thus means "all land is repatriated and all settlers become landless" (Tuck and Yang 2012: 27) such that "settler colonialism and its decolonization implicates and unsettles everyone" (2012: 7).

Although anti-colonialism and decolonization have international forms, they also have forms specific to the context of the lands occupied by Canada and forms specific to one's social location. Debates about terms like anti-colonialism and decolonization can seem in some ways like academic exercises, while front-line activists are often more concerned with doing the work than with what the work should be called. However, I think focusing both terms on the present structures of settler colonialism, in the ways the above definitions accomplish this, can be helpful. It may assist activists in keeping priorities such as land repatriation and Indigenous sovereignty as central to our work and to the struggle. Anti-colonialism and decolonization have a long history and multiple manifestations originating with Indigenous Peoples and communities here, on lands occupied by the Canadian state. For me, both anti-colonialism and decolonization will prioritize, support, and complement Indigenous resistance and resurgence. Both seek to resist, challenge, undo, change, transform, and transcend settler colonialism on personal, relational, institutional, structural, political, and national levels. Ultimately these processes must occur in dialogue with Indigenous Peoples and within Indigenous sovereignty.

Because I view anti-colonialism and decolonization in ways that are closely aligned if not interchangeable, in this book I tend to include both terms. Some of the people whose stories are in this book frame their work in either one or both ways, while others use terms such as solidarity, support, or allyship to describe their work. I respect the diversity of terminology used in these discussions and make every effort to forefront the terminology used by the participant or scholar in question.

INDIGENOUS AND INDIGENOUS-LED RESISTANCE

When examining and learning about anti-colonialism and decolonization, it is imperative to understand that from the time of initial contact with Europeans, Indigenous Peoples on these lands have been engaged with contesting colonialism and with decolonization (LaRocque 2010). Therefore, on these lands, decolonization and anti-colonialism originated with Indigenous Peoples. This is an especially crucial context for this book that focuses on settler roles and processes of decolonization and puts this work into perspective.

For Simpson (2017: 9), an "intense love of land, of family, and of our nations ... has always been the spine of Indigenous resistance." The resistance and resurgence of Indigenous Peoples has taken place in both large and small everyday ways, and it has been ongoing. Ladner (2010: 306) writes that when specific issues and opportunities arise, "The masses mobilize, 'kitchen table' networks are engaged, wider networks are rekindled and the movement becomes organized." This mobilization may occur on different levels, in different domains, and using different methods, and yet Ladner notes that throughout history, the same basic issues have been addressed: "Indigenous Peoples have taken up matters of citizenship, territoriality, development and Canadian sovereignty. The issues at hand have not changed. Indigenous struggles have been and will continue to be defined by or predicated on considerations of nation-hood and decolonization" (2010: 306–307). Ladner lists many acts of Indigenous resistance:

> Little things like Mistahimaskwa refusing treaty, citing the need for meaningful and trustworthy consultation and negotiation and reminding the representatives of the Crown that the Nehiyaw are a sovereign people who will not (and have not) ceded their right to self-determination nor their territories, which they agreed to share with the newcomers. Little things like the women … who refused to leave and/or returned to their reserves after they had married non-status men, gotten divorced or been widowed and who brought this gendered inequity to the streets, the Canadian Courts, the constitutional talks, the United Nations and the International Court of Justice. Little things like all of those parents and grandparents who refused to allow the state/church to take their kids to residential school and fought tirelessly for day schools, access to high school, integration and band-controlled education. Little things like Frank Calder and the Nisga'a Nation taking the Canadian Government to court in the 1970s in defense of their land rights and Aboriginal Title. Little things like all those fisherman (and women) like Dorothy Van Der Peet and Donald Marshall Jr. who struggled for years on their rivers, their lakes and their oceans to maintain their fisheries despite being told that they were "fishing illegally" and knowing that they would end up in Canadian jails and courts. Little things like the Dene Declaration of 1975 and the corresponding mobilization of the nation in defense of their homelands. (2010: 300)

A large flashpoint resistance of which many Canadians of a certain age would be aware is the resistance at Kanehsatà:ke, which many refer to as the Oka Crisis. The resistance at Kanehsatà:ke can be seen as a wake-up call for Canada (Ladner 2010), as it drew attention from people around the world and resulted in the Royal Commission on Aboriginal Peoples. In fact, a number of people whose narratives are featured in this book specifically mention the role of the Oka Crisis in their consciousness-raising and early motivation for decolonization work. Ladner describes the resistance:

> There were blockades. There were rocks. There were tanks, guns, bayonets, helicopters, snipers and anything else that the Canadian army and the Québec paramilitary provincial police force could imagine. There were Elders and children who had their cars pelted with rocks or who were beaten (even bayoneted) as they attempted to leave their communities. And then, of course, there were the people who stood on their lands protesting the development of their lands (a commons which held the trees their ancestors planted and the bones of their Ancestors) for yet another golf course and parking lot. They were the people — the women, children, Elders and men — behind the blockades and on our television sets every night talking about their Ancestors, the treaties that they signed with the newcomers, their lands/the Pines and the violence that besieged them on the blockades, in the neighboring towns, by the Québécois, Canadians, their army and the Sûreté du Québec (the SQ). (2010: 303)

The Grassy Narrows blockade, beginning in 2002, has been operational now for almost two decades. The blockade was in response to mercury pollution found in the water in 1972 (as a result of a paper mill dumping mercury into the water since 1952) and in response to clear-cutting in the area (Da Silva 2010).

A recent and international movement began several years ago in Canada, in the fall of 2012. The Idle No More movement is Indigenous-led and started with a teach-in organized by Sylvia McAdam, Nina Wilson, Jess Gordan, and Sheelah McLean about the removal of environmental protections and lack of consultation with Indigenous Peoples. This inspired "a continent-wide movement with hundreds of thousands of people from Indigenous communities and urban centres participating in sharing sessions, protests, blockades and round dances in public spaces and on the land, in our homelands, and in sacred spaces" (Kino-nda-niimi Collective 2014: 21). The movement grew to incorporate Indigenous

Rights, Indigenous resurgence, land protection, and education-related efforts, and it has continued in a number of ways over the years.

During the revisions of this book, much happened by way of Indigenous resistance. Wet'suwet'en land defenders have continued their years of resistance to pipeline development on their territories occupied by British Columbia, all the while the RCMP protect and facilitate Coastal GasLink's efforts to build the pipeline (Unist'ot'en Camp 2017). Meanwhile, in southwestern Ontario, members of Six Nations of the Grand River and their allies reoccupy their sovereign territories in opposition to the Mackenzie Meadows housing development project being built on Haudenosaunee lands bordering Caledonia and the Six Nations reserve (Forester 2020a). In connection with this reoccupation, Ontario Provincial Police have attacked and arrested community members at the 1492 Land Back Lane camp (Forester 2020b). Simultaneously, non-Indigenous commercial fishers terrorize Mi'kmaw fishers when they exercise their Treaty Right to a moderate livelihood while the RCMP stand by (Bilefsky 2020; Googoo 2020), sparking protests across Canada (Idle No More 2020). Concurrently, Algonquin-Anishinaabe peoples are calling for a moratorium on moose hunting in La Verendrye Park, Québec, as the moose population declines. They have established non-violent camps and checkpoints to draw attention to the need to protect the health and sustainability of the moose population (Deer 2020).

I want to close this section by emphasizing that Indigenous resistance has been multifaceted. Wherever Indigenous Peoples live, work, and engage, they may be involved in anti-colonial and decolonizing practice. Indigenous Peoples in their anti-colonialism, decolonization, and resistance efforts have been, according to Palmater (2015), portrayed as angry and violent criminals by mainstream media, supporting their continued exploitation by government and corporations. Although, as LaRocque (2010: 19) says, "Native people resisted European oppressions long before they took up the English alphabet," part of the anti-colonial mobilization on the part of Indigenous Peoples has been in written scholarly or academic forms. Certainly, academia is a growing site of Indigenous activism. Many are also involved in spiritual activism, including reclamation of ceremonies and Traditional Knowledge, which often undergirds their structural and epistemic activism. Taiaiake Alfred's (2005) description of an effective anti-colonial movement among Indigenous Peoples is one that rests on a number of conditions, including the condition that it have the support and co-operation of allies in the settler society. It is to an exploration of the decolonization and anti-colonialism of settlers that I now turn.

FRAMING WHITE SETTLER DECOLONIZATION AND ANTI-COLONIALISM

What do decolonization and anti-colonialism look like for white settlers? Are they even possible given our colonial structures, histories, and socialization? What will our lives look like in the new world toward which we are working? Are there historical examples of white settlers doing this work? It is questions like these that I take up in this section.

McCaslin and Breton (2008: 519) argue, "This, then, is the core challenge: We cannot practice justice as a way of life and remain colonizers. We cannot avoid confronting the colonizing cage — a cage that traps both Indigenous and non-Indigenous people." They explain further:

> Colonizers need to learn the ways of decolonization that teach respect and the honouring of all relationships. What is destructive and catastrophic to the well-being of one cannot be good for the other.… We cannot get to a good society or a good relationship between peoples as long as colonialism is the dominant model. (McCaslin and Breton 2008: 513)

Hart, Straka, and Rowe emphasize that there are different roles for Indigenous and non-Indigenous peoples in anti-colonialism:

> To be anti-colonial, Settlers have to ensure that their actions do not reinforce colonial oppression, such as when they claim they are doing "what is right" for the colonized. Their actions must always support Indigenous peoples' self-determination, and it is always Indigenous people who determine "what is right" as anti-colonial action.… People of the colonizing group thus have to recognize the complex dynamics of colonialism, how they are implicated, how they may replicate the power dynamics in their relationships, and how they can use their power to challenge the oppression. (2016: 2–3)

In the context of Minnesotans and the colonization of Dakota peoples, Waziyatawin writes about what decolonization might look like:

> Decolonization requires the creation of a new social order, but
> this would ideally be a social order in which non-Dakota would
> also live as liberated peoples in a system that is just to everyone,
> including the land and all the beings of the land. (2008: 174)

Many white settlers worry that such a new social order would not have a
place for us, or that in such a world, we would be oppressed as Indigenous
Peoples are oppressed now (Memmi 1965). Waziyatawin answers this fear:

> *Wasicu* [white] people need not fear the empowerment of Dakota
> people. When we are lifted up and our humanity is recognized,
> everyone will be lifted up. Those of us clinging to traditional
> Dakota values are not interested in turning the tables and claiming
> a position as oppressor, as colonizer, or of ruthlessly exploiting
> the environment for profit. (2008: 174)

This sounds like a wonderful future. However, it is a future that requires
our work. Waziyatawin calls upon white settlers to "help repair its tremendous harms ... and restore the integrity of the land and people" (2008:
175). She emphasizes that this vision cannot move forward as long as
Minnesotans deny or celebrate the Dakota genocide and dispossession
from which settlers have benefited. Waziyatawin's words emphasize the
interrelatedness of Indigenous and settler decolonization work. As Alfred
writes,

> While we are envisioning a new relationship between
> Onkwehonwe [original peoples] and the land, we are at the same
> time offering a decolonized alternative to the Settler society by
> inviting them to share our vision of respect and peaceful coexist-
> ence. The non-indigenous will be shown a new path and offered
> the chance to join in a renewed relationship between the peoples
> and places of this land, which we occupy together. (2005: 35)

Biermann (2011) points to a number of motivations for non-Indigenous
people to work toward decolonization. First, there is an ethical imperative
to respond to structures of injustice and oppression and to make every
effort to dismantle these. Second, he says, "there is the realization that
colonial systems of oppression diminish everyone's humanity, including
and especially the oppressor's, necessitating resistance by those who are
systematically privileged, for example, by whiteness" (2011: 387). The

final motivation described by Biermann is mutual benefit, which has been amply described by Alfred (2005), McCaslin and Breton (2008), and Waziyatawin (2008). Despite the privilege and material advantages of colonizing, there are spiritual, ethical, and emotional reasons to decolonize. But can we?

Can Settlers Be Anti-Colonial/Decolonial?

Both Dei (2009) and Memmi (1965) raise questions about the ability of people from the colonizing group to be anti-colonial, but for different reasons. For Dei, anti-colonialism comes out of the experiences, histories, and epistemologies of colonized Indigenous Peoples, and he questions whether white settlers, socialized within Eurocentric frameworks, can engage in deep ways. Memmi, on the other hand (although within the context of Algeria rather than Canada or the U.S.), emphasizes that refusing to be a colonizer means either leaving the colonizing setting or fighting to overthrow the colonial conditions that benefit him and thus overthrowing his own existence as a colonizer, which is an impossible situation. While both scholars seem to foreclose the possibility of anti-colonial settlers, both leave open a crack in the door.

For Dei (2006, 2009), white settlers need to recognize that their anti-colonial thought will be limited. He argues that the colonizer will often "remain oblivious to the sites of oppression/domination (thereby showing limitations in knowledge and knowing) … [because] the site from which we oppress is the site on which we least cast our gaze" (2006: 11). Dei challenges those who engage in anti-colonial practices to consider the question of "whether the dominant/colonizer should know and critique colonialism, imperialism and oppression without the input of those who have received, and continue to receive the brunt of the colonial encounter and its violence" (2006: 11). Thus, in the end, white settlers who wish to deepen our anti-colonial understanding need do so in relationship and dialogue with Indigenous Peoples (Carlson 2017). This is one reason why I have invited many Indigenous scholars, activists, and Knowledge Holders to walk with me while engaging in the research and writing of this book. For Memmi, the possibility lies in a deep transformation or rebirth. He writes that the colonizer who refuses his colonizing situation

> certainly does not conceive … of a deep transformation of his own situation and of his own personality.… He invokes the end

of colonization, but refuses to conceive that this revolution can result in the overthrow of his situation and himself. For it is too much to ask one's imagination to visualize one's own end, even if it be in order to be reborn another; especially if, like the colonizer, one can hardly evaluate such a rebirth. (1965: 40–41)

Although they are discouraging for many white settlers, I believe Memmi's words here are essential. As concepts of reconciliation, nation-to-nation relationships, and decolonization are catapulted into the public purview, as has happened in Canada in the last ten years, many worry that they are being engaged in superficial ways. This is certainly my observation. Memmi reminds us of the complete reordering of our foundations and very selves; of our every thought and action, and of our emotional and spiritual selves, that is necessary for anti-colonial and decolonial work — for living in Indigenous sovereignty. Anything less is window dressing.

Returning to the question that animated this section, *can settlers can be anti-colonial or decolonial?*, my answer is *we must*. Hart and Rowe (2014: 37) write, "Relationships involve at least two parties. As such, both the oppressed and privileged in the colonial relationship must be involved in decolonization processes." Kempf writes:

> While anticolonialism is in many ways a language of resistance for and from the oppressed (see Dei and Asgharzadeh 2001), the dominant must also participate in the anticolonial struggle.... Where anticolonialism is a tool used to invoke resistance for the colonized, it is a tool used to invoke accountability for the colonizer. (2009: 14)

Although we will do this work in limited and imperfect ways, with numerous blind spots, reproducing colonialism even as we make strides towards resistance and transformation, we must try. To do otherwise would mean more harm. It would mean accepting our role as colonizer and continuing to reproduce this dynamic in the same ways we always have and as fully as we always have. With all this being said, as we engage in anti-colonialism, our work must have — as its foundation — the epistemological mirrors we receive in text and dialogue as gifts from Indigenous and colonized peoples, as best as we can understand them. Because of our limitations (our Eurocentric lenses, fears, and defence mechanisms such as denial), it will be important to have input from Indigenous Peoples into our work at multiple levels. And although we must engage in a journey of continual growth, we will never understand fully enough or engage in transformation completely. Humility is in order (Carlson 2017). We will never be fully anti-colonial.

With increasing attention to decolonization and reconciliation within Canadian discourse, one might wonder if settler anti-colonialism and decolonization are new. History, in fact, offers us myriad examples of settler individuals and movements that struggled against colonialism in both Europe and the Americas. However, they were never widespread or complete enough to effectively and fully intervene in colonialism in Canada or the U.S. in a way that significantly changed the trajectory for the better. In sometimes obvious and sometimes subtle ways, many of these have reinforced colonial dynamics even as they sought to disrupt them. LaRocque (2010) and Young (2001) note the many anti-colonial dissidents and visionaries who abhorred colonial cruelty, such as Francisco de Vitoria and Bartolomé de Las Casas in the 1500s. Young also describes a radical anti-colonial tradition in Europe in the eighteenth and nineteenth centuries. Examples in Canada of settlers who, in the 1800s and early 1900s, protested cruelty and injustice toward Indigenous Peoples have been outlined by Freeman (2000): John Eliot, Governor General Charles Thompson, and Frank Oliver. More recently, settlers in Canada have supported Indigenous-led resistance during flashpoint events such as Burnt Church (1999–2002), the Oka Crisis (the resistance at Kanehsatà:ke) in 1990, the resistance of the Chippewas of Nawash in the 1990s, and the long-standing blockade of the Anishinaabe of Grassy Narrows, which started in 2002 (Da Silva 2010) and continues. John and Dave, whose narratives appear in Chapter 15 and 17 of this book, describe the role of the resistance at Kanehsatà:ke in the early growth of their anti-colonial awareness. In Chapter 11 of this book, Susanne McCrea describes her support work of the Grassy Narrows blockade and the great number of people who developed as allies under the guidance of Judy Da Silva of Grassy Narrows First Nation. These also include John and Rick, whose stories are told in Chapter 15 and 13 of this book, respectively. The list of Indigenous-led struggles that have been supported by settlers goes on and on, from the Six Nations reclamation in 2006 (Keefer 2010); to Idle No More in 2012, which was co-founded by Sheelah McLean (2018), a white settler; to the current Wet'suwet'en land defence, struggle for Mi'kmaw fishers' rights, and the 1492 Land Back Lane reclamation at Six Nations in 2020 and beyond.

Sharing these examples is not meant, in any way, to overshadow the role of Indigenous resistance in what changes have been made. Clearly, Indigenous anti-colonialism has a very long and effective history and has provided direction and knowledge that has informed settler solidarity work and resistance. Examples of European and Euro-American approaches to anti-colonialism are important, however, because they represent elements of a counter-narrative (at least partial) to settler participation in colonialism and can be instructive, providing inspiration and allowing us to learn from both their successes and their shortcomings. It remains important for white settler people to have models of doing emancipatory work.

State of the Colonizer

As colonizers, our participation and complicity in colonialism in the places we occupy has diverted and polluted our best energies: "For if colonization destroys the colonized, it also rots the colonizer" (Memmi 1965: xvii). Whether or not we wish it, as Euro-Canadians, we are turned into colonizers (Memmi 1965), which means occupying positions and reproducing practices of colonial privilege. These privileges draw settlers to colonies where there are jobs, high wages, and profitable businesses. However, colonial privilege comes at the expense of Indigenous dispossession. Memmi (2000: ii) writes, "The economic aspect of colonialism is fundamental ... the deprivations of the colonized are the almost direct result of the advantages secured to the colonizer." The effects of colonization, Sartre (1965) asserts, are the alienation and dehumanization of not only the oppressed, but also the oppressor. Here, I refer the reader to Heaslip's (2017) in-depth exploration of this alienation through her psychology of settler privilege and socialization, which is unfortunately beyond the scope of this book. For our purposes, it is important to understand that to be able to harm others, one must objectify life, harden one's heart, and think hierarchically (McCaslin and Breton 2008; Sartre 1965). A close mentor to me, Kelly Lovelace (Anishinaabe) shared her understanding:

> Something had to have happened in their history that they would forget who they are, their ancestors, that disconnection ... there's a lot of white people that are disconnected from themselves ... who are suffering in the mind. And they're looking for something but

they're either afraid, unwilling, or don't have the ability to go back to find who they are. (Personal communication, February 4, 2002)

The journeys of many Euro-descended families who reside in Canada are characterized by fractures: the fracture between our ancestors who emigrated and family who stayed, and the fracture from our ancestral homelands. One reason many settlers insist that Canada is their homeland is because of this fracture. Day shares,

> I know I am not really of the land, anywhere. Just as I am land-less, it is also very unclear who are my people, other than, as I've already mentioned, that I am some kind of European settler … a nomad wanderer, with fragments of a family, a few friends widely dispersed, many contacts, but no real community, no one, other than my two boys, whose fate I share, whether I like it or not … can there be a true community of the homeless and landless? (2010: 267–268)

Carey narrates that as a non-Aboriginal woman living in the settler state of Australia, she has also been unable to find belonging in the land of her ancestors:

> I went to Ireland when I was 19, to check if I was Irish. A bus driver in Limerick set me straight. He said the Americans were tourists and Australians were guests. At first I thought he was flattering me. It soon clicked though that he thought I was only margin-ally higher up in the pecking order than those loud Americans who developed sudden penchants for wearing tweed caps and walking with the aid of a blackthorn stick. I was just a guest. An Australian guest. (2008: 3)

Make no mistake, this type of suffering is incomparable with the genocide experienced by Indigenous Peoples in settler states, and it is accompa-nied by all kinds of material advantages and privileges; it is suffering nonetheless.

Our status as colonizers and occupiers is difficult to face, not only because of the alienation that accompanies it, but also because of the harm we have caused. Many settlers wonder whether they are to blame for the genocide of Indigenous Peoples. Freeman (2000) takes up this question through her research regarding the role of her ancestors in Canadian and

U.S. colonialism. She asks, "Just who is responsible for what has happened? Are colonization, land theft, and cultural obliteration the work of certain morally reprehensible individuals or a collective guilt?" (Freeman 2000: 452). In light of her research, Freeman concludes,

> The colonization of North America has been the result of millions of actions, or non-actions, great and small, by thousands, even millions, of people over hundreds of years.... Ordinary people have been part and parcel of the process, making decisions that deny another people's being or that allow a destructive process to continue. Within the norms of a culture, "decent people" can do indecent things; they are conditioned to be insensitive to another people's pain. With regard to the taking of Native land, the breaking of treaties, and cultural genocide, Canada as a whole is implicated — as is the United States. Everyone benefited except the indigenous people. It was, and to a very large degree remains, a culturally sanctioned injustice. (2000: 452)

When settlers become aware of this, they are "often bogged down in paralyzing and patronizing feelings and behaviours, including both a 'fascination and guilt' with our privileged position, as well as shame and despair" (Wilmot 2005: 15). An appropriate response to wrongdoing and colonial complicity, *guilt* is part of the settler condition. The fear and avoidance of intense emotions such as guilt is what may keep many non-Indigenous people from engaging with Indigenous Peoples and sovereignty (Freeman n.d.).

The intense emotions of white settlers may also result in the engagement of defences that function to restore status quo equilibrium rather than engaging change. Defence mechanisms such as denial, minimization, justification, repression, and projection are common in settlers when it comes to colonialism. Williams (2008: 249) aptly writes, "If we live in dread of guilt, we must construct a temple of illusions." Alfred (2005: 107) says that denying the truth is "an essential cultural and psychological process in Settler society":

> I am convinced that most Settlers are in denial. They know that the foundations of their countries are corrupt, and they know that their countries are "colonial" in historical terms, but still they refuse to see and accept the fact that there can be no rhetorical

transcendence and retelling of the past to make it right without making fundamental changes to their government, society, and the way they live. For no other reason than a selfish attachment to the economic and political privileges they have collectively inherited as the dominant people in a colonial relationship, they, by cultural instinct and imperative, deny the truth. (2005: 107)

Regan describes an instance of her own internal personal campaign of defensive self-justification:

On the way to the meeting place, I find myself recounting all the reasons I am not a colonizer: I am working for social justice and change from within my own dominant-culture institutions; I am enlightened and empathetic; my intentions are good; I am committed to finding a just solution … I have Indigenous colleagues and friends; I grew up in a single-parent, low-income family in an ethnically diverse East Vancouver neighbourhood; I am not one of those racist white upper- or middle-class people raised in insular privilege! (2010: 171)

Projection, another defence mechanism, is described by Memmi (2000) as scapegoating, whereby the colonized and racially marginalized are blamed for things that are not of their making, which is a dynamic of racism. Memmi (2000: 64) says, "to exteriorize evil by incarnating it in another separates it from society and renders it less threatening … at the individual level, one destroys in the other what one would like to destroy in oneself, by imputing to that other one's own faults." Thus, the racist is left to feel innocent and pure, given "self-absolution" (2000: 65).

Another strategy used to retreat from the guilt, sadness, and rage one may experience upon being confronted with one's role in colonialism is to seek to return to the status quo by asking, "what can we do about it?" (Day 2010: 265). Tuck and Fine (2007: 153) discuss this dynamic of colonizer's guilt through which the "acknowledgement of oppression and the simultaneous retreat from responsibility for change" occur. They describe the dynamics that inevitably emerge in Q and A discussions of Indigenous scholars with mostly white audiences:

There is a moment and a string of moments when members of the audience begin to feel implicated, personally responsible for the ongoing colonization of indigenous peoples. And so one person stands and says, "What can I possibly do?" And that response, although frustrating (… because it is so quick to get that big guilt off its back, to shift from being under the eye of scrutiny) is understandable only because it is so typical. Understandable if the audience misunderstands/takes the indigenous project as swapping one agenda for another … sliding a new checklist beneath the academy's waiting pen.… This question, steeped in the privilege of white ideology, reeking of false generosity, asks me to do the work of the question poser. An element of white privilege is to reduce someone's theoretical work to a honey-do list for white people. (Tuck and Fine 2007: 153–154)

Yet another set of strategies used to avoid painful emotion and responsibility are *moves to innocence*. When faced with "the relentlessness of settler guilt and haunting" (Tuck and Yang 2012: 9), settlers thus hurry toward any reprieve through these moves. One of the moves to innocence described by Tuck and Yang (2012) is that of *colonial equivocation*, in which settlers try to alleviate their guilt by focusing on the ways that they have been oppressed, and then conflate these with being colonized so that they can position themselves as colonized rather than settlers. *Settler nativism* is another move to innocence involving locating or inventing a "long-lost ancestor who is rumored to have had 'Indian blood,' [so] they use this claim to mark themselves as blameless in the attempted eradications of Indigenous peoples" (Tuck and Yang 2012: 10). *Fantasizing adoption*, as a move to innocence, functions to "spin a fantasy that an individual settler can become innocent, indeed heroic and indigenized, against a backdrop of national guilt" (Tuck and Yang 2012: 14) by conceptualizing themselves as adopted by Indigenous communities. Tuck and Yang do not take issue with the appropriateness or legitimacy of actual adoptions but note that the representations and claims by settlers to be adopted by Indigenous Peoples "far exceeds the actual occurrences of adoptions" (2012: 14). Ultimately, all of these moves are attempts to "deflect a settler identity, while continuing to enjoy settler privilege and occupying stolen land" (2012: 10). In the end, engaging these defences or moves to innocence detracts from "what a real/an ethical conversation about ongoing colonization and ongoing decolonization requires: preparedness, listening, reflection, and reparation" (Tuck and Fine 2007: 155).

Much of the critical whiteness and anti-racism literature suggests that guilt is not helpful for white people; that it is immobilizing and an exercise in narcissism (e.g., Dyer 1997). As white settler occupiers, we may conflate guilt and shame, believing that if we do wrong or hurtful things this means we are bad people; this is a conceptualization that makes it psychologically difficult to view anything we have done as bad. I contrast this with Byron Matwewinin's (personal correspondence, October 1, 2010) Anishinaabe/ Cree teachings about guilt. Matwewinin shared that his father always taught him that guilt is a sacred teaching: it tells us what not to do. When we have done something wrong and we feel bad, we learn about ourselves and what that feels like so that we won't be like that a second time. He shared, "You get yourself up and continue taking that walk."

Grief also affects white settlers who are willing to come face to face with colonial realities. Freeman says, "It's appropriate to grieve because it's a pretty horrible history, a lot of it. It's really sad. And a lot of people died, and a lot of lives were wasted. And grief is something we can share" (n.d.: 5:11–5:35). Tuck and Fine write,

> These dynamics are aged, living in the bodies of those who have survived and those who have been sacrificed; these dynamics also carried through the bodies of those who believe themselves unaffected ... what David Eng calls racial melancholia for white people. (2007: 146)

Rather than defending against or fleeing these settler emotions, Freeman (n.d.) recommends feeling them and working through them. She says,

> If you can allow yourself to feel what's there, including the grief, it passes. It doesn't mean it's over, it doesn't mean that, okay now everything is fine, but it's a working through, it's an acknowledgement of how bad it was. And in my experience, unless you come to that acknowledgement, it's going to be pretty hard for you to work with Indigenous people and for Indigenous people to trust you.... Where your heart is, is really important, and I think that unless we do open our hearts and let our hearts grieve, and feel even a smidgen of the pain of what's happened, which Indigenous people had to live with, we can't really connect honestly. We're avoiding it. (Freeman n.d.: 5:35–6:27, 6:50–7:15)

As someone who has worked for many years as a therapist, and who has also undertaken my own work around settler emotions like guilt and grief, I find Freeman's words important and reflective of my own experience. Working through these emotions has not changed the reality of my implication in colonialism, but it has lessened the intensity of the pain and has helped me to work alongside Indigenous Peoples without needing to centre my own emotion. I have been able to come to enough peace with myself that I can do the work more wholeheartedly and with greater energy and joy. The dynamics and characteristics of the conditions of white colonial settlers living on Indigenous Lands are important as they interface with our ability to engage well in decolonization and anti-colonial activism. The narratives presented throughout this book demonstrate many examples of working through these dynamics in a way that allows one to move forward, to engage in anti-colonial and decolonial work, and to begin to live in Indigenous sovereignty.

CHAPTER 3

INTRODUCING THE NARRATIVES

*Elizabeth Carlson-Manathara with Aimée Craft,
Dawnis Kennedy, Leona Star, and Chickadee Richard*

The stories presented in the following chapters do not exist in a vacuum. The shapes the stories have taken have had many influences. These stories are primarily based on research interviews that occurred in 2014 and 2015. The narratives represent only a portion of the interviews, and the interviews represent only a portion and representation — what was shared — about the lives and work of those interviewed. Traditional academic researchers often conduct studies individually and make sense of the information their studies yield on their own. In fact, this is still a requirement for doctoral research studies in many universities. Relational accountability features prominently in Indigenous methodologies, and it recognizes that each researcher's perceptions are shaped by the many relationships through which ideas have been shared with them and emphasizes the importance of remaining connected and in dialogue with communities impacted by the research. It means that the priorities, values, and needs of these communities shape the way the research is done and the process of making sense of the information gathered by the research. As a settler researcher, I knew that my values, priorities, and practices remain heavily influenced by settler colonialism, even if against my wishes. Thus, I had to figure out a way to adjust my lens. Remaining in dialogue and relationship with the Indigenous scholars, activists, and community members in my life became a valued and necessary way to do this, informing the decolonizing and anti-colonial practices and goals of the study.

In keeping with these principles, choices were involved in prioritizing the portions of the stories shared with me in the narratives that follow, many of which involved relational accountability with Indigenous Peoples and the land in accordance with the "Orienting toward Indigenous Sovereignty" chapter of this book. Although these stories were shaped by a consultation process and by priorities articulated in Indigenous scholarship, as a researcher, I nonetheless had a role in shaping the stories through the questions I asked and the answers I emphasized. The one or two interviews upon which each story was initially based ranged from 1.5 hours to 2.5 hours, during which much beautiful, painful, and inspiring content was shared.

The narratives were static; the humans who shared them are not. Since 2014–2015, much has changed in the world and in Canada and much has stayed the same. Since then, much has potentially changed in the lives of those interviewed, and perhaps some things have stayed the same. Many of those interviewed have undertaken substantial anti-colonial initiatives since and/or have had significant shifts in their understandings. Thus, a number of them have updated or added prologues or postscripts to their original narratives to reflect this, while others have significantly rewritten their stories. Some chose to keep their stories as they had been written and view their narratives as a snapshot of their former selves.

As I prepare to share these stories, I wish to reiterate some of the context through which the stories have come forward. The research began with an idea borne of my experience and the mentorship and teachings that had been shared with me up to that point. As someone who has struggled to deepen my anti-racism, anti-colonial, and decolonial work over two decades, I know what a lonely journey this can be, especially from my early work. I knew how much I would have benefited from hearing the stories of a variety of people who had been doing the work longer than I had and in different ways than I had. I felt hearing these stories would have helped me to feel less alone and to know that others have struggled with similar challenges in their work. Also, I felt the stories would have helped to enhance my ethical practice in the work, along with my under-standing of the work and the varying ways it can be and has been done, and would have provided guidance in the ways I might move forward in deepening and focusing my engagement.

There is certainly a danger of misrepresentation and of re-colonization in centring stories of white settler occupiers within the context of decoloni-zation movements. Such movements have been largely initiated and led by Indigenous Peoples, with white settler occupiers having peripheral roles. There is also a danger of reinforcing the hero/saviour complex (Flaherty

2016) deeply embedded within colonial culture, which has held that white European-descended people could save their cultural, racial, and/or geographic others from "savagery," from hell, from poverty, and from uncivilized backwardness. Now we would save them from the effects of the colonial genocide initiated by our collective ancestors and perpetuated by our generation.

It was my sense as the interviewer that there were times those I interviewed were aware of these dangers, and they wished to maintain a stance of humility, sharing information about their work conservatively. There were times that information was shared only after a fair bit of nudging. Some seemed to feel uncomfortable listing examples of their decolonization work and discussing in detail the emotional struggles they encountered in their work. How can these compare with centuries of Indigenous suffering and resistance? *They cannot.* Comparison is not the purpose of this book. Neither is it the purpose to draw attention away from Indigenous resistance and resurgence, which clearly must be centred. It is not my purpose to celebrate Euro-Canadian accomplishments and activists as white saviours emerging out of the ruins of our colonial disaster. Rather, it is my hope that these stories be read as the narratives of those who have imperfectly travelled a challenging road and have been willing to share their mistakes, learnings, insights, and journeys with others who wish to consider, initiate, or deepen their own decolonial engagement. It is hoped that the collective set of lifeways shared in this research provide a glimpse into some of the possibilities and options of how the work can be done, and perhaps how similar mistakes can be avoided. Rather than being seen as appeals for pity, it is hoped that the detailed descriptions of emotional processes be read as spaces that provide guidance and support for settlers struggling with the emotions of the journey so that care of settler emotion need not fall on Indigenous Peoples.

As I prepared to compile the interviewee's stories, I reflected on some inspiring words. For example, Chickadee Richard (personal communication, August 17, 2013) shared, "There are seven billion ways to decolonize. All are valid and valuable, and all form part of the whole." I also had an opportunity to sit with Aimée Craft, Dawnis Kennedy, and Leona Star, and I was gifted with words that offered beautiful ways to approach the narratives. Aimée Craft (personal communication, April 9, 2016) questioned whether people doing good decolonization work need to be strong in all areas of the work, while Dawnis Kennedy (personal communication,

April 9, 2016) explained that some people will be really strong in one area while others will carry a little bit of everything. She said, "That has to do with their walk, what they have, and what they need for the work that they're called to do." Aimée Craft (personal communication, April 9, 2016) reminded me that as I hold up the work of those I interviewed, readers can take away what fits for them, what they need to work on, and/ or what they lack. Leona Star (personal communication, April 9, 2016) added that we're not going to take everything of what we read, but rather bits and pieces for our bundle. Aimée Craft (personal communication, January 10, 2020) expanded on these important themes:

> We are all in constant evolution. That is the beauty of how we tell stories to ourselves and to others, for ourselves and for others. We tell them not so much to recount a truth or a fact, but rather to be of service. We tell them so that the listener can take what they need from the story. In fact, Elders will often tell us stories that are an indirect response to a question. They probe us to think beyond the story, to work for the "answer" in the context that we find ourselves in. In many ways it's analogous to the journey (of reasoning through something) being more important than the destination (or answer to the question). It also allows for the journey to continue, for your thinking and learning to evolve. I often think back on stories that I was told when I come to under-stand another aspect of the stories' meanings based on what I am currently experiencing or because of something new that I have learned. In this way, we are constantly carrying with us a suitcase (or bundle) of stories that can help us process, or help us help those around us through, around, or into something.
>
> This is why relational accountability is so important. The story evolves, the person evolves, the context evolves. And this means that we must continue to loop back into the circle of relation-ship, check in, and take responsibility. We are accountable for our contributions to what has been placed into the circle that represents that relationship, as well as to its ripple effects onto other relationships.

Craft's words are a good reminder that although this work has received a great deal of guidance from Indigenous authored literature, and orally from Indigenous scholars and activists, I bear full responsibility for the ways in which I have interpreted and applied this guidance, including any misinterpretations and misrepresentations.

Ultimately, I encourage readers to view the content of these thirteen narratives as points of engagement, and as ways in which particular people, each with their distinct experiences, knowledges, and values, have done some of their work. I encourage readers to pick up what feels important to you and to leave the rest, knowing that some of it may find its usefulness for you in the future, or perhaps not.

CHAPTER 4

MONIQUE WORONIAK

Monique Woroniak and Elizabeth Carlson-Manathara

IDENTITY AND EARLY INFLUENCES

"What is he doing?" eleven-year-old Monique had asked her father when she saw Elijah Harper holding up a feather on CBC news, blocking the Meech Lake Accord. Monique says,

> I didn't understand how he was alive, because I thought all "Indians" had died. The only other people that my father could point to who were Indigenous and who were alive were the individuals that we drove past when we went to go visit my grandmother on Boyd, which is off of North Main.... Until that point, [to me] all Indigenous people were dead, and then at that point, there was Elijah Harper who was alive, and individuals who were having a very difficult time on Main Street.

Monique's elementary school education had depicted Indigenous Peoples as living in the 1800s, and her experience as a child demonstrated that

> society is not set up for an Indigenous person and [a] non-Indigenous person to have a friendship, it's just not. It's not supportive in that way.... [There are] sets of privileges, and sometimes geographic distance, and not-shared histories.... I grew up in a place where it was ensured that I would never see anybody Indigenous, or, at least that I knew were.

Monique, now in her thirties, is a settler Canadian woman of Ukrainian and French ancestry who was born and raised in Winnipeg. The daughter of a teacher-librarian and a Canada Post worker, Monique grew up in a working-class family whose ancestors had been farmers in Canada, struggling in relative poverty with little education. Monique's family socialization taught her that "if you work really hard, the things you achieve are what you deserve," which she refers to as her *hard work* and *you deserve it* baggage.

LEARNING

Her interest in Canadian history and politics would lead Monique to do undergraduate work in political studies with most of her electives in Native studies, because she "knew enough as an eighteen-year-old to know ... you weren't going to understand anything about Canada unless you understood something about that." As she learned about Treaty Land Entitlement, the Royal Commission on Aboriginal Peoples, and read more, Monique began to feel angry at the public education system of her youth. She was "somebody who liked information, so [she] was just angry at not having been told the full picture." Monique also began to realize that rather than simply deserving their status because of hard work, her family had benefited from being on and working "land that, of course, was effectively stolen from other people." Later, she would understand that her *hard work* and *you deserve it* baggage "makes no sense ... because I see members of the [Indigenous] community work so incredibly hard, and don't have the things I have." By the time Monique went to graduate school in order to become a librarian, it had become clear to her that her career would be infused with Indigenous solidarity work. When she returned to Winnipeg, she found a position in the public library system that allowed her to work directly with the Indigenous community.

SOLIDARITY WORK AND CONTINUED LEARNING

Monique feels that her solidarity work began in 2012, when she began to hear about and attend memorial events, vigils, and community gatherings related to missing and murdered Indigenous women. Monique says, "I knew from the beginning that my affinity would be around solidarity work with Indigenous women. That's sort of the bedrock for all of this for me." Attending gatherings of "community members coming together around honouring their missing sisters and wives and friends" made a big impression on Monique, who reflects:

I remember being witness to just astonishing strength and bravery. I have no reference point for that kind of strength in my own life, even though I thought my own personal family has been through a lot. I just had no reference point for what these women had been through and how generous they were with inviting others in.

Monique would show up at events, introduce herself, and offer to help. She would look for a moment when she could approach someone, and she might say, "My name is Monique, and I know so and so," sharing her response to the event. She'd say, "If you see me around and you see something that I can do to help, please let me know." She was surprised and grateful when her offers eventually led to invitations and opportunities to assist with the planning and support of events and initiatives, opportunities that were precious to her. She would help with logistics, material support, and with getting the word out; all within her skill set and knowledge base. At such events, people need to be fed and things need to be carried around — all things she could help with so that event leaders would be able concentrate on other things. Monique's efforts meant that she was exposed to "large amounts of pain and people that have been through just really horrendous stuff." She listened to and witnessed this pain. Her deepening solidarity work with Indigenous women brought about a new wave of anger about the apartheid she experienced as a child:

I just think [about] all these people that I've missed out on — that maybe I could've met different kinds of people. It's like this whole swath of society was not there for me. So mostly I was angry, and I still am, depending on the day.

Monique has come to see her work as connected to relationships, which "make everything possible." With the advent of the Idle No More movement, her circle of relationships widened:

Everyone's sort of figuring each other out — who's going to do what, and trying to get to know each other on a personal level at least a bit because it makes the work easier and also more joyful. That was my approach around Idle No More — and it was pretty easy in terms of being open to listening to what people were asking that you do, because everything happened so quickly. All of a sudden a round dance was called in and so there were ways to help, and then, something else was called so there were ways to help with that.

Monique says, "January 28, 2013 — I'll never forget that. I was just really honoured to be asked to speak at the Leg[islature] at one of the round dances." Her work has also involved pushing information out into the community through social media, using her librarian/information skills to put together educational resources for the Idle No More Manitoba website, responding to information requests, and working on an educational website for settlers.

In addition to Monique's affinity for history, she carries gifts that have served her in her work. She has a "helping personality" and hates to see people in pain, although she is conscious to not try to fix or solve something or operate out of a "white savior complex." She is also "generally very curious about people" and likes to hear and share stories. Monique also loves literature, books, and writers. She says, "We're in a Golden age for Indigenous authors being published, so you learn a whole other set of stories from fiction and poetry and other work." Monique also says,

> I like organizing things, I like things to be in order. I'm a librarian, so to the extent that pieces have been needed at certain moments, certain individuals in the community have come to see me as somebody that can help out with logistics and maybe getting something done quickly, or research — that kind of thing. I care about children very much, that's something I see as a fundamental priority as a movement — finding out ways we can support families.

Monique thinks about the children who attend events and actions and has hope that what they learn by attending events might enable them to create a different reality in the future.

A focus on "the land [I'm] living on now and who lived there before, and what exactly transpired to make it so that they are not living here now in the ways in which they did previously" has anchored Monique's work. She says, "I can't separate the work in the movement from that, because so much of the oppression that's going on today, and what was wrought upon Indigenous people historically, was about displacing them off of the land." Monique emphasizes,

> I don't see how anybody can do Indigenous solidarity work and

not be asking those questions about the history and learning about it. Because what we're doing every day in the work is we're interacting with the descendants of the people who were here.... They're here because their ancestors made it through enormous obstacles. It's astonishing! And now we have these fellow community members.

Monique has thought frequently about her relationship to the displacement of Indigenous Peoples:

> Whatever flier made its way to the Ukraine that got someone on a boat, saying that there's free land in Canada for whoever wanted to work it — they worked their butts off, fine. No one's going to say they didn't, but they were able to do that on land that was effectively stolen from other people. So, now I'm here, four or five generations later, and still have my nice little parcel of land I'm living on. It's a very difficult thing to reconcile.

Monique discovered that she lives on land that is very near the borders of Rooster Town, "a primarily Métis community that was here from the early 1900s to the late 1950s, and then was forcibly removed and displaced by the municipal government." Monique acknowledges, "It really localized it for me." She says,

> For me, the next step of all of this is what to do with that actuality.... All of it's linked back to reading that Treaty, and reading Treaty histories, knowing more and more about the histories of the Métis populations that lived on those lands, and talking to people.... I think it helps inform some specific choices on what to focus on or not.

For Monique, solidarity work involves listening, asking questions, and taking direction through "projects or ideas that come from Indigenous Peoples themselves." She states,

> There's all kinds of non-Indigenous activists that can think up a hundred ideas to do — we could blockade over here, we could demonstrate in front of this building, we could throw this potluck, we could bring in this speaker. And it's not to say that they're bad ideas, but place and person matters in this. I think what works is

supporting the ideas that are already in the [Indigenous] community and that are coming out of the [Indigenous] community.

It is an "extraordinary amount of listening" that is required, Monique explains:

> White non-Indigenous people are generally not socialized to be quiet ... I think it has to start there, whether you listen by reading a lot of things, that's a way of listening — choosing to read things that you wouldn't normally read. Or whether it's when you're actually in spaces with Indigenous Peoples and you listen.... And you listen to the broad range. I think it's a very natural thing to want to hear those Indigenous voices that you feel you have more of an affinity with, then you don't really listen as much to the other ones. I find myself guilty of this at times, hear[ing] an Indigenous individual advocating for a particular choice, cause, or decision that is not where my politics are at and doesn't feel good to me as an individual. I just think it's really important to listen to that and understand where that's coming from.... When it comes to the Indigenous community, I just think that there's just been too much silencing, and whenever I've chosen to not listen to something, it inevitably ends up feeling wrong later, maybe [I] missed some information that would've been good to know. I think that listening and keeping an open mind, particularly if you're someone that comes in with a set of politics or passion for your own politics.

Monique asks for direction in her work, "and if people say, 'Oh, no, you're helping, you make your decision about how you'd like to do it, you just need to get that done,' great, that's [her] direction." Other times, "there's very specific direction, not just related to cultural Protocols, [but] related to strategy." Monique says, "Another way of listening is to ask questions." She asks about anything, from what will be most helpful to how to sit during a ceremony. She says, "[It's] never gone wrong, and it goes back to the generosity, you immediately get an answer — 'We could really just use 100 plates,' or 'Monique, just tap into your heart.'" Monique explains, "It always ends up in a better place. As soon as you stop asking questions, everything falls apart. That's been my experience."

Monique believes it is a responsibility of white non-Indigenous allies to be involved in educating the Canadian public. This, she says "is a massive, massive project, and it involves everything from mainstream lobbying, policy work, and getting curriculum changed, to some really in-your-face street interactions around issues as they come up." She says, "I think [education is] the key issue. I think after that, everything else starts falling into place, but it's impossible without it … I just don't see how it moves forward without it."

Monique has encountered a few areas of struggle in her solidarity work. Although her book learning taught her that going into a solidarity situation and trying to control things in the way she was socialized to do "is just replicating the type of behaviour that [Indigenous people have] suffered under for generations," giving up control is not always easy for her. She says,

> I definitely got the controlling thing, got it from society and got it from family too.… In my work life, and even as a kid growing up, I tended to be in leadership roles, I think I was doubly socialized, and you think you can see solutions after sitting in a room for an hour. "So those two people need to talk, because they've got it, what they said 20 minutes ago. We should be doing something around that."… As somebody that was always encouraged to see those things and then take it and run with it — you can't do that.

Because she is aware of her personality and her socialization, Monique has been "just very cognizant" of issues of control. Monique explains,

> The way in which it influences my work is that probably in some moments, I think I pull back or hold back when I probably shouldn't have, where I pulled back too much, where there's something I could have offered in a moment, where it would've been okay to leap in a little bit more, that there was enough of a relationship there that it would have been okay. But I find myself sort of second guessing.… I act very differently around some of the organizing when I'm with a group of strictly non-Indigenous women. I'm way more game for putting up my hand and saying "Yeah I'll take that! Give me that chunk, I'll lead it!"

Monique considers,

> There have been other times too, though, that in my head I feel

like — "Oh, it would be better if we did *this* — I think it would work better," and I've failed to pull back on that. And instead, will try to couch it as a suggestion — "Well what if we did *this*?" And if it's not getting picked up by the group, and I'm having what I call a particularly "weak day," because it's a weakness, I'll find myself forty-five minutes later in the meeting just rephrasing the same thing. I know it's just not mine to remember, it's not mine to drive.

Concern about avoiding taking control should not, however, become an excuse for non-Indigenous people to do nothing. According to Monique, this creates the effect "that the Indigenous folks are doing all the heavy lifting, and there is no actual solidarity work happening, because everyone non-Indigenous is just thinking 'Well, it's just not my place.'" Monique also struggles with feeling that she isn't doing enough to create change:

> It's sort of like [I] count up the hours in a week and I think, "Well, how many hours did you spend really?" And I always think it's not enough.... I wish I could quit my job, and then I think, "Well, maybe you *should* quit your job — like why are you scared of quitting your job? You just won't have as much money — well that's a pretty stupid reason to be scared of quitting your job, in relation to the work needing to be done."

Monique has given time, money, and energy to the work. She wants to be able to give materially for a long time and says, "I guess my limit there is I do it as much as I possibly can without depleting things so that I can keep doing it." If the conditions were right and she felt it would significantly advance a revolutionary change, Monique would also consider going to prison for the work. Monique struggles with the idea of giving up land for decolonizing change:

> I'm not brave enough to give up my piece of property here in Winnipeg — it's the honest answer right now. In my head I can see that it's the right thing to do, it makes sense to me when certain segments of the Indigenous population talk not about reconciliation, but about restitution as being the prerequisite to any kind of reconciliation. And part of that restitution being just to give the damn land back.... But if there was a knock on the door half an hour from now and certain parties to Treaty 1 said, "We need this land back now!" I don't know what I would

do…. If somebody came in and said, "We've got an opportunity here to turn over parts of Treaty 1 that were never delivered, and we decided to start with your eight square blocks" — well I'd be terrified, because I'd be without a home.

Exploring creative land sharing solutions and land justice strategies are a next step of learning and growth. For Monique, "the land question … just sort of hangs there." She says,

I think it comes back to that education piece, because what non-Indigenous Canadians could do, if they did understand the issues, they could create situations where they could place enormous amounts of pressure on whoever needed that pressure. I think in most ways, as difficult as it is and as important as it is to get people to even know that residential schools existed and the impacts; this one is a whole other ball game. You need to understand, depending on where you are in the country, the problematic nature of your being on the land that you're on. Especially in a society that prioritizes owning things. Not that all non-Indigenous Canadians own land, because many don't, [but] we still benefit from being able to rent it. That one is not happening without education…. I don't see non-Indigenous Canadians applying any pressure without even understanding what happened in the first place. Then I think after that education piece happens, then we can talk about that and maybe now we're in a position to listen respectfully to what Indigenous people living in [the] Canadian state want.

Monique has heard "stories with individuals having, usually, rural land and giving it back." She explains,

There's a lot of restitution to be done here, so that Indigenous Peoples can enjoy the benefits of a land base that they haven't had for generations. And I have no idea what that would look like. I'm sure there are members of the Indigenous community that have an idea of exactly what that would look like, and I think listening to that en masse as, particularly white, settlers would be a pretty amazing thing. It will look different everywhere in Canada, because again it goes back to that "what happened on the land that you live on?" Restitution leading to reconciliation is going to look different everywhere in Canada, because [of] the nature of the oppression.... The specific nature of the oppression and the specific tools of the oppression played in just slightly and sometimes not-so-slightly different ways across the country. So the reparations, at least in my head, I would think are going to look different.... It looks different depending on where you are — in the North or in the South. We talk about Crown land; we talk about private land. And it really depends on what individual Indigenous communities and nations will push for.... I feel like someday, whoever is living where we are sitting right now, we're going to get to a place where there's a discussion about who should be living here, I think that's where it's headed.... It's going to look different and depending on who's making the claim and what they want. Or maybe it will be more of a resource-sharing thing, or whatever it is Indigenous people want. I do think [the land question] is so fundamental. I mean the wealth of this country is in this land, and we just can't get away from it.

Although Monique has heard messages given in activist circles that guilt is "not a particularly useful emotion," she believes it can be an instructive reminder. Guilt is a reminder that "I'm in this house because someone's not in this house. Colonialism is an ongoing, active form of violence, and I benefit from it." She says, "I don't think it's inappropriate to feel guilty." Rather than eliminating or denying feelings of guilt, Monique is interested in figuring out how to work with it and find balance so as not to get paralyzed or to crumble under the weight of it.

Monique also experiences profound sadness in her work, "especially around issues around missing and murdered women, and certainly residential schools ... disbelief and sadness." "But the flip side of it," she says, "is great hope, because of the fact that horrendous things happen, and the community remains strong and focused."

In order to be able to continue over the long haul, Monique finds that there are periods when she has had to do a bit less — especially when she is having a tough time in other areas of her life. She receives the support of her long-time activist partner. She feels that she has gotten back so much more than she has given in her solidarity work. Hearing Indigenous women speak "so clearly and so bravely about things that they had been through" has given Monique "more courage or sense of urgency around being honest with things that [she] had been through in [her] life." The work has also gifted her with the ability to give up control, and she has seen benefits when she has let go a bit.

Monique's vision of the just future she is working towards is one in which Indigenous voices are at the centre, leading and sharing. She can't see justice without "some kind of mass return of lands," and without the revitalization and resurgence of a diversity and range of Indigenous governance structures. It is a future in which the environment is privileged over development, and the relationships between Indigenous and non-Indigenous people happen on the terms of Indigenous communities. Monique has been told that if non-Indigenous Manitobans are able to "come to the table with really open hearts and curious minds and a lot of kindness, knowing some good facts and a good sense of history," there would be a place for them. Whatever process leads to this just future, Monique believes it has to go beyond the official leadership and "be born out of the very, very Grassroots, of the most Grassroots level."

Monique is involved in her work because of the injustices she sees. She feels that it is easy for well-meaning non-Indigenous people to be insulated from seeing the injustice and to not be motivated to action. Relationships with Indigenous Peoples also motivate her. She says,

> Unless you have relationships with people, and those people matter to you, you don't really have a sense of how wrong it is … when there's something that unjust, that wrong, happening to somebody they care about, they're motivated to do something.

When Monique learns more about the specifics of history, "those individual stories and instances of what happened," as opposed to "just knowing that the land was stolen in general," "it just fuels that motivation fire." Monique aspires to do work "for the Indigenous Peoples … for their ancestors, and what happened to them and what they were prevented from having, and for all these children that are to come." Monique looks forward to a day when non-Indigenous people have deep, solid relationships with the First Peoples of this land. Her work is also for the future generations in her family: "I want them to grow up in a land that looks different than the one I grew up in … and that's going to be a great thing for everybody."

POSTSCRIPT, 2019

Several years have passed since Liz and I spent an evening and subsequent afternoon talking. It is late 2019 as I write and the oppressions that spring from settler colonialism and plant themselves wherever there is land, wherever there are Indigenous Peoples, continue to thrive. In some ways, and in a direct response to Indigenous Peoples' resistance, they have grown deeper roots.

Because of this I am both more and less hopeful than I was at the time of the interview. I never fully trusted the concept of reconciliation and particularly not a process driven by the needs of the Canadian state and its levels of settler government. But closing in on five years from the release of *The Final Report of the Truth and Reconciliation Commission of Canada*, and also after *The Final Report of the National Inquiry into Missing and Murdered Indigenous Women and Girls*, I trust the reconciliation project not one bit. It is a Canadian project, centred on the needs of the Canadian state in general, and the most privileged of its settler populations in particular.

In this interview I expressed that I wanted to be involved in Indigenous solidarity work for the "long haul." I remember saying this, remember thinking it, and remember thinking how pauses would likely be necessary to keep up the work and relationships for as long as I would be here. I know now that I did not understand just how hard it would be to stay active. The lessons I am still learning come from the urgent echoes of Indigenous voices I worked hard to listen to earlier this decade.

Land and courage; art and expression; honesty and no shortcuts; humility and justice — at all costs. Those voices are still here, mixed in with new community voices, and are insisting: keep your promises.

CHAPTER 5

MURRAY ANGUS

Murray Angus and Elizabeth Carlson-Manathara

IDENTITY AND EARLY INFLUENCES

Murray Angus is a fifth-generation Canadian whose Scottish ancestors populated lands after the signing of Treaties in southern Ontario. "They were living on treated land," Murray says, and "when the kids got bigger, they wanted their own land, so there was a subsequent migration, my grandfather, out to Manitoba." There they established the town of Angusville. Murray himself grew up in the only white family that lived on the reserve side of the river on the outskirts of Thunder Bay, Ontario, in a small log cabin with no running water. He says,

> My neighbours were all the people on the reserve, Fort William
> First Nation. Those are the people I grew up with, as much as I
> grew up with people in the white town. And that was probably
> one of the two most formative things shaping my life, because as
> I grew up, I had one foot in both worlds, literally, daily — back
> and forth, and I fit into both.

As a child, Murray's only neighbours were a nearby family on the reserve:

> They had eleven kids and their house was teeming, but there
> was always room for me. So that was my other home. I grew up
> mostly with three of the oldest boys.

Murray reflects on the way they had grown up with the land. He says,

> It was the best place in the world to have grown up. We had Lake
> Superior in front of us and miles and miles of bush behind us, all
> reserve land. We lived *on that land*. Our footprints were on *that
> particular place*, and I can go back there and I walk through the

area, and run my hand over it because there's a memory behind every rock that sticks out of the ground, and every tree, literally. I've never had friendships that were so integrated with the land. When one of those friends passed away a few years ago, it made me reflect on the fact that we had all become who we were because of what we had done on that land, and because of our relationship to it. A wonderful thing to realize. It gave me a glimpse into what people must feel who live their entire lives, and have for generations lived in relationship to a certain piece of land. It was that first experience of my own, of seeing how it could be impossible to have an identity that is separate from that piece of land. It was on that land and out of that land that we became the people we were, and I love that. I can still go back there and walk through it and stand on the place where my own father died ... my roots go really deep in that place.

Murray credits his mother for his most important foundational values. He says,

On the surface, she was the most compliant, deferential person to all around her, unless her core principles were at stake. One of the principles that I saw her live out most clearly was that people deserve to be treated with equal respect, irrespective of their background.... That left a deep impression on me. When there was a difficult decision to be made, she would not base her response on what would be best for her; rather, she acted on the basis of what she felt was the right thing to do, based on her beliefs and her faith.

As he was growing up, Murray absorbed attitudes from the dominant white society around him. He says, "Even before we've had our own experiences in life, our attitudes are shaped by the world around us." Growing up in northwestern Ontario culture, "soaked in racism," Murray found

there were no messages in my white society that carried as much weight in terms of the number of places you heard it from, [and] the consistency of the message, than messages about Indians.... What were the messages? There were two. One is *Indians are at the bottom.* Well, you could just look around you and that was verifiable, economically and socially.... They were noticeably living in poorer conditions than people across the river in the city.… But the second message was *That's where they deserve to be.* That was embedded in everything, and it was in the air.… You would inhale it. You couldn't not inhale it if you were white. There was consensus on that point. *Indians were on the bottom, and that's where they deserve to be.* They were less valuable, that's the inference.

The difference for Murray, was that at the same time as he was getting these messages from his own white society, he was having his own real-life experiences of people and families on the reserve. He says, "As I began to tune into things in the world, going back and forth between the reserve and white community every day, I became very conscious of the fact that those messages about Indians in my white world didn't square with my experience."

Murray was not unaffected by the racism around him, however. Like other children, he engaged in racial and ethnic jokes and put-downs and rarely challenged his white peers. At that stage in his life, it was his primary goal to blend in and belong. He says, "There would be occasions when, in my relationships with people on the reserve, I would see the white attitudes coming out in me … and it would make me feel horrible." He recalls being ashamed as a middle school student to be on the "Indian school bus," to the point where he would wait for the bus on the "far end of the block, away from the school." He wouldn't invite his white friends home. He says, "I couldn't bring the two worlds together just because I was conscious of it, and it didn't meet the standards of the white society." The internal and external conflicts waged. Murray says,

Sooner or later, something had to give. The messages I was getting in my white society, i.e., that "Indians aren't worth as much as us," was something that I just couldn't buy into.… I knew people too much for that to be true. I respected and cared for my friends on the reserve, and it offended me that they were being looked down upon. And I remember reaching a crisis point where I had to personally make a decision for myself: What am I going to believe here? Am I going to trust my own experience or am I going to concede to all those powerful messages that were dominant in my white society?

Murray remembers the moment when he decided, "I'm going to trust my experience here, over and against all the messages that [are] coming at me from my white world."

LEARNING AND EARLY ACTIVISM

Murray sees this moment as "the beginning of [his] critical consciousness," which sent him on a ten-year journey of seeking answers for himself about the messages in his society: "Why are those messages out there? Why are they pervasive? Why are they consistent? Why are they being perpetuated?" Another major turning point for Murray in becoming an activist occurred in 1973, when he reflected on the question, "What was the attitude of people in my white world, northwestern Ontario, towards the Treaties?" The people of Fort William First Nation had signed the Robinson-Superior Treaty in 1850, which "locked them in and set in place a degree of marginalization that they were still living out." Murray wondered how people in his own society "account for [themselves] in relation to that." He saw that Treaties represented our "one kick at the can" as a society to define a just relationship with Indigenous Peoples. He says,

> Nobody in the white community would ever pretend that the Indians had gotten a good deal in that Treaty. People were willing to admit that we'd gotten the best of them, but it was something that had been done in the past, and so it wasn't on us, not on our hands. So yes, we're benefiting today, but we can't do anything about it because that was previous generations. The inference was that, if a Treaty was being done today, we would do it differently, and more fairly. That was how people absolved themselves of guilt and any kind of societal accountability for the relationship that was forged with the Treaty.

However, for Murray, this stance was "blown totally out of the water" when

> Robert Bourassa, in 1971 announced the project of the century in Quebec — to dam up the rivers into James Bay, flood vast areas, generate hydroelectricity, [and] sell it to the States. The Cree that were going to be flooded weren't even told — they heard about it on the radio. And that just taught me something so important. *In our time, we'd do it again.* And that was all the proof that anybody

would need. It's one thing to say people don't matter. It's another thing to say people don't even friggen exist. That's the way that the Cree were handled, as if they weren't even there. How much more racist can a society get?... It still outrages me just to recall that, and our society was going to prove no better than people that sold the Treaties 100 years earlier.

Murray watched the "explosion of oil and gas exploration in the western Arctic," major plans for development in Canada's North in the 1970s, and the fact that nobody was talking with the Indigenous people out there. "So, I became an activist in the '70s as a student," says Murray. He says, "Back in '75, '76, we had a local group here in Ottawa that was formed just to hold public meetings and meet with MPs, just representing the local constituents." His first summer job was working for the Canadian Association in Support of Native Peoples (CASNP), doing research and assisting with lobbying during the Mackenzie Valley Pipeline Inquiry.

When Murray went back to school, he used his degrees as a vehicle to continue to work through and find answers to his core questions. While working on a master's in religious studies at Carleton, he took on his church, unpacking his own faith tradition in a critical bent. After completing this degree, Murray began a master of social work program at Carleton and focused on the federal government's Land Claims Policy of 1973. He knew "the relationships forged in Treaties or land claim agreements last forever," and Murray did not like the way "mainstream Canadian society had been choosing to deal with the people it encounters in the northern parts of the country that have not been treatied." He was "piecing together how the world worked to account for *why Indians were at the bottom and kept there*," and his search for answers revealed, "those values and those attitudes towards Indians couldn't be sustained unless somebody was benefiting from their continuation." He says, "If we think of some people as less valuable than ourselves, then their interests are less important, their needs are less important." This means "we can behave towards them in ways that we would not find acceptable towards people like ourselves." Murray concluded,

That's the payoff for sustaining those kinds of attitudes toward people. It gives us licence to abuse them economically, cultur-ally.... That's the core of it, the unethical core. And what does that translate into? Land. Resources. We can take from them because

they're not as important as we are. That gives us our moral permission. Well, that's [a] pretty self-serving morality. But it allows
us to do it.... And we need those resources — we'll decide. And
that provides a distorted moral justification. It's not said explicitly
in those terms, but that's what those attitudes create room to do.

Murray connected this unethical core and "the relationship between the
corporate world and the government's function to create the conditions
that ensure a profitable private sector." He says, "In a capitalist economy,
that's what you do. You give yourself over to that as the engine for society,
and you have to ensure that it has what it needs."

DECOLONIZATION WORK AND CONTINUED LEARNING

Much of Murray's decolonization work has occurred within the context
of his thirty-year career as a co-founder and long-time staff member of
Nunavut Sivuniksavut (NS), an Ottawa-based college program that serves
Inuit youth. During his time working for the CASNP, Murray had contact
with Inuit leaders, and he had intentionally followed development and
land claim issues related to the Inuit, Dene, and Yukon First Nations. In
1981, he was hired by Peter Ittinuar, the first Inuk member of Parliament,
and he attended meetings on Parliament Hill and sat in on land claims
negotiations concerning the Inuit. He did work supporting land claims
because he sees them as a primary point of leverage where "Aboriginal
people get to negotiate their relationship to the rest of the country." It
has to be done right, Murray says, "in a way that treats people with great
respect, honours the fact that they have their relationship with the land,
and it's not just ours to exploit." He explains,

> It's one of those places where I will do what I can to stand in the
> way of my own government doing something that I disagree
> with, that will intentionally or effectively end up marginalizing
> people. Because you can't go back. That's the story of land claims
> and Treaties, you can't redo them.

Soon after he left his position with Peter Ittinuar, Murray was approached
to teach young Inuit and prepare them to negotiate and implement land
claims, work that would evolve into the Nunavut Sivuniksavut program.
At NS, Murray says,

We're not neutral, we're very clear on that. The whole function of what we do is to affirm the Inuit experience historically, politically, economically — and that's always satisfying, because that's what I want. I want Canada to understand that point of view. We're in a situation where we can affirm it for young Inuit, because they grow up in a world that's quite ambivalent about the legitimacy of their own point of view.... They leave NS with renewed confidence that their own experiences and viewpoints matter ... and they'll never look back, they'll never back down. And that to me is decolonization, where they own their own life, their own story, and they leave determined to keep making their own story.... They understand their own experience of colonialism and appreciate the efforts [of] the previous generation to react to that history of colonialism in the Arctic ... negotiating a land claim settlement — the largest in Canadian history — negotiating a new political territory for themselves, negotiating Aboriginal rights in the constitution, negotiating space on the satellite to be able to broadcast television in their own language. What's been accomplished in one generation has been, in my view, one of the most impressive stories in Canadian history ... where Inuit as a whole have come, in terms of all of the successive waves of Europeans that have come into the North — beginning with explorers and whalers, and missionaries, traders, RCMP, the military, government administration — and all the ways that those outsiders have ended up taking away power of one kind or another from people themselves.... This was the last generation that was born on the land in igloos, after the Second World War. But they took on the Canadian system and decolonized it. They pushed back.

Nunavut Sivuniksavut helps "young Inuit learn about the dominant society so that they're more equipped to negotiate the relationship with it that they want." It also offers young people just out of high school a year of personal and collective identity formation and empowerment. They learn about Inuit political organizing in the face of colonization. Murray says, "When the land was threatened, people started acting. They just felt they had to act because the land was everything."

NS students have been involved in cultural performances, attend standing committees to support Inuit organizations on Parliament Hill, and engage in counter-demonstrations when animal rights groups do not take into account Indigenous hunting rights and practices. After completing the eight-month program they go home "determined to contribute in one way or another to the Nunavut project." "They're so passionate about home and their own territory because they're so impressed with their own people," says Murray. He has lived and breathed the NS program. He says, "Virtually all my energy has been confined to the Inuit world and to this program in particular." Murray was named to the Order of Canada in 2009 "for his varied contributions to building awareness and respect for Canada's Native people and their traditions, and for the role he has played in empowering Inuit youth as founder of Nunavut Sivuniksavut."

Murray's work has also involved educating others through his writing and church work. In 1991, he published a book, *And the Last Shall be First: Native Policy in an Era of Cutbacks*. He has also written a number of articles, including two pieces published in the book *Nation to Nation: Aboriginal Sovereignty and the Future of Canada* (Bird, Land, and Murray 2002). Now a member of the United Church and one of the most progressive congregations in Ottawa, Murray is involved with the Right Relations Group. This group works to raise consciousness among the congregation in an ongoing way through films, speakers, and literature. They network with other churches, connect with and support TRC events, and raise funds for justice initiatives. They "keep each other informed about things going on, opportunities for relationship building, and participation in Aboriginal events, lobbying, and education."

Murray believes Euro-Canadian people have a responsibility "to recognize [racism] within ourselves and be responsible for managing it." In doing his work, Murray has learned to "listen more than talk." This is difficult for Euro-Canadians because "we're so full of answers before anybody asks us the question." Murray points out, "We're very good at filling space, that's our cultural norm." "A certain humility can go a hell of a long way in giving people space," Murray says, "If you want to be in a relationship that rights the balance, just shut up for a while." He emphasizes, "It's relationship, it's not management." Murray believes that, as a society, listening to Indigenous Peoples, "who actually have a relationship with the land," is crucial to our survival.

During his early days as an activist, Murray observed that in solidarity groups there seemed to be white people who did not like their own culture, did not like their own identity, wanted to be like Indigenous people, and wanted to appropriate Indigenous cultures for themselves. Murray was uncomfortable with them as "people who don't know, or like, who they are." He believes in white people owning who they are and using their power to create change. He says,

> If you're a middle-class white guy, use your power! It's *your* government! Don't try to be an Indian, they don't need it! That's meeting your own need.... White should be white. I just think we have to recognize where we fit in the system and deploy our resources and our power to the greatest effect.... Governments listen to people like me more than many other people. Don't throw away your power, own who you are. Use it to effect the change that you want.

Having worked for most of his life with the NS program, Murray wonders whether his views have narrowed. He has "the ultimate best of both worlds ... circumstances that are quite luxurious, while still doing something that [he believes] is making a difference." He says, "I'm extremely thankful for that, but it has made me wonder at times how much of an activist I am anymore, and just what is the impact of being so bloody comfortable." He asks himself, "Would I be doing things differently out there in the world, taking more chances, having a more critical view of things than I currently do?" and, "Has the comfort associated with this career reduced my motivation to do more radical things?" In the early years of the program, he and his colleague did make sacrifices, working twenty-four hours a day and taking home low wages so as not to look like they were "feathering [their] own nest." But later, when NS was incorporated and affiliated with Algonquin College, they no longer had control of their salaries and the pay scale shot up. Now, Murray feels he's "not being tested very much in terms of sacrifice." Murray wonders what things will look like when he retires soon and has less income and more time.

New developments on the land where he grew up have caused reflection for Murray. In 1919 there had been a transaction that led to a strip of Fort William First Nation lands being turned into city-owned parkland. Cottagers, including his family, were allowed to lease some of this land. These cottages are now being knocked down and the leases closed off, and the band may be taking steps to reclaim the land. Murray would be happy to see it returned. However, he says,

> If I was still living there, I can't say for sure I wouldn't have mixed

feelings about that. Because I know the people on the reserve, it wouldn't be as threatening ... but still, it would mean losing control, which is, well, that's the way it should be. So, I won't be there to be in that kind of dynamic, but I can't begrudge it. That should be how it is.

One of Murray's big regrets is not having learned Inuktitut. He says, "My whole work was a reaction to how much my society was running over them, intruding into every nook and cranny of their society." He thought, "One of their few remaining safe havens, where they can have privacy and keep us out, is language." Murray says, "Years later, I had to humbly accept that I was wrong," because "people have more respect for outsiders that want to make the effort to come inside their world and not just intrude on it without knowing it." He says,

> If I had been smarter and more respectful, I would've made every effort to pick up the language, because I could've, every day I was with people who spoke it. That was laziness on my part, that was not showing the kind of effort and kind of respect that a good person would've done.

Anger continues to be a motivating factor for Murray's work. He says,

> It's my great lasting motivator.... That's what has spurred me on — a sense of outrage at the way my own society treats Indigenous people, both in terms of attitudes and behaviour. And how our government's actions reflect that. I just find it outrageous for me, in terms of my own sense of fairness. So that has never really left me as my reason for being involved.

One of the most painful aspects of Murray's journey has been finding racism in himself. He says, "It was always one of those instances that you wish you could just rewind the tape." Although it would "hurt like hell," he has been "able to be forgiving of [himself]" because he believes racism is in all Euro-Canadians and "that's what we inhale from the moment of birth." But mostly, Murray's work has been characterized by passion for the content of the courses they teach at NS and deep satisfaction about the work they do and the impact it has on Inuit youth. He says,

> If you want a reason for hoping for the future, you can just pay

attention to what some of these young people are doing, just exuding talent ... doing wonderful, amazing things, and they're doing it very purposefully, with a full understanding of the historical context for it.

Murray's vision for the future is a just situation in the context of Nunavut. His work is "motivated by that original belief that we're all equal in the eyes of God." When he sees Indigenous Peoples "being treated as less equal than others," he takes spiritual offence. Murray says, "I'll stand against that every day of my life ... I can't fix that, but I can use my life to stand against it."

CHAPTER 6

STEVE HEINRICHS

Steve Heinrichs and Elizabeth Carlson-Manathara

IDENTITY AND EARLY INFLUENCES

Steve Heinrichs is a thirty-nine-year-old Russian Mennonite, white set-tler, Canadian husband and father who was born and raised on unceded Coast Salish Territory in a part of Vancouver that was heavily populated by Euro- and Asian-Canadian peoples. As a child, Steve remembers staring out onto an ocean inlet, wondering about peoples who were there before him, with little thought about living Indigenous Peoples. When he asked about Indigenous Peoples, "there were no responses around the table," and Steve says, "The news didn't talk about Indigenous Peoples unless it was a fishing controversy in B.C., or a blockade, or the Gustafsen Lake reclama-tion when I was a teenager." Steve would listen to family conversations and was troubled by aspects of his family's history, particularly the *Mennonite myth* that said, "We were a persecuted people that went to lands that were empty, and we were a blessing to the larger community there because we were hard-working and we were able to create breadbasket farmland for people." When Steve asked, "But who was there when we went into those spaces?" his grandparents seemed to take the attitude of "We don't go there." Steve now lives in Winnipeg, Manitoba: Treaty 1 Territory on the traditional lands of the Anishinaabe, Cree, and Dakota Peoples, and homeland of the Métis Nation. He is a "first generation immigrant kid," a human being, and a Treaty person with Treaty responsibilities. He works with Mennonite Church Canada as the Indigenous-settler relations direc-tor and is a "follower of the Jesus way."

LEARNING AND EARLY ACTIVISM

Steve has been grappling with the realities of colonialism in Canada for over ten years. An early point of transformation in this journey was being taught by Professor Dave Diewart in seminary, who raised issues of settler colonialism with colleagues and students. Dave operated a 'for-the-community space' in the Downtown Eastside where, among other things, he held classes connecting Biblical traditions to international and Canadian realities of genocide and colonialism, inviting grassroots Indigenous activists and settler allies to present in his class. Steve says, "For a bunch of evangelical Christian kids ... it was earth-shaking stuff."

When Steve began working with Palestinian Muslims through Christian Peacemaker Teams, something he would do for several weeks every winter for six years, he was exposed to "language and frameworks that [he'd] never heard before coming out of [his] Christian milieu, like *undoing racism* [and] *anti-oppression*." Steve says, "I don't know how anyone can do work in the West Bank, where you're dealing with concrete realities of settler takeover of Indigenous people's lands, and not have their eyes open to realities in other places." He recalls being with "Palestinian shepherds who were trying to protect their land from being expropriated by armed Jewish settlers with AK-47s" and being struck with the thought:

> This is B.C.! Sure, we can't map everything from one situation onto another, but that's what happened in this British Columbus land that I name as home. It was the politics of domination and violent expropriation that removed peoples from their lands, and that's what's happened in this place that I call home.

In 2005, Steve and his partner, Ann, became more intentional about learning the colonial history of Canada. In this time they also became "the proud parents of this beautiful Stó:lō girl [Abby]." Upon adopting Abby, Steve and Ann determined that,

> in order to be good parents to Abby, we knew we had to go on a journey, that this was going to be a life's work of building relation-ships. We couldn't be parents to a Native child if we didn't have peers around us who are Indigenous who could speak into our own lives, who could be aunties and uncles and friends to Abby.

They relocated to northern B.C., and Steve took a job as a pastor in a small, mostly white mining community in Yinka Dene Territory that was located right next to a First Nation reserve. The neighbouring Indigenous community welcomed Steve's attempts to build relationships, and Steve came wanting to "learn the history and learn how I can be a good neighbour." His work revealed the blatant face of racism in some of his white parishioners, many of whom treated the handful of Indigenous parishioners differently, adhering to "dirty Indian" racist stereotypes, and even making violent statements such as "Custer had the right idea, we should just get rid of them all." Steve came to realize that most parishioners did not know "the history of why our relationships were like they were." They observed "alarming socioeconomic factors [common in] Indigenous communities," but had no idea what was causing these and had no desire to learn.

Steve's work in northern B.C. was complex, and he made mistakes as he sought to navigate difficult terrain. The church partnered with young adults from Vancouver who wanted to "serve the Native community" by leading Vacation Bible School programs for Indigenous youth and children. Worried about some parallels with residential school dynamics, Steve sought guidance from the (largely self-professed Christian) Indigenous community. When the community expressed its desire for the program to continue, Steve was troubled by the dynamic of "young, white Christian folks hanging out with even younger brown children doing basically an evangelization program." Steve wrestled (and continues to wrestle) with how to "honour Indigenous Peoples and communities that name themselves as Christian, recognizing the fact that many wouldn't, if it wasn't for the heavy hand of colonialism." In the end, Steve arranged that the white teens from Vancouver spend their afternoons "with the Elders, hearing their stories, watching documentary videos such as *Muffins for Granny* ... hearing the story of Babine Lake First Nation — how they were dispossessed of language, culture, lands." Steve's biggest regret of that experience was that he had neglected to invite the Indigenous parishioners, Elders, and parents to be a fuller part of the children's programming, resulting in the reification of the colonial pattern of predominantly white leadership. At times, Steve tried too hard and led in a way that exemplified his stereotypes of what Indigenous people would want, rather than following their lead. When Steve sought to bring together Indigenous and non-Indigenous men to hear each other's stories over breakfast, he played Indigenous flute music through a sound system and, on one occasion, led the circle in a song about the Creator using a drum. While some appreciated his efforts to embrace Indigenous culture, others gently teased him: "This is great music! I feel like I'm back in rehab," or "You're more Indian than us!" Steve realized this was their way of saying:

> Just take us where we're at. Respect us where we're at. So some of us like to wear cowboy hats and cowboy boots, and we listen to Johnny Cash, and we like Pentecostal Christianity, and we don't do traditional stuff right now ... and we're still Indians, right?

DECOLONIZATION WORK AND CONTINUED LEARNING

Steve views his work as both decolonization and Treaty relationship work where he seeks renewed relationships with both Indigenous Peoples and with the land. Steve's decolonization journey is largely one of education. He seeks to educate himself, to engage with his family's education process, and to inspire significant pockets of the Mennonite Church community through education that embraces decolonization and relationships of solidarity. As the parents of "three kids, two of whom are Indigenous — one Stó:lō, one Nuu-chah-nulth," Steve and Ann work as a family to explore their respective roles and experiences with regards to colonialism. They attend Indigenous-led activist events, expose their children to Indigenous-authored children's books, and engage their children's questions and emotions. This work is "an offering to our kids," saying, "we are taking you seriously, your stories. We are coming to a greater awareness that you two beautiful Indigenous kids would not be in our home if it wasn't for colonialism." Steve and Ann want to learn more about their daughters' communities in order to explore what it means for Abby and Isabelle to grow up Stó:lō and Nuu-chah-nulth. They try "to figure out ways to be in deeper relationship with their birth families ... to do that respectfully and well ... [and get] to know their stories and share their stories with them." As Steve and Ann learn more about their histories as settlers, they "invite Aiden [their biological son] into that so that he can have pride in the good stories that are there, but a deep awareness ... around the stories that are not life-giving." In their process of learning, Steve has discovered that his ancestors and his daughter Abby's ancestors are woven together in a history of dispossession and settlement:

In the 1920s, they were contemplating draining a lake in between Abbotsford and Sardis — Sumas Lake — in order to make farmland.... And the local Stó:lō Peoples were resisting that and saying, "No, this is where we live." They had villages around the lake. They even had homes and fishing sites built on that lake on stilts. And that's where my daughter's great-great-grandparents lived — right on that lake. And so they were dispossessed, removed — no doubt many of them ended up at Coqualeetza Residential School right there in Sardis. And then my family is welcomed in half a generation later to that place by Mennonites who were already there and settled that land in 1929, when there was no lake.

In his current role with the Mennonite Church, Steve aims to include "a critical lens." He says, "That's working on justice pieces ... [and] finding ways to carve out space for Indigenous voices to speak into our work." He raises awareness in the Mennonite community in a number of ways. He has organized learning tours around events such as the Truth and Reconciliation Commission on Indian Residential Schools and has engaged Mennonites in exploring Indigenous theologies and how these can challenge Western Christian traditions. He has supported Indigenous-led actions and engaged in conversations with Survivors of day schools, who were not included in the residential school settlement. Steve's denomination had two day schools in Manitoba, and he found "people were reluctant to talk about it" due to their fears of legal and economic reprisals. After conversations, though, they decided that rather than privileging themselves, they would need to do the right thing and centre Indigenous Peoples by attending gatherings and conferences to learn about the day schools and support movements for reparation.

Steve has worked on producing short educational films specific to the Mennonite community. For instance, he and others accompanied Ovide Mercredi, former Grand Chief of the Assembly of First Nations, and a small delegation to London, England, around the anniversary of the Royal Proclamation to make a statement about recognizing Indigenous sovereignty and jurisdiction over lands. They filmed the journey and created an educational video about Indigenous sovereignty.

Steve aims to deconstruct dominant Mennonite myths and help Mennonites to understand that "we too actually were involved in dispossessing Indigenous Peoples from lands." He says, "I see myself as a facilitator trying to gather people, small pockets from different places, to be present in circles where Indigenous voices are privileged and we can learn, ask questions, and be in this conversation together." Steve helps to mobilize action groups in various churches that focus on growing awareness, attending Idle No More rallies, and building relationships with Indigenous communities. One set of relationships that inspires Steve is the relationship that some Mennonites have cultivated with the Young Chippewayan Cree over a number of years:

> Sometime back in the 1870s, the Dominion Government allotted a piece of land [to the Young Chippewayan Cree as a reserve] just south of Laird, Saskatchewan, and that place had ties to the Young Chippewayan traditionally — there were sacred burial grounds and gathering places there. In the late 1880s ... the Young Chippewayan Cree were looking for food, they were starving, and so they went off to potentially find some of the last remaining buffalo in southeast Saskatchewan. While they were off, the government expropriated that land and gave it to Mennonite settlers.... That story wasn't known to the Mennonite settlers until the 1970s when a friend of mine, Leonard Doell, was trying to nurture relationships with the Young Chippewayan Cree. [He found there was a need to] deal with the concrete land injustice that the Young Chippewayan Cree have experienced and that the Mennonites have actually benefited from.

The two communities built trust and had a covenanting ceremony in the early 2000s, agreeing to work towards healing and concrete land justice. So, a group of Mennonites and Lutherans have raised "some tens of thousands of dollars to do a genealogical survey to support the land claim of the Young Chippewayan Cree." Although "there hasn't been any concrete land transaction that's gone on yet," Steve says, "they're working towards that." Land reparation is "one of the most difficult conversations to have ... the fears are most pronounced because right away they're running to 'Am I going to have to give my land back?'" But Steve sees this work as very hopeful. And there are pockets of people within his church community who will talk about reparations. He says, "I know someone in a community who has fifty acres of land, who is in conversation with Mi'kmaw folk on the East Coast about returning all that land except for half an acre so that he can be in relationship with the people." In 1992, the Mennonite Church had established a "Jubilee Fund based on the Biblical call to redistribute the land." Each year, the fund contributes $5,000 to support the land reclamation efforts of an Indigenous community. For example, recently an Ontario community used the grant to buy a plotter to map out their Traditional Territory.

Through his position with the church, Steve has facilitated the publication of a book and numerous pamphlets, magazines, and study guides. He edits a quarterly magazine called *Intotemak*, which aims to inspire Mennonites to explore "our stories, our history, why we have the relationships we have with host peoples." It extends the conversation beyond "decolonizing relationship[s] with Indigenous communities [to] the land itself." It has contained articles, for instance, about the Enbridge pipeline and about Shoal Lake as Winnipeg's water source. With input from Indigenous and settler peoples, Steve created a *Paths for Peacemaking with Host Peoples* (2015) booklet offering practical how-tos for Christian settlers new in the journey. The book *Buffalo Shout, Salmon Cry* (2013), which Steve edited, brings together Indigenous and settler voices to address settler colonial legacies of fractured Indigenous communities and the fracture of Indigenous Lands, and it takes seriously Indigenous knowledges, bringing "Indigenous ways of knowing and being into the conversation." The study guides Steve develops are intended for small group study, with the hope of leading to action.

Steve has provided leadership towards structural changes within his organization. When he started in his position, it was called Native Ministry. Steve advocated for a change in title to Indigenous–Settler Relations in order to reflect mutuality. Steve was asked to assist with visioning statements for the Mennonite Church Canada, and the board approved wording such as:

> Foster in our church an awareness of Indigenous Peoples and settler identities; that is the history, the problems, and the promise of our relationships both past and present…. Equipping our churches to begin important peace initiatives relating to past and present Christian colonialism of Indigenous nations, for example residential and day schools, [and] the failure to honour covenants and Treaties…. Receiving and seeking ways, as a national church, to be an ambassador of Indigenous-settler reconciliation through the larger church and mainstream society…. Fostering inter-cultural and inter-religious dialogue with Indigenous lifeways, respectfully finding ways to receive good news from traditional

circles so that our Christian faiths can be refined and rooted in this land.

Steve is thankful that his church has been willing to name decolonization and make such changes that may not seem radical to some ears but are fairly unique within the context of church institutions. However, because much of the work Steve is doing with the church is educational, Steve hesitates to see this work as benefiting Indigenous communities. He says, "Until we're at the place where we're really redistributing power and privilege and resources ... we're not there."

Steve's personal passion is "to do more activist kind of front-line work." Issues around "Indigenous Peoples renewing, revitalizing, and regaining jurisdictional control on lands" resonate strongly with Steve. He is inspired by Justice Murray Sinclair's challenge to settlers: "Your responsibility is to repair what was broken, to return what was lost." He hears "so many Indigenous voices saying, 'All this other stuff flows from the land, flows from a relationship with the land.'" He says,

> Within my Christian community we resist that with all our might ... even though we will reap all the economic benefits of that land to the high heavens ... that's where I would like to see my church go more, to animate pockets of non-violent militant Mennonites who are able to support that work.

Steve is also exploring ways to connect with the land in his own personal life. A friend taught him, "You can't love the land unless you actually know the land, and you can't know the land unless you learn from the land and listen to the land." He is learning:

> The stories of a variety of creatures who have called this place home ... what are the Cree and Anishinaabe, Dakota, Métis stories in this place? Getting to know the land via their stories, their lenses ... getting to know the bioregions, the actual diversity of life that's present here. Taking time to be on the land and ask questions — "what is the land saying?"

Steve has been taught by Indigenous friends and Elders to view himself "first as a human being, as a creature in relationship with other creatures before the Creator." He is taught he's interconnected with non-human nations, and that it is important to learn the Treaty relationships of the particular place where he lives. He says, "Leanne Simpson talks about Treaties being made not only by the Anishinaabe and other Indigenous communities and nations, but actually with the fish nations there." Steve says, "This land has a spirituality." He explains,

> When I ride my bike and I go to work, I stop just over Omand's Creek at the bridge there, and I stand and I pray and I listen. And I don't simply ask, "God, what are you saying to me through the land?" I do something which seems very foreign to me — is coming from Indigenous teachers who are telling me, "Ask the water! Ask the river, what's it saying?" And so I'm just trying to be quiet and listen.... So I need to cultivate spiritual disciplines that reconnect me to the land, and I don't know what that all means.... We are so disconnected from the land, especially my people because we've been hopping around from land to land, to land — that's part of our spirituality, we're aliens and strangers. So I feel that disconnection, and many of us settlers do. In our desire to reconnect we screw up a lot of the time.... This feeling of dislocation that settlers generally have and the many different ways that we go into finding roots in these spaces, or conversely to downplay our lack of roots, to numb ourselves to the fact that we are so rootless in these spaces, with our continual moving. I think my soul is impacted by the fact that I don't recognize that I'm in promised space, that stories of beginnings come from these very places.

Steve is quick to acknowledge there is "so much happiness and joy and laughter that comes in the midst of doing this work," and "whole worlds have been opened to me as I've gone on this journey." Nonetheless, his work can also be incredibly difficult. Steve faces anxiety when going to predominantly Indigenous gatherings, and says he often has "to give [himself] a little pep talk: Don't be so insecure, don't be scared, this is good work, and you always find welcome." He believes this reflects not only his introverted personality, but also his worries about messing up. He also gets anxious he says, "when I'm going to my predominantly white church, and I fear the kinds of questions that are going to be asked — that I'm going to be expected to be an expert on Indigenous-settler realities, which is so far from the truth." He says, "In some ways the work that I'm doing cuts against my personality ... [but] it's the right thing to do.... It's not about simply finding your gift, it's that we need to fill gaps as well ... sometimes this work is hard." He says, "There's a bit of a cost to [this work], and you can have more fun and success, and a [higher] salary doing other work." The work "can fracture personal and collective relationships where I'm not as popular as I once was within my own community." Steve admits,

> I feel angry because within even the dominant community that I have, you're seen as a shit disturber, and you're seen as sometimes a troublemaker for trying to narrate a different past and present. It was within my very first month that I took on this job, I was invited to Steinbach to speak at Grace Mennonite Church. They asked me, "[T]ell us about the kind of work that you're doing." And I decided that instead ... I'm going to talk about the local history of this space and how we were given an East and West Reserve by the Canadian government as the expense of Cree and Métis people. That is going to be my sermon for this morning, and tie it to a Biblical text.... The pastor responded as soon as I sat down and said, "Thanks for screwing up my Sunday!" in front of everyone, but he did it with a bit of laughter. And I find out [later] that he is one of the allies of the community that's saying we'll take this seriously.

He continues,

> But there is a lot of negative feedback that you have to deal with.... I spoke a couple of weeks ago at a community and there were a few folks that have decided to no longer go to that church, because they allowed me to come and speak there on the issues that I spoke on. I hear that, and I feel crappy about that. You can feel alone in the work that you do.

He advises those coming into the work to "grab onto the hope, get some good friends, [and] learn a sense of humour." When things get difficult, Steve takes "solace in the story of Jesus ... [who] was an Indigenous Palestinian born in occupied Jerusalem, [and] was resisting and proclaiming liberation for the captives." Steve is guided in his work by the "prophetic tradition of the Judeo-Christian scriptures," which describes "radical equity and radical sharing [and] has concrete sociopolitical ramifications that the land is shared, and there is no want." He is also guided by the Treaty vision. Steve says,

There are no notions of cede or surrender within Indigenous Elders' understanding of what Treaty was all about in respect to the land. Michael Asch [in his book, *On Being Here to Stay* (2014)] says it's not about attaining shared jurisdiction of the land, it's actually living where Indigenous Peoples have jurisdiction and governance, and we are following their lead.... [This has] very tangible sociopolitical ramifications — it means that there should be more funding for Indigenous languages than there is for French Immersion programs. It means the Canadian nation will obligate corporations within this nation-state to respect the duty to consult.

Steve feels it is a function of colonialism that he speaks English and not Halq'eméylem, the language of the Stó:lō people, on whose lands he was raised.

Steve is engaged in decolonizing and Treaty relationship work because it's the right thing to do, and because the God he wishes to emulate

is more concerned about decolonization than anyone, is more concerned about issues about oppression and injustice, and 17 different pipelines flowing from Fort McMurray, or Hydro dams at Big Falls, or the 70 plus percent in CFS [child and family services] being Indigenous kids. That gives me hope and animates my personality, coming from a deep spiritual well.

Steve believes, "God is like a mama bear who sticks up for the children that are getting hurt." He says, "God is for just relationships and wants people living in equity and radical respect." He does his work out of a felt personal and spiritual obligation to his girls and their communities. He says, "I want my girls and my son to be able to look at us — Ann and I, when we're older and say, 'We're proud that you tried.'"

CHAPTER 7

FRANKLIN JONES

Elizabeth Carlson-Manathara and Anonymous

IDENTITY AND EARLY INFLUENCES

Franklin Jones is a white settler Canadian student and musician in his thirties. He grew up in a white, lower-middle-class monoculture suburb of a prairie province city. He is a "cis-gendered heterosexual, able-bodied … son, family member, friend, partner … and a bit of a black sheep" who says he "never really felt like [he] belonged anywhere." Franklin's right-wing neighbourhood was known as a centre for the Canadian chapter of the KKK in the eighties, with a culture in which "it was cool to be racist." As a child, he witnessed violent anti-Indigenous sentiment and discrimination. "The true history of what happened on Turtle Island" was never taught in school or at home. Franklin recalls being seven during the Oka Crisis and says,

> My dad [told] me "the Natives are rising up!" And he was scared. He was like "they said they were going to poison the water supply!" This is from my dad, who I've never heard say an overtly racist thing, but at the same time his mind was blown at the possibility.… I remember that being told to me as a little kid and I was terrified.

When more Indigenous people moved into his neighbourhood following the opening of subsidized housing, "It was not met warmly. A lot of people felt there was more crime that came in." Franklin says, "Anything that happened in the neighbourhood that was wrong, someone got jumped, or someone's car got broken into … those folks got blamed for everything." He was a child who felt strongly and connected through his heart. Being subject to male socialization against emotion and vulnerability meant "there were people that tried to beat that out of [him]." He says, "I had to deal with a lot of abuse for that, but they couldn't take that away, it's just like part of who I am." As a result of the abuse, Franklin experienced being "pretty numb ... [and he] battled with a lot of depression and thoughts of inferiority." As someone who has always questioned things, Franklin's teenage involvement with music accompanied a rebellion against the conservative right-wing mentality around him:

> A lot of the bands in the '80s from the UK had a very anti-authoritarian, left-leaning radical message about opposing racism, and I remember when I heard that, it really struck a chord with me — I realized that something was very wrong with my neighbourhood. I started playing in bands, started thinking differently. There's a lot of things that you witness as a kid that you know in your heart are wrong, but until you actually read something or hear something [different] ... so I had to reach outside the neighbourhood for that in terms of media, film, and music.

LEARNING AND EARLY ACTIVISM

Franklin left his neighbourhood and began working at a leftist bookstore. He says,

> That was definitely a life-changing period for me ... my mind was just opening to a whole new way of thinking.... They had speaking events, and the whole environment was operated collectively.... So I started reading books by Ward Churchill and Dee Brown, like *Bury My Heart at Wounded Knee*, and Gord Hill, and reading about historic and ongoing acts of resistance against colonialism.

While working at the bookstore, Franklin "got to know quite well a group of about five or six Indigenous men that lived on the streets and the various shelters in the wintertime." He reminisces,

> [I'd] take smoke breaks with them ... and hear their story and hear what's been going on with them. At the time I started to romanticize it because I had [been] so sheltered — it wasn't until I was a teenager that I actually realized there was poverty. I never saw it.... Develop[ing] relationships with them really, really changed my life.

Franklin naively thought, "Oh we're equal friends and there's no power difference, we can just cast aside all the things that make us different." He says, "I didn't know how to be an effective supporter, or an effective ally. I didn't know anything really." He says,

> There weren't a lot of boundaries in place and some of the relationships became quite dependent … unstable and unhealthy. People are in very real need and real crisis and you have more means than they do, and you care about them and they care about you, and you want to help them and they need help.… You have a group of Indigenous folks who are really just getting by, and there was lots of violence, lots of addiction, problems with other gangs, problems with the police.

During one instance, Franklin and his Indigenous friend were outside when police came to address someone they knew who had passed out and was asleep on the sidewalk. When Franklin and his friend tried to intervene after police had escalated the situation, Franklin was told by police to go back inside while his friend was threatened with arrest. He says, "They very visibly treated us completely different based on who we were … it fully clicked in my mind." Most of these friends have passed on now due to overdose, suicide, and extreme winter temperatures. Franklin says, "I'll never forget those guys, I miss them." His time with them shifted his focus toward anti-colonial activism. He learned, "If you're going to organize or resist the way things are in this world … Indigenous struggles are at the forefront."

ANTI-COLONIAL WORK AND CONTINUED LEARNING

Franklin's friendships inspired him to become involved with anti-police brutality activism and prisoner support and literacy programs within a psychiatric lockdown facility, spaces that would reveal "first-hand the disproportionate amount of Indigenous prisoners and what they were going through." They met with mothers and recorded them reading books to their kids. They would then rip a CD, add a message to their kid, wrap the book and CD, and bring it to their kids "so that they can read along with their mom in jail." When he began to see that "one of the ongoing or visible effects of colonization is resource extraction without informed consent," Franklin attended demonstrations in support of Indigenous-led resistance to resource extraction. He and his band began to raise funds for legal fees for Indigenous groups that "were arrested or came in conflict with the law" due to blocking resource extraction on their lands, including the Tyendinaga Mohawk, Grassy Narrows Anishinaabe, and Elsipogtog Mi'kmaq. While on tour, they used their time on stage with the microphone to speak about the blockades, the roles that settlers can have, and about missing and murdered Indigenous women in Canada. Franklin says,

> We had these rich conversations with people after ... this exchange of energy and ideas. By the end of the tour, we [had] raised something like $800 from those shows to send to the legal defence, and that felt good.... That felt like a good use of privilege.

As someone who has been unfairly granted "an easier, safer life, and at the expense of the original people of this land" through colonialism, Franklin says, "I always just want to feel like a respectful guest, that's how I want to walk as a settler on this land, and to not ever feel that sense of entitlement." Franklin feels colonialism has taken from him "the ability to connect to this land in a real way." He seeks to respect territory and respect land, learning whose Traditional Territories he is on and acknowledging this publicly, with feeling. He says, "I don't know where else I can go right now, so how can I be where I am right now in the best way I can be?"

Franklin is involved in a lifelong learning process. His understandings of white privilege and of his role in the colonial oppression of Indigenous Peoples have grown. He has sought to deconstruct and analyze "the tone in which things were shared with us or the misinformation we were fed as children." He says, "It was important for me to understand my role that I was playing in the oppression of Indigenous people." Franklin is a student in an access-based bachelor of social work program that has helped to deepen his anti-colonial understanding.

Franklin believes white settlers have a powerful role to play in decolonization by educating other white people. Working through relationships with friends, family, colleagues, and communities, Franklin tries to push "for deeper understanding of colonialism and tr[ies] to involve people in the struggle against it." He notes that many white people are "used to getting everything and not thinking about where it comes from." "Having grown up with that and having been told that they deserve that, that's a part of their identity," he says. When Franklin addresses racism in his conversations with friends, family, and co-workers, it is within the context of love and respect in an effort to share more of who he is. When those close to him say racist things, it puts up a wall in the relationship, and Franklin cares enough about them to talk to them in an effort to bring the wall down. Nonetheless, in these discussions, he may notice a change of tone or added tension. It has altered some relationships. Sometimes this has meant losing friends or opportunities, and yet it remains important to Franklin to "not take the day off because it feels inconvenient." If settlers would become informed on the real history of what happened on this land and its continuing impact, and "could actually just really just open up our hearts to each other, and try to deprogram the socialization that we've had," Franklin says, "it's nice [to] try and imagine what kind of a world we'd live in." If we increasingly see "a settler population that's well-informed of the history of colonialism, a real history of what happened on this land and how it continues to impact things," then "a social movement [will] happen."

Franklin has gone to "as many Idle No More protests as possible." He says, "When there's a protest or when there's a rally and they're asking for people to come, I can do that." Franklin's experience of round dancing at a busy city intersection during rush hour was life changing. At one of the rallies, Franklin and other white settlers took a pledge at the legislative building to "do something when you see racism, to not let it go." He took this pledge very seriously.

Franklin has been invited to take part in Indigenous ceremonies, which have become a part of his decolonization practice. He supports the ceremonies by helping to set up, giving people rides, and working as a *scabe* (helper). As he attended, he says, "I started to feel things that I couldn't explain … there was something bigger at play.… It was of this land, and it was coming from the land." His ceremonial involvement has awakened spiritual and relational aspects of himself and has given him a sense of belonging and connection that has been healing:

> The relationships I've developed through ceremony, the feeling of connecting with people in a real way, to feel welcomed … I feel like it provides me with this knowledge of myself, and knowledge of my place on this path I'm on.… Realizing that mistakes happen in terms of the greater struggle of how to do effective support work, I know that involving myself and being invited to ceremonies, it keeps my heart good, and it keeps my spirit good.

Rather than working from his head based on what he has read in anti-colonial books, Franklin's relationships have led him to work from his heart. He says,

> I've developed a lot of really amazing personal relationships that I value so highly, and a system of support — the feeling of just complete love in my heart for folks. When a white activist is trying to do this work without any sort of personal or emotional tie to it, I think there's so many more mistakes that can happen. It's hard to describe the difference I feel now. I feel like it's become way more personal.

His participation brought a greater commitment to the struggle and has helped him to become a better man to himself. He says, "I'm treating myself better … it's brought me a lot more compassion towards myself, and it's let me be more gentle and warmer and kinder in my life." His participation has also brought a sense of peace he has not previously known. He says,

> I felt I was walking in a better way.… I was communicating through my heart, and I was living my life with more courage, and I wasn't afraid of what people thought about me in the same way.… It's something that's such a hugely positive protective factor that's now my life, which is a guiding force in how I try and do everything, [how] I try to be in my relationships and in my activism.

Franklin's ceremonial relationships have also helped him to heal emotionally from issues related to his male socialization. He now had a community that felt safe. He explains,

> Part of my decolonization work is … giving myself permission to feel things and to communicate my feelings, to do that with other men in my life and show them that they can do that around me. I have experienced a lot of trauma from men in my life, like through violence, peer-to-peer violence. I grew up that way, so I've had a hard time developing close relationships with men. I realize that sometimes I start putting on a guise around other men, because I feel like I need to protect myself. And I feel like in the last few years especially, I felt like I could have these really

amazing emotional connections with other men, and that's something that's new, that I've never really felt comfortable doing ...
so decolonizing as part of me is also recognizing that emotional
part of who I am and the nurturing side — the compassionate
side. And those parts always existed, but sometimes I felt like I
needed to keep them locked away.

Some of Franklin's white activist friends have criticized his participation in Indigenous ceremonies, saying he is appropriating another culture.
There have been times when Franklin himself has hesitated when invited
to participate because of his own fears of appropriating. Once, after having
helped to build a Sundance arbor, people had gathered to drum. When he
was encouraged to drum with them, he said, "Oh, I can't. I can't do that.
That wouldn't be right." The person who invited him "laughed at [him]
so hard, [and said] 'It's just hitting a drum! That's so funny.'" He says he is
careful not to "do something I wasn't invited to do ... pass teachings off
as my own or share them without permission." Franklin does not wish to
use his ceremonial participation "for any kind of instrumental gain," such
as trying to absolve himself of his complicity in colonialism, as a strategy
to develop relationships, or a shortcut to gaining the trust of Indigenous
Peoples. He has seen white activists "wear the ceremonies they go to like a
badge on their sleeve ... 'I did this, I did that' and just inject it ... 'Hey I'm
cool, don't worry, I'm not one of the shitty white people, I go to sweats!'"
Franklin is careful to "be 100% up front" about who he is, and when he
shares anything about the ceremonies, he speaks of his own experience
and journey. He says, "You never forget, nor should you, that you're a
white person, and I don't ever want to forget that. But that doesn't mean
that you can't experience things in an emotional or spiritual way within
ceremony." Franklin understands that "what you've been invited to do by
somebody might rub somebody else the wrong way." He uses his heart
to feel what is right for him and remains open to criticism, feedback,
and questioning. He believes that as long as it's done with respect, his
participation is part of him being on a good path. While it used to get to
him, now, he says, "When I encounter other white people that are very
critical of me going to ceremonies, I understand that it's actually part of
their process and has nothing to do with me."

"When you're doing this kind of work you need to be humble," Franklin
says, "walk soft and show your worth by being really solid, doing what you
say you're going to do, not overstretching or over-committing yourself, not

taking up a bunch of space or feeling like you have an answer." Franklin believes that solutions need to come from the grassroots, with settlers taking direction from Indigenous Peoples about how to proceed. This can be tricky with "so many different ideas on how to move forward from different Indigenous individuals, communities, and groups." Also, he says, "Sometimes [Indigenous] folks get really tired of having to tell white people what to do all the time. Just like, 'What do I do now? What do I do now? Did I do a good job?'" It is good to find something to do "that doesn't always necessarily require really intense direction, but you know it's welcome." Sometimes this means taking initiative to work with other settlers, or responding to calls from Indigenous Peoples such as, "'We need people at this blockade,' or 'We need this many people at this protest.'" Different types of support work require different levels of risk. Franklin recalls a march he attended in support of land defenders out east with forty others downtown during rush-hour traffic. He says,

> Nobody external to that could have dragged me away from being there. They would've needed to arrest me to get me to leave, because I knew in my heart that that's where I needed to be at that moment in time. There's a lot of factors that contribute to that. Potentially it's who you're with, and what's going on, and where you are with your life at that moment. But I think unless people with privilege are willing to put themselves [at] risk, nothing will change. That could mean losing job opportunities because you're the shit disturber at work, or it could mean being arrested at a blockade. If people aren't willing to do those things, then it'll just continue.

"What are you willing to give to change a system that is destroying the entire world?" he asks. "What will you say to your kids? What will you say to your grandkids about what you did?"

"I think it's really important that we defer to Indigenous types of knowledge [and] ways of being; perhaps especially when they come into conflict with where we're coming from. And that's part of our work," Franklin says. Having been a vegan for over a decade, he has particular beliefs about animal treatment and has opposed hunts. Reading the book *Night Spirits* (Bussidor 2000) invoked a struggle within Franklin as he began to understand that Indigenous Peoples have their own hunting practices based on their own knowledges, which he had not taken into account.

He realizes, "I live in such a way that is completely disconnected from the land, and I'm disconnected from how food is procured … that's actually part of my socialization." When Franklin has travelled to Indigenous communities, as "someone that doesn't eat meat or dairy typically," the issue has manifested itself when he has been offered food. He says,

> I turned down food once. That was a mistake.… And it's such a privileged thing to be a vegan, especially when you're going up north. That's a clear example, but I think it's fairly symbolic of holding on to your rationale, understanding of the world, and feeling like it's superior even when you don't want to imply that.… I would never refuse food now. I've had relationships begin with me refusing food, and that's so significant, to have someone as a guest and you're giving them food that you made, you hunted, or that you got from the store, and someone can't eat it because they think it's wrong to do that.

Part of Franklin's internal work has involved processing the guilt he has felt as he has learned more about colonialism, his own mistakes, and the colonial dynamics he has enacted often out of obliviousness due to his own privilege. He says,

> At some point, you learn things and then you feel that, and you're like "Holy Shit!" When you actually learn what actually happened, you continue to learn what happened, and then you look up, and you actually learn what's happening now, it is — it is actually staggering to open your heart to that, and it's very important to do.

He feels it becomes counterproductive when supporters "internalize [guilt] to such a degree that they just hate themselves … and potentially remove themselves from the struggle." Yet, he says, "Guilt is an important thing to feel, at some point, for what we're implicated in. And if you don't allow yourself to feel that, you're probably never going to do anything." Franklin's implication in multiple forms of oppression has caused him to go "through large periods of just really hating who I am." He says, "I think when you hate yourself, you're actually less effective as an activist and you're not treating others well … you're not taking care of yourself, [and] you can't really do much for anyone else, or any cause." Understanding the structural reasons for what is wrong in society has helped Franklin to cope with guilt, and his participation in Indigenous ceremonies has also helped him to work through these feelings. Anger is another feeling Franklin has been working through, anger towards police and politicians, and "anger at these institutions and what they're doing to the world — doing to people and the land." He wavers between hope and hopelessness "because you see the world on such a frightening and disturbing course," and yet, "you also see people resisting that, people that always have resisted that, and those victories.... It makes you want to try to have more courage and to struggle harder, to stop certain things."

Humour and humility have helped Franklin in situations where his work has brought him face to face with the feeling of being "other." When he attends particular ceremonies or travels to Indigenous communities, he may be the only white person present and he becomes hyper-aware of feeling very white. After a Sundance meeting one year, everyone was dancing. He says, "It would've been wrong not to dance, but we didn't know how, so we just looked like complete idiots, and everyone was laughing at us." He says, "Humour is such a huge part of it. It feels good to make people laugh with my ignorance or stupidity sometimes, as long as people always know it's never intentional." Nonetheless, "fear[s] of being — of feeling 'other' are very real for settlers and white people, and it's a real barrier for them to actually put themselves out there." "They're scared because they don't want to do the wrong thing," but, he says, "I think doing something, and making a mistake as a supporter is still better than doing nothing." He advises,

> I think that we should face that fear. It's okay to be uncomfortable.... You're going to feel "other" — and you're going to feel silly, and you're not going to know what to do and you're going to feel like the dumb white person, which is what you are. And that's okay, and that's an important thing to feel, we never feel that ... we're so used to being the dominant group, and the dominant group is rarely questioned.... As long as you're there with respect and humbleness, you've come to be there in a good way; [I]f you don't know what to do, people will tell you what to do.

Because he only goes where invited, he says, "When I experience those feelings of doubt, I fall back on 'I've been invited to be here, it's ok.'"

Franklin believes the way of life of white settlers causes "a loss of hope, a loss of connection, and a loss of purpose," resulting in mental health struggles. He explains,

> I think a lot of people that struggle with those things are drawn to activism.… For me, there have been different times in my life where [I] have dealt with a lot of anxiety, depression, thoughts of suicide. I think having things to feel connected to … has brought me a lot of strength and connection.

Being involved with activism gives him something to believe in. He says, "Being with a group of people that are trying to do the right thing can save people, can save their lives." He emphasizes,

> Being at a demo[nstration], or a protest for something that you believe [in], being with other people feeling the same things, on our own paths that brought us there that day or that night. That feeling of marching down the street. We've lost that — that feeling of actually being free. Those moments bring a lot of hope and a lot of love.

Franklin says he sometimes wonders "what my life would have been if I had just gotten a job at the hammer factory and had a truck and two kids." He suspects that "the older you get and the more pressures that are put on you, the easier it is to walk away from things." "We'll always have that, as white people, as an option with this struggle, is to walk away from it," he says. Yet, "once you know the things that you know and you open your heart to them, you can't turn your back on it." It becomes, "actually the struggle for your soul." Franklin says, "I'm most definitely a product of this colonial culture that I've been socialized in, so I need to actively resist that." He says he does his work because "I have so much privilege that by doing nothing, I'm actually causing harm." Franklin says, "To be a decent person, to look in the mirror, I have to be involved in this. There's no option." "I think it's really a question of what kind of world you want to live in." He thinks of children growing up into the hate, inequality, and fear of systemic and individual racism. "To try to be a part of the solution rather than the problem is really deeply ingrained in who [I am]," he says. "I don't see that ever changing, I see that actually deepening over time."

CHAPTER 8

ORIENTING TOWARD
INDIGENOUS SOVEREIGNTY

Elizabeth Carlson-Manathara

Just before Covid-19 took the international stage, in Canada all eyes were on Wet'suwet'en (Fornier 2020; Unist'ot'en Camp 2020). For a number of years, Wet'suwet'en land defenders have been standing against the invasion of their lands by Coastal GasLink, whose efforts to build a pipeline through Wet'suwet'en lands are being supported by the government and the RCMP. The struggle intensified again in February 2020, when, facilitated by a court injunction, RCMP officers arrested and removed Wet'suwet'en land defenders from Wet'suwet'en lands for resisting the pipeline (Crawford 2020).

In solidarity with Wet'suwet'en land defenders, Kanien'kehá:ka (Mohawk) activists camped near CN rail tracks, resulting in CN shutting down rail service in parts of Canada and impacting the economy (Pashagumskum 2020). Of the action, Tehonikonrathe (in Pashagumskum 2020: para. 2) said, "This is our [Mohawk] country. We are sovereign. We've taken away our permission to pass trains through our lands."

As a result of these events, Indigenous sovereignty and Indigenous law have become part of the national dialogue. For example, a CTV news story asked what is revealed by the Wet'suwet'en case about Canadian courts' engagement with Indigenous law (Smart 2020a) while a *Canadian Press* article, duplicated in *The National Post* (Smart 2020b: para. 7), described a current "national debate over Indigenous land rights and sovereignty." In her *National Observer* article, Rita Wong (2019), citing Tait and Spice (2018), pointed out that Anuk Nu'at'en (Wet'suwet'en law) predates Canadian and provincial law. Also, MP Paul Manly (2020) affirmed Wet'suwet'en hereditary law and Wet'suwet'en sovereignty in a *Canadian Dimension* article.

Earlier in the book, I shared my framing of *living in Indigenous sovereignty* as living in an awareness that we are on Indigenous Lands containing their own stories, relationships, laws, Protocols, obligations, and opportunities, which have been understood and practised by Indigenous Peoples since time immemorial. As Canada increasingly grapples with its relationship to Indigenous law and Indigenous sovereignty, settlers who wish to live in Indigenous sovereignty are engaging in a process of reorienting our lives toward Indigenous Lands, stories, relationships, laws, governance, resurgence, Treaties, prophecies, and Protocols; or, as Dawnis Kennedy said, thinking of ourselves as characters in the stories of Indigenous Peoples. But what are these stories? How do we learn about them so that we can orient to them? This is a process of courageous listening, and while it can start, as it does here, with the words of Indigenous scholars, Knowledge Holders, and activists, it must soon move off of the page and into relationship.

Aaron Mills (2016: para. 27) urges settlers to live "not merely making space for indigenous voices but acting, choosing, thinking, feeling as if what those voices say about this land and how to be on it really matters." But what do Indigenous voices say? Certainly they are varied, as there are over fifty Indigenous nations and fifty Indigenous languages in Canada alone. In this chapter, I engage with Indigenous knowledges and relations to listen to what just some of the voices of Indigenous scholars, activists, and Knowledge Holders are saying about white settler occupiers living ethically on Indigenous Lands among Indigenous Peoples, in Indigenous sovereignty. In recognizing the diversity among Indigenous nations, communities, and individuals in what they are saying, I make no claim that what I engage here represents the fullness of this diversity. The authors and scholars I draw from tend to be well respected and esteemed within circles of people working in these areas and, in some cases, are people I know and with whom I have nurtured relationships. What I present here is influenced by my own choices based on where I have lived (Indigenous Lands occupied by Winnipeg and now Sudbury), my connections with Indigenous communities, and my focus on decolonization, activist, and anti-colonial Indigenous literatures. I focus, in part, locally. As Ritskes contends, the terms of engagement with Indigenous nationhood "depend on the Indigenous land and culture that you are co-existing and co-resisting with" (2014: 261).

Earlier in the book, I described the words Dawnis Kennedy shared with me: she understood my research to be guided by questions around what I needed to know in order to live in Indigenous sovereignty. She understood that within my process I would look at the literature and that I would go out and find people, Elders, and mentors that I would learn from who would help me fill my bundle with what I would need to live this question. In this chapter, I share some elements of my bundle. I draw from sources such as oral and written literature, knowledge shared at community gatherings, and knowledge shared by traditional Knowledge Holders from whom I have sought specific guidance using traditional Protocols. What follows are areas of learning that I feel are crucial and foundational for settlers as they seek to reorient their lives. There are frequent and sometimes lengthy quotes from Indigenous activists, scholars, and Knowledge Holders in this section, and indeed throughout much of the book, and I would encourage the reader to take time with these as an act of listening. As has been noted, striving to live in Indigenous sovereignty is fraught with tensions, contestations, and seemingly opposing perspectives. These dynamics are certainly present in this chapter, and I generally view these as parts of the whole and as threads to be woven and balanced. Thus, as I point out these divergent perspectives, I do not always articulate a preference or answer. However, there are places where a clear message does emerge, where those from which I learn indicate a stronger consensus, and/or where particular perspectives are borne out in my experience.

Here, it is important to keep in mind that although it is worthwhile to read foundational knowledge for living in Indigenous sovereignty, this is not all that is required. Aimée Craft (personal communication, April 9, 2016) shared that settler decolonial work

> isn't going to happen in just one way, and it isn't formulaic.... In any ally relationship, you can check all the boxes and somehow it's always gone wrong.... Being in relationship is something very different than just checking a box in these categories.

She said, "It's about the continuing dialogue about common goals and objectives, so that idea of grounding in a relationship is important. How much are you actually listening, and dialoguing, and continuing to check in with Indigenous partners?" I note these words in order to advise the reader that the ideas in this chapter are not meant to be seen as a checklist for knowledge in action, but rather as areas to consider for settlers engaging in anti-colonial and decolonial work. Craft says, "What you might take away at one point in time is actually what you need to work on, what you lack" (personal communication, April 9, 2016).

ENGAGEMENT WITH THE LAND

Mills (2019: 209) writes that "in order to reconcile themselves with one another, indigenous and settler peoples must first reconcile themselves with the earth." He emphasizes that "a [rooted] way of understanding the earth ... and one's relationship to and within it ... [is] available not only to indigenous peoples, but to everyone on Mikinaakominis [Turtle Island]" (2019: 270). As will be described in this chapter, Indigenous sovereignty and Indigenous law are relational, emphasizing kinship with not only humans, but also the Earth and the non-human beings of the Earth. If we are to fit into Indigenous law and orient to Indigenous sovereignty, as settlers we must begin to learn a new way of relating to land. Mills' (2019) writings reflect back the idea of settler relational agency — the understanding that settler orientations toward living in Indigenous sovereignty need not be fully mediated by the state. He writes, "Canada the nation state isn't living and isn't capable of earth connection, mutual aid or kinship. It isn't capable of being-with us [Indigenous Peoples], so we turn away, engaging it only strategically. However, the same can't be said of its settler" (Mills 2019: 279–280).

What can we learn from Indigenous Peoples' relationships to their lands? One important dimension is that Indigenous Peoples have been connected to their lands for a very long time. Dakota Elder Eva McKay (1999: 293) says, "Our ancestors say we were always here, this is where we always were." The connection is intimate, and more literal than many settlers can imagine: "Tribal territory is important," writes Little Bear (2000: 78), "because the Earth is our Mother (and this is not a metaphor: it is real). The Earth cannot be separated from the actual being of Indians." The connection is relational, with humans being part of, and not higher than the land. Little Bear (1994: 7) describes the relationships of Indigenous Peoples to the land as manifest "through a complex inter relational network with all of creation which sees humans as simply a part of creation and not above it, and which has as its goal balance and harmony ... accomplished through constant renewal." Thus, the land shapes Indigenous laws and Protocols immensely. McAdam (2015: 23) writes, "*nêhiyaw* laws are in the songs, the ceremonies, and in all the sacred sites. The land is intertwined in a most profound manner, so to separate the two would mean death to many aspects of *nêhiyaw* culture." With land profoundly constituting the legal, cultural, and relational dimensions of Indigenous communities, the dispossession of Indigenous Peoples from their Traditional Territories has had a profound impact. McKay describes the fallout of such disconnection:

> There are lots of farms here, no one can trap and hunt for liveli-
> hood, so we are in a tight spot here. There is nothing much left.
> We cannot live off the land anymore. The generation today has
> lost their culture, so they are suffering. You see them in jails,
> they are people without a culture, they have nothing. (1999: 307)

Because, as Leanne Simpson says, the root of the [colonial] problem is "the dispossession of Indigenous Peoples from our homeland" (2013b: 9:40–9:43), a root of decolonization is "land and how we're going to share it" (2013b: 9:45–9:47). But as peoples with a comparatively very short history on these lands, what is our status in relation to Indigenous Lands? What can our experiential, spiritual, and emotional connections with the land look like? And what are our responsibilities to these lands?

Status on the Land

It is important to reckon with the reality that our presence on these lands "interrupts [Indigenous Peoples'] ways of being in this world" (Simpson 2013a: 56). Understanding our status on these lands can serve to reorient our relationships to the land and to the people of the land (Ward 2015). Ward (2015) discusses examples of status on the land, starting with his own story as Mi'kmaw from Esgenoopetitj (Burnt Church) First Nation, having married into and resided in Shxw'ow'hamel First Nation (Stó:lō Territory). His status has been that of a guest, which determines how one behaves when on someone else's land:

> You respect their laws, you respect their customs, you respect their
> rules, you respect their norms, you respect their way of life.... You
> become aware that it's their land, not yours. They have rules that
> were developed specifically from their relationship to the land.
> You must learn to put yourself under that, you've got to humble
> yourself so that you're willing to accept those laws, those rules,

and your status within it.... Don't forget who you are. You are who you are, but at the same time you have to respect the people whose land you're in.... As a guest ... you have certain limits and certain restrictions, that you can't just exceed those limits. You can't just somehow impose your ideas, your behaviours, your conduct. (Ward 2015: 1:45–3:25, used with permission)

Even if our position was that of guest, this would be very difficult for white settler occupiers to do, since it involves relearning habits, patterns, and ways of being. Whiteness, and the socialization of white peoples, is known for its ontological expansiveness, the tendency to "act and think as if all spaces — whether geographical, psychical, linguistic, economic, spiritual, bodily, or otherwise — are or should be available for them to move in and out of as they wish" (Sullivan 2006: 10). The ability to "restrain personal power as a way of demonstrating respect and ... conform our behaviours within that status" (Ward 2015: 4:15–4:25, used with permission), to rec- ognize our limitations and responsibilities, may require practice. Another hallmark of white socialization that makes it difficult to live within our status on the land is thinking we know what is best for others and thus trying to give advice, influence, or even coerce others into saying or doing as we see fit (Good Tracks 1973). Ward addresses this and what it means for the role of guest:

I don't have a right to be on this land.... I don't have the right to tell the people of this land what to do. I don't somehow have this political equality to the people of this land.... I am not to assume I know better about how to relate to this land. I've been here [Stó:lō Territory] what — just a little bit over a decade? And I can assume that I know more than people who have been here for tens of thousands of years? That I can tell them how to relate to the land better?... I am in a role of being a helper and a sup- porter. (2015: 3:40–5:45, used with permission)

All of this applies even more so to settlers. Ward, as Mi'kmaw, sees himself as a guest on Stó:lō lands, but he contrasts this with the status of *xwelítem,* a Stó:lō word for the colonizing group:

We do not have the same status here on this land.... As xwelítem, you carry the legacy of the colonial crimes of your forefathers up to now.... Right up to the inclusion of the very Canadian system that occupies these territories. As xwelítem, you're a part of that, that's what you carry with you as baggage, every single time you encounter an Indigenous person. Every second you're standing on Indigenous soil, that's the baggage you carry with you, and that's how your status is formed here.... Guests don't invade your lands. Guests don't declare sovereignty — absolute control over your nation. Guests don't come in with gunboats, armed personnel, and the first things they construct are forts. Guests don't settle the land for the sake of gaining your resources, displacing you from your own territory. Guests don't bring in their families, their friends, and your slaves to take over your land and take those resources. Guests don't disrupt and destabilize your society or your political institutions. Guests don't forcibly change your religion. Guests don't usurp your traditional government. Guests don't replace it with a puppet regime. So I hope that's clear enough, that your status is not a guest. (2015: 16:25–18:45, used with permission)

As has been noted, Ward (2015) believes the status of xwelítem on the land to be that of an occupier. He argues that acknowledging our status as occupiers reflects a truthful rethinking of our status on these lands, which is an important element of decolonial work.

Experiential, Spiritual, and Emotional Connection

Relating to land deeply in experiential, spiritual, and emotional ways as settlers can be exceedingly difficult as it often challenges the foundational worldviews of our socialization. Many settlers are raised to see the land as an object — as a resource to be used for progress and financial wealth. What's more, reading about new ways to relate to the land often results in an intellectual understanding that may not go deep enough to transform our very beings. In the first chapter, I shared a dream that helped to deepen my transformation. I shared that prior to the dream, as much as I had heard Indigenous Peoples talk about their relationships with land, my understanding was a world away. One Indigenous scholar whose work reminds me so much of my dream, and who shares profoundly impactful writings about respecting and relating to land is Robin Wall Kimmerer (n.d., 2020). I would refer the reader to her essay "The Serviceberry: An Economy of Abundance" and to her book *Braiding Sweetgrass* for additional learning despite my belief that book learning around this only goes so far. Even now, my understanding is still very limited. And yet I strongly believe that the dream I had was only possible because of my relationships with Indigenous Peoples and because of the prayers and intention I had sent out as a result. All of this is to say that while I believe important ideas about experiential, spiritual, and emotional connections to land are shared in this chapter, I also believe in the importance of relationships with Indigenous communities and peoples in facilitating this learning at a deeper level.

Desiring to relate to land can also seem contradictory. If we are working toward the return of Indigenous territories to Indigenous nations, is it not counterproductive to attach to these lands? Leanne Simpson describes some of what the colonizing presence of settlers on the land has cost Indigenous Peoples:

> Over the past two hundred years, without our permission and without our consent, we have been systematically removed and dispossessed from most of our territory. We have watched as our homeland has been cleared, subdivided, and sold to settlers from Toronto. We have watched our waterfronts disappear behind monster cottages ... our most sacred places have been made into provincial parks for tourists, with concrete buildings over our teaching rocks.... The land, our Mother, has largely been taken from us. (2013a: 51)

Note Simpson's reference to cottages and provincial parks, which often provide the backdrop of settler attempts to connect with land, while settlers live in ignorance of what this means for Indigenous Peoples. Waziyatawin (2009) explains that due to colonial regulation, Dakota Peoples today continue to be prevented from living as Dakota on their homelands. She says, "We are not in control of caring for our land base ... we are still denied access to sacred sites, lands, and waters that are central to our spiritual traditions. Consequently, we grieve the losses we have suffered and continue to suffer" (Waziyatawin 2009: 154). What if we recognized the sovereignty of Indigenous Peoples over their lands and sought to connect through their guidance — through Indigenous sovereignty? This would certainly be more widely practised if Canada recognized Indigenous sovereignty such that Indigenous Peoples had access to and control of their lands; until then, we can choose to live in a way that supports this. Benally (2013) explains that to avoid perpetuating settler privilege and colonialism, non-Indigenous persons seeking to connect with Indigenous Land should consult with Indigenous Peoples. He suggests listening to Indigenous people who are still here and have had connection with the land since time immemorial. Kennedy (personal communication, April 9, 2016) says,

> We're the ones who were placed here on this Earth [Turtle Island]. So yes, we're the ones who are responsible to be able to speak for the land here, to have Protocols in place. That's our responsibility. And yes, that positions us differently. But we are also just human as well.

A number of Indigenous Peoples are asking non-Indigenous people to understand Indigenous Peoples' connection to the land and to learn to connect to and love the land themselves so that they will be able to more effectively support Indigenous efforts to protect the land. Melody Andrews describes the connection of Stó:lō to their territories:

> Being *Hwulmuhw* [an Indigenous person] ... is about understanding your connection to the land, where you come from, and knowing the origin stories of the land and the sacred responsibility for defending your territories from destruction and exploitation.... A Hwulmuhw person knows how to interact with the land in such a way that it guarantees a future for upcoming generations. It is a way of thinking that utilizes deep respect as a tool to place limits on our capability to take from nature. This restraint ensures a healthy, sustainable way of life for generations yet to come. To be Hwulmuhw on this land means to be Stó:lō. Stó:lō means people of the river.... The river has always taken care of us for thousands of years. Our villages are located along the river, we sustain our lives from the river.... The land develops you as a person. It provides places, specific experiences, and wisdom for a person as they grow. (2015: 7:07–8:25)

Andrews says, "As a xwelítem, you need to understand the connection to the land, and the importance of our sacred sites so that [you] too can get behind the Stó:lō and have the sacred responsibility to protect these lands for the next seven generations" (2015: 9:23–10:00). Nii Gaani Aki Inini (Dave Courchene) says,

The reality of the Red Man is one of connection to the land —
having a close and sacred relationship with the land ... in the sense
of relationship like that of a child to its mother. Mother Earth
has been the true teacher for our ancestors. It was through her
natural laws we found balance and harmony.... Her abundance
comes with the full spirit of love that she has for all life — a love
that we feel in the food, the medicines, the natural materials we
use in our homes and in our cooking, and most importantly,
in the teachings, natural laws and connection she brings us....
Relationship begins with the land.... For us, the Earth is the face
of the Creator. (2016b: para. 11, 12, 13, 21, 24)

According to Nii Gaani Aki Inini (Dave Courchene), this relationship is
based on love, just like in my dream. Dawnis Kennedy explains,

We love our mother [Earth]. That's why we want to be responsible in our relationship with her, because we love her. And she
loves us.... That's the heart of that relationship. The heart of our
[Anishinaabe] law is that. And a lot of the colonial, anti-colonial
literature isn't about love. It's just about responsibility. And it's only
about humans.... But our connection to each other is through our
mother, the Earth. And that's where the heart comes. That's where
the love comes. There's a purpose to decolonization and respectful
relationships that has nothing to do with human beings. We as
human beings have obligations to all our relations in creation.
(Personal communication, April 9, 2016)

This idea of the Earth as mother is spoken by many of the Indigenous
scholars and Knowledge Holders I have learned from. Nii Gaani Aki
Inini (Dave Courchene) speaks to both Indigenous and non-Indigenous
peoples with his invitation to learn and to transform:

It is only in returning to the mother that we will be reminded of
our true purpose as human beings. The only thing that can lift
us out of this insanity is love, a love that comes from the land....
When we are able to sit on the land is when we have our best
chance of feeling the love expressed by the Earth.... It will be the
great love of the Earth that will take us to the heart. We need a
change of heart if we hope to survive.... This is a personal journey
that we must each make. It is a journey to discover your own spirit

that will define your purpose and bring meaning to your life. When we are able to truly feel the land is when change will happen, because we will be directed by the spirit in the land.... Our homeland is filled with the spirit of our ancestors, who walked for tens of thousands of years, taking care of the land. They continue to walk in spirit to help those who will be willing to accept the duties and responsibilities required in taking care of the land. We are willing to share what has helped our ancestors to take care of the land. We want to step forward and fulfill our leadership in our homeland, teaching those that want to learn why we love the land so much, and hopefully you will join us as we take care and love the land together, for the sake of all children. (2016a: para. 7, 25, 28, 31, 32, 84, 85)

Responsibility to the Land

As has been noted, one of the reasons for settlers to learn to understand and embody a connection to the Earth is that it will strengthen their support of Indigenous efforts to defend their lands. In fact, a number of Indigenous scholars maintain that connecting with and defending the land is also a Treaty obligation of the Crown and those represented by the Crown on Treaty lands (settlers). Tasha Hubbard shares that, based on Treaties,

we [Indigenous Peoples] understood that we would share information back and forth, that we would share [with settlers] that ethic of mutual responsibility of giving back, of the obligations that we all have to this land and to the inhabitants of this land. And not just humans. We tend to think it's always just about us. It's all about people. But it's not. It's about our other relatives. And just imagine how different this land would be if people had come, and been open, and understood that we are in relationship with everything that lives on this land. They are our relatives, and we need to think about them and their wellbeing. (2013: 45:00–45:35)

N.J. Sinclair (2014) speaks of Treaties made between the Anishinaabe and a number of animal nations represented by the Clan System. When Anishinaabe people signed Treaties with the newcomers, they often signed with their Clan symbols, demonstrating that the newcomers were signing into responsibilities to those Clan animals, and thereby to the natural world where they live: "In the water, in the land, in the sky, in the sun, in the moon; in a long chain and network of relationships" (Sinclair 2014: 44:30–44:45). Therefore, the Treaty reflects the obligations of non-Indigenous people to also care for and relate to the waters, the land, and the animals. Simpson shares insights she has gained from Elder Robin Greene, who says that from Nishnaabeg perspectives,

> humans should be taking as little as possible and giving up as much as possible to promote sustainability and promote *mino bimaadiziwin* in the coming generations. We should be as gentle as possible with our Mother. We should be taking the bare minimum to ensure our survival. He talked about how we need to manage ourselves so that life can promote more life. How much are you willing to give up to promote sustainability? We need to make different decisions. (2013a: 55)

Greene's perspective emphasizes the great shift in values that is required of settlers. I have sometimes thought of this in relation to my propensity for bargain shopping. I have greatly excelled in my embodiment of some of the capitalist, consumerist values of my socialization, and those who know me sometimes remark at my ability to get a good bargain. But, seen differently, what does this mean? It means I value getting more while giving less. This is in sharp contrast to Greene's words about taking the minimum necessary and giving as much as possible. They remind me of a teaching that was shared with me by Lorraine (Whitecrow) Derman (Anishinaabe from Seine River First Nation). I was preparing the gifts and tobacco that I would offer when asking a question of a Knowledge Holder. Lorraine shared, "How much it means to you is how high you pile the gifts" (personal communication, 1999).

A number of those whose narratives appear in this book articulate a connection to land. Silvia experienced being shaped by the forests of northern Ontario and experiencing a deep connection there, while still acknowledging the difficulty of rooting in stolen land (see Chapter 16). Steve, in Chapter 6, describes offering prayers, being quiet, and listening to what the land is telling him in an effort to reconnect. Susanne has done extensive environmental and land protection work, and she has had profound spiritual experiences on Indigenous Lands. She connects to land through the Earth-based spirituality of her European ancestors (see Chapter 11).

ENGAGING WITH INDIGENOUS PEOPLES

Engaging in relationship with Indigenous Peoples and communities is so foundational to decolonial and anti-colonial work, and yet this relational work is fraught with challenges from both sides. Some of this has to do with settler socialization. Taiaiake Alfred writes,

> There is a great danger in attempting to negotiate structural changes to our relationships before our minds and hearts are cleansed of the stains of colonialism. In the absence of mental and spiritual decolonization, any effort to theorize or to implement a model of a 'new' Onkwehonwe [Original Peoples]–Settler relationship is counter-productive to the objectives of justice and the achievement of a long-term relationship of peaceful coexistence between our peoples. (2005: 180)

Sakej Ward addresses this from his perspective as Mi'kmaw:

> We can't have a relationship if you insist on being the colonizer. We can't have a relationship if you're still going to be the occupier. That part of that identity has to be acknowledged, and there has to be work to change that. I am not going to be in relationship with anybody who insists they're superior to me, that insists they have the right to control me, they have sovereignty over me; that insists that because of our race they have a right to take away my nation, my land, my kids. The only relationship we're going to have is a hostile one. (2015: 24:40–25:20, used with permission)

My observation is that many settler occupiers stay away from engagement with Indigenous communities out of fear that they will say or do the wrong thing and cause harm, but even more so, I think this comes out of a fear of facing Indigenous anger and refusal and a fear of being humiliated. It is justified when Indigenous Peoples are angry in the face of colonialism and settler occupiers. Dispossession and colonization, Flowers (2015: 34) says, "are the primary obstacles to even beginning to imagine the co-existence of settlers with Indigenous peoples." She wonders, "How might such a gulf be bridged and solidarity be created?" (2015: 34), especially when "Indigenous peoples have no desire to build a future that is still grounded on a colonial relationship" (2015: 35). Flowers writes, "maybe some Indigenous people don't want or need settler co-resistance because we don't trust them.... For many Indigenous peoples the settler never ceases to be the enemy; the settler cultivates righteous anger within the colonized" (2015: 38).

In this context, Flowers' work addresses the justified right of Indigenous Peoples to refuse, in this case, settlers; and the inverse, that the "settler too must demonstrate a willingness to be refused" (2015: 34). As I emphasize the importance of engagement with Indigenous Peoples and communities for settlers who wish to live in Indigenous sovereignty, the question arises: what if Indigenous Peoples refuse this engagement? In this case, Flowers (2015: 34) writes, the "labor of settlers should be to imagine alternative ways to be in relation with Indigenous peoples." Therefore, it is crucial that white setters engage in the hard work of becoming safer, better humans with which Indigenous Peoples may choose to engage. It is typical for many white settlers to have the view that they are kind and benevolent people without having gone through the painstaking process of identifying their colonial socialization and ways of relating. A first step to the mental and spiritual decolonization Alfred (2005) describes, then, may be the recognition that we do indeed carry colonial ways of being and relating. We may then engage in a continual process of identifying, addressing, and transforming these elements of ourselves.

Engagement with Indigenous Peoples also needs to be realistic. Tuck and Fine (2007: 155), citing Vine Deloria, "reprove that romanticized vision of the Indian guide, that noble savage leading the white folks into the clearing, the earth and brook that will make real again the sterility of modernity." Dawnis Kennedy (personal communication, April 9, 2016) sees Anishinaabe Peoples as "an unsteady touchstone, because we're just as human." She says,

> Anishinaabe people, we may have been the first ones here among the human people, but we aren't the first ones here [on Indigenous Lands]. As members of the human people, we're like twins [of non-Indigenous people] born a second before. But we have so many relatives that came before, and our mother [Earth], and the spirit who created us all. So looking at only just this one little human relationship, we don't have any wisdom. We're just as human as anyone else.... It's not our knowledge. It's from the plants, it's our relatives, the animals, they showed us all of that.... We can't be a measure of anyone else's success because we're trying to walk and live and learn life just the same way everybody else is.

Our people have almost destroyed ourselves numerous times with nobody's interference. (Personal communication, April 9, 2016)

Treaty Relatives

Treaties are important agreements around the relationships between Indigenous and settler peoples. Indigenous perspectives on Treaty relationships provide guidance towards framing these relationships around kinship. Indigenous sovereignty originates from the Creator; Treaties, "through spiritual ceremonies conducted during the negotiations, expanded the First Nations sovereign circle, bringing in and embracing the British Crown within their sovereign circle" (Cardinal and Hildebrandt 2000: 41). The political relationship established by Treaties, which creates obligations of both sides, is mutually beneficial and reciprocal (Office of the Treaty Commissioner 2007), but also enacted within many Treaties is the making of relatives. Harold Johnson says,

> It was in accordance with the law of adoption that my family took your ancestors as relatives. We solemnized the adoption with a sacred pipe.... This adoption ceremony is what we refer to when we talk about the treaty.... We expected that you would behave like relatives and help us in hard times, just as we took the responsibility to help you if you needed it. We expected to keep living as a family with a new family in the neighborhood.... You became my relative at treaty, you are my relative today, and our children and grandchildren and great-great-grandchildren, and so on, will be relatives in the future. (2007: 29–31)

Sylvia McAdam (2015: 41) affirms that Treaties are a ceremonial covenant of adoption: "During the Treaty 6 making process, the *nêhiyawak* understood it was adoption of the Queen and her descendants, binding the two nations together for all time. We became relatives." For the Treaty 1 relationship: "the Anishinabe kinship norms invoked duties of love, care, kindness, and equal treatment of all children" (Craft 2013: 16). Further, Craft (2013: 113) says, "In Anishinabe inaakonigewin [law], relationships never end. They are constantly fostered, re-defined, re-examined, and re-negotiated. They must be tended, fuelled, nurtured, or simmered." "Treaties are the fabric of creation," N.J. Sinclair (2015: 10) similarly writes,

binding all living things together in a vast and complete network of relationships. They are intricate ties that must be visited and re-visited, maintained and fortified, and can — with enough care and concern — be virtually indestructible. This is why treaties produce family, not friends. Family is for life.... Treaties are the template Indigenous people follow in creating and maintaining relationships.

N.J. Sinclair says: "Treaties are about trying to figure each other out for the rest of our lives. Forever" (2014: 32:25–32:30). As can be understood, these kinship bonds must be carefully nurtured.

Solidarity and Activist Relationships

In solidarity and anti-colonial activism, the ideal relationship is sometimes framed as that of *accomplices* (Indigenous Action Media 2014). *Accompliceship*s are accountable relationships built of trust and mutual consent in which non-Indigenous activists are at the side of Indigenous activists, complicit in their work, taking the same risks on the front lines. The creation of these meaningful relationships while attending marches and rallies, however, does not mean that non-Indigenous supporters are viewed by Indigenous Peoples as "one of us" (Xhopakelxhit 2014: 5) or that non-Indigenous people become universally accepted. Friendships between Indigenous Peoples and non-Indigenous people who are working toward decolonization can nonetheless become powerful sites of transformation. Dorothy Christian and Victoria Freeman (2010: 367) describe "how [friendship] can build or deepen our commitment to work for social change, and how powerful friendships can be in changing both parties — actually helping people to decolonize at a personal level." Such relationships are not always easy. Christian writes of the amount of energy it sometimes takes to be around non-Indigenous people, and of some of Freeman's colonizing behaviours. In the end, Freeman warns that

> friendship between Aboriginal and non-Aboriginal people is certainly not all that is required for decolonization. There are entrenched systemic issues of inequality, prejudice, violence, poverty, and theft of land that will take years of political action to address. But the relationship between our peoples does not exist only on a political level; it exists on every level, including the most personal. All of us are part of this relationship; all of us make it what it is. Working things through at a personal level can

prepare and strengthen us for other kinds of more public work. The tricky part is to understand what in the personal is political or social in origin. (Christian and Freeman 2010: 38)

A number of those whose narratives are included in this book credited the role of relationships with Indigenous Peoples in their work. In addition to Freeman, who also describes her friendship with Dorothy Christian in Chapter 18, John, in Chapter 15, says that his close friendships mean that he is more invested in anti-racism action and decolonial justice work, and Franklin, in Chapter 7, describes the support and love he experiences in his relationships that help him feel more connected and enable him to do anti-colonial work from the heart. Similarly, Monique, in Chapter 4, says that when you have relationships that matter to you, it motivates you to do something about the injustices your friends are facing.

ENGAGING WITH INDIGENOUS STORIES

In the opening of this book, we described a challenge issued by Dawnis Kennedy (personal communication, June 19, 2016): that non-Indigenous people see and understand ourselves within the stories of Indigenous Peoples rather than seeing ourselves solely as main characters in our own stories. This involves a process of decentring ourselves and learning to fit within Indigenous sovereignty. In order to do this, we need to begin to listen to Indigenous Peoples when they share their stories. After all, the failure of white peoples to "engage with the reality of Indigenous sovereignty" (Nicoll 2004: 370) is related to the "persistent failure of white people to respond appropriately to the true stories of Indigenous people" (2004: 370). These true stories of Indigenous Peoples may take many forms, including oral and written scholarship. Engaging with Indigenous literatures is, perhaps, an easy first step. LaRocque (2010: 14) writes of the "rapidly growing, consciously alert, decolonizing scholarship" of Indigenous Peoples. When settler scholars have trouble thinking beyond colonial mentalities, Indigenous scholars may not (Alfred 2008). While some Indigenous scholars and activists have expressed a weariness of settler expectations that Indigenous Peoples educate us and do the work of figuring out how we should engage in decolonization and solidarity efforts, Indigenous scholars who publish their work have chosen to make their ideas accessible. Their written scholarship is available for us to learn from if we are willing to put forth effort to locate and explore it. I personally have learned so much about living in Indigenous sovereignty this way. In recommending that settlers orient to the true stories of Indigenous Peoples, I frame stories broadly: What are true Indigenous stories related to prophecy? Treaty perspectives? Laws and teachings? Practices, Protocols, and ceremonies? Indigenous nationhood, governance, sovereignty, resurgence, and decolonization? And how do we fit within these? Already in this chapter, I have shared the words of some Indigenous scholars and Knowledge Holders regarding their stories about settler relationships with Indigenous Lands and Indigenous Peoples. Now, I share some stories related to these other elements.

Prophecies

At an Anishinaabe water law gathering, Dawnis Kennedy (personal communication, June 19, 2015) explained that Anishinaabe foresaw and considered a way for non-Indigenous people to belong here before we came to Turtle Island. Elder Peter Waskahat, Nêhiyawak (Cree) from Frog Lake First Nation, Treaty 6, says:

> Long before the arrival of the White man, the First Nations discussed how they would live with the White man. There were extensive discussions to determine how the First Nations could peacefully co-exist with the newcomers. The Elders say they knew the White man was coming across the sea from places where there was much bloodshed. On the island of the new world created by Wisahkecahk, that way of life could not prevail. The island of North America was created so that peace could prevail. When the newcomers arrived, peace treaties would need to be negotiated. It was decided long before the White man arrived that the First Nations would treat the newcomers as relatives, as brothers and sisters. The First Nations had decided they would live in peace and that they would share the land with these newcomers. (Cardinal and Hildebrandt 2000: 31)

Simpson (2011) describes the Seven Fires Prophecy as an epic narrative related to colonialism, decolonization, and resurgence. She says, "Many Nishnaabeg thinkers believe we are in the time of the Seventh Fire" (2011: 66), a time when the Oshkimaadiziig, or new people, will "pick up the pieces of our lifeways, collectivize them, and build a political and cultural renaissance and resurgence ... [that] has the power to transform settler society" (2011: 66). There is also an Eighth Fire Anishinaabe Prophecy, described by Bone, Copenace, Courchene, et al.:

> The 8th fire prophecy shares that a time will come when Mother Earth will enter into a change and rebirth, a time of a "New Life".... At that time all cultures of the world will gather here at the centre of Turtle Island to share their teachings and knowledge and collectively seek a vision that would create a "New People" representing all races of humanity. The New People will find a way to unite and create a new understanding of how to live in peace and care for the Earth ... we believe this time all the races of humankind will walk with us. Our prophecies have told us that it will be our people, the Red People who will lead this movement of return. (2012: 38, 44–45)

These powerful prophecies include settlers in what was foreseen, and provide a role for us in following the lead of Indigenous Peoples toward transformation. Simpson writes,

> In order for the Eighth fire to be lit, settler society must also choose to change their ways, to decolonize their relationships with the land and Indigenous Nations, and to join us in building a sustainable future based on mutual recognition, justice, and respect. (2008: 14)

Treaty Perspectives

As has already been described, many Indigenous Treaty perspectives focus on the sacred and ceremonial nature of Treaties, on the establishment of kinship relationships, on the sharing of land, and on mutual benefits and obligations. The use of Anishinaabe laws and Protocols inform "the substantive expectations of the treaty [One]" (Craft 2013: 16). Craft (2013: 16) says, "Anishinaabe law is all about relationships: relationships among and between ourselves, relationships with other animate beings. These relationships give rise to rights, obligations, and responsibilities." Thus, she writes, "kinship relationships, the obligations derived from them, and a sense of the sacred obligations involved in treaty making informed the agreement that was made between the parties" (2013: 13). A critically important point for settlers to understand and support is that Indigenous perspectives consistently affirm that Indigenous nations, during Treaty negotiations, did not cede, surrender, or agree to the extinguishment of their titles to their Traditional Territories (Craft 2013; Hubbard 2013; Johnson 2007; McAdam 2015). The Office of the Treaty Commissioner, Saskatoon, Saskatchewan, writes, "Elders firmly believe that the land was to be shared with the newcomers but that did not mean a loss of ownership" (2007: 18). This true Treaty story helps set the stage for our orientation toward Indigenous sovereignty because it shows us that, contrary to Crown perspectives on Treaty, Indigenous Peoples remain sovereign on Treaty lands. Craft (2013: 16) says, "Anishinaabe understandings of their relationship to Mother Earth informed what could be negotiated in terms of sharing the land with the incoming settlers." Craft notes, "It may have been that each party had a different understanding of what sharing the land actually entailed" (2013: 11). She writes,

> Anishinabe expected they would not be limited in their movements or their sustenance activities…. Neither an owner or a seller, the Anishinabe used the land and cared for it. The Anishinabe retained control over the land, subject to sharing it with the White settlers for the limited purpose of sustenance. (Craft 2013: 112)

Johnson also explains,

> When your family arrived here, *Kiciwamanawak*, we expected that you would join the families already here, and, in time, learn to live like us. No one thought you would try to take everything for yourselves, and that we would have to beg for leftovers. We thought we would live as before, and that you would share your technology with us. We thought that maybe, if you watched how we lived, you might learn how to live in balance in this territory. (2007: 21)

Certainly, Treaties did not establish Crown, or settler sovereignty, and "did not give [us] the right to impose [our] law, [our] customs, and [our] religion" (Johnson 2007: 66).

According to Kennedy (personal communication, June 19, 2015), in order to belong here, non-Indigenous people also need to learn to respectfully observe, belong to, and fit into the pre-contact Treaties of Anishinaabe law. As has been noted, pre-contact Treaties included Treaties with other-than-human life as well as Treaties between Indigenous nations. Spiritual Protocols and assistance were invoked during the making of Treaties, making them eternal and spiritually binding (Johnson 2007; McAdam 2015). Following the teachings of Haudenosaunee scholar and orator Dan Longboat, Leanne Simpson (2011: 21) says, "treaties are not just for governments, they are for the citizens as well. The people also have to act in a manner that is consistent with the relationships set out in the treaty negotiation process." Craft writes,

> My hope is that a better understanding of Anishinabe normative values and principles will assist in rebuilding the treaty relationship and allow us to honour its original spirit and intent. The core purpose of treaty was to create relationships, not to cede land — which was the way that it was understood by the Anishinabe and endorsed by the creator. (2013: 114)

Already having read the above perspectives by Indigenous scholars, I had begun to think of myself as a Treaty relative. When I moved to Sudbury in 2017, I immediately set to work trying to learn about the Robinson-Huron Treaty of 1850. I attended educational events, listened to Knowledge Holders speak about the Treaty, and began to follow the Robinson-Huron Treaty annuity case that was taking place in the courts after the twenty-one Robinson-Huron Treaty First Nations filed a Statement of Claim; in the Treaty, Canada had promised annual compensation for the sharing of land and resources that was to be increased as economic circumstances allowed. Yet the compensation had not increased since 1874. I attended some of the court sessions and Robinson-Huron Treaty gatherings, learning more about the Treaty and the case. After Justice Patricia Hennessy found in favour of the First Nations in the first two of three phases of the case, the province of Ontario filed an appeal. At a Treaty gathering, I heard how disappointed the First Nations members were about this, and I was angered that an elected government, said to represent me, would spend tax dollars to fight against having to uphold its Treaty obligations. I wondered what to do, and eventually, in consultation with organizations of the twenty-one First Nations, myself and two students in a course I was teaching started online and paper petitions demanding that Ontario drop its appeals. The petitions coincided with other events being held by the Robinson-Huron Treaty First Nations for Treaty Recognition Week in Ontario. Others whose narratives appear in this book have also engaged with Indigenous Treaty perspectives. In

Chapter 12, Kathi describes her Treaty research, helping to organize a Treaty 3 gathering, educating others about Treaty, and her involvement with fighting for Aboriginal Treaty Rights. Steve, in Chapter 6, shares that he views his work as both decolonization and Treaty relationship work, and that he has pursued more knowledge around Indigenous Elders' Treaty perspectives. Indeed, Indigenous Treaty perspectives are powerful true stories we need to know and place ourselves within.

Laws and Teachings

These stories overlap. True Treaty stories are not separate from true Indigenous legal stories and teachings. McAdam writes,

> In the spirit and intent of Indigenous sovereignty and treaty, and honouring Indigenous relationships; non-Indigenous people must begin supporting and encouraging Indigenous laws and teachings, in every aspect, and by whatever means possible. How this might look is up to the Indigenous nations working alongside these systems to intervene in colonial narratives, laws, and policies, and collectively work toward dismantling destructive and oppressive systems which have been imposed on Indigenous peoples through colonization. (2015: 36)

But what is Indigenous law? Borrows (2005: 190) writes, "Indigenous peoples in what is now Canada developed various spiritual, political and social customs and conventions to guide their relationships. These diverse customs and conventions became the foundation for many complex systems of law." These laws, according to Borrows, have often been recorded and communicated through oral histories, Elders, ceremonies, and wisdom keepers, and have been preserved using memory devices such as "wampum belts, masks, totem poles, medicine bundles, culturally modified trees, birch bark scrolls, petroglyphs, button blankets, land forms, crests, and more" (2005: 190). Nii Gaani Aki Inini (Dave Courchene) says, "Everyone and everything is held together and governed by Spiritual Laws and Natural Laws — laws that are woven into the fabric of Creation and written upon the Earth. We refer to this as *Okichitibakonikaywin* — The Great Binding Law" (2016a: para. 5). Johnson (2007: 27) says, "When your ancestors came to this territory, *Kiciwamanawak* [my cousin], our law applied." McAdam (2015) emphasizes the necessity of non-Indigenous people following the laws of the Indigenous Peoples on whose land we are staying. She describes a number of *nêhiyaw* laws including laws of transgression against other human beings (*Pâstâhowin),* and laws of transgression against other-than-human beings (*Ohcinêwin)* in which the people are instructed not to cause pain or suffering to animals, waste animal products, over-harvest trees, or pollute the environment. She writes, "No relationship could be developed without the *nêhiyaw law of miyo-wîcêhtowin*" (2015: 47), which refers to having good relations and "originates in the laws and relationships that their nation has with the creator" (2015: 47). As Xhopakelxhit (2014: 5) indicates, "saying you are in solidarity with indigenous people and sovereignty means you accept our laws and reject the illegal laws of the military state that is actively occupying our lands." But respecting and fitting into Indigenous law does not mean that we need see ourselves as less sacred or worthy than Indigenous Peoples. Recall Mills' words:

> It truly is important to recognize that one is a settler but that should never be an impediment to the practise of Anishinaabe law on Anishinaabe territory and that means standing within creation, not taking a dejected step back from it. (2016: para. 27)

Connected to true Indigenous laws are Indigenous teachings:

> Those teachings have evolved over thousands of years to get to a point to understand how best to relate to that land so it can be there for the next generations. Those teachings become the culture of this area. They become the basis for natural law in this area, in this particular nation, and that's important. We have to understand that land develops culture.... My ability to interact with my homeland, my ability to be Indigenous in my homeland, requires certain skills, certain understandings and certain teachings ... we have to see that the land will inform us, the land will tell us, the land will let us know how best to live here. And we in turn have to learn those rules, and those behaviours of how best to live with the land. When we don't abide by those rules, when we no longer respect the land we live on, we start to extract, we start to destroy, we start to commodify, we take. To the point where that land can no longer take care of you. (Ward 2015: 7:33–11:15, used with permission)

It is easy to see from Ward's words how our unwillingness to learn and follow Indigenous law has led to much of the destruction around us.

Practices, Protocols, and Ceremonies

The true stories of Indigenous practices, Protocols, and ceremonies are diverse and localized. Further, there are diverse views about the ways that settlers can fit into and orient towards these. Different nations and Knowledge Holders may hold differing views related to a host of issues, including the participation of non-Indigenous people in Indigenous spiritual and cultural Protocols and practices. There are historical, political, and structural contexts that shape views shared by Waziyatawin (2009), Mills (2017), and Graveline (2012) regarding white colonizers' participation. In emphasizing the importance of settlers learning about and living within Indigenous legal systems, Mills (2017: 24) is careful to point out that this does not mean he is inviting settlers "to participate in our ceremonies (and certainly not to perform them!); to visit our sacred sites; to wear, repurpose, or reproduce our sacred things; or to participate in any other form of cultural appropriation." He views these actions as a violation of Indigenous law. Fyre Jean Graveline (2012: 79) defines appropriation as "the process of taking land, ceremonies, stories, images and ideas without giving acknowledgement or benefits to the person or people who originally had it or came up with them," which leaves space for settlers to participate respectfully without taking and misrepresenting these.

However, Waziyatawin points out that such participation can also be offensive to many: As has been previously noted, "most Dakota people today are prevented, still, from living as Dakota people in our homeland" (2009: 154). This means they are unable to practise their traditional spirituality due, in part to being "denied access to sacred sites, lands, and waters that are central to [their] spiritual traditions" (2009: 154). She says, "Our spirituality remains inaccessible to most of our community members because our people do not know where or how to begin practicing the traditions that were stripped from us" (2009: 154). Therefore, she asks,

> What does it mean when white colonizers practice aspects of our culture while that privilege is still denied to us, or remains inaccessible for a variety of reasons? It is deeply offensive to most of us. White people coming to our ceremonies do not carry the traumatic history that we do. Instead, they come with a sense of

entitlement.… When Indigenous people object to their theft of our traditions, they dismiss those objections as hateful, angry, and un-spiritual. Yet, those individuals have appropriated our inheritance. They are practicing what has been denied our ancestors and what our children have yet to recover. It is just another assault on our spirit. (2009: 154)

She cautions that appropriation is "not a good way to build solidarity with the Indigenous struggle" (2009: 154). In light of these political and structural contexts, Waziyatawin suggests that at this time, a more helpful approach, rather than adopting Indigenous practices, would be to "work to ensure that Dakota people are able to practice Dakota ways of being" (2009: 155). Nonetheless, Waziyatawin states that this does not mean "others should never engage in Indigenous ways of being (2009: 154). Waziyatawin writes,

If we are struggling for Indigenous liberation on Indigenous lands, all people are going to have to practice Indigenous ways of being in some form. We will all need to engage in sustainable living practices and Indigenous cultures, including Dakota culture, offer excellent models for all people. That does not mean former-colonizers can appropriate our spirituality and ceremonial life, but it will mean they need to embrace Indigenous values such as balance and reciprocity. (2009: 154–155)

Mills (2019) describes an *earthway* praxis of the natural world and the connection of humans within it, pointing out that this is available to everyone, not just to Indigenous Peoples. However, Indigenous law and earthway understandings cannot be learned from the current liberal standpoints of settlers or through literature and mental engagement alone (Mills 2019). Thus, he nuances his perspective on appropriation:

Rooted systems of law can't be understood without a much larger commitment being undertaken.… One must be prepared to enter into, even if not to accept, the indigenous people's lifeworld. This requires a subjectivity reckoning, ordinarily accomplished in immersive whole-self experiences: again, one must be the law. A common starting point is the sweat lodge. One must learn how to learn indigenous law, which is to say that one must first learn about that indigenous people's lifeway, lifeworld, and legal traditions. This is no small endeavour and it isn't one which settler peoples (or anyone else) have a right to. That being said, if invited to participate and learn, settlers and indigenous peoples from other communities can certainly come to understand and practise indigenous law. (Mills 2019: 270)

This ties in with Nii Gaani Aki Inini's (Dave Courchene's) (2016b) belief that Anishinaabe prophecies place Indigenous Peoples as the true leaders of the land and urges that Indigenous Peoples return to their sacred lodges, awaiting the arrival of the newcomers who will come to seek advice. Concluding this discussion regarding Indigenous ceremony and appropriation, it is critical that engagement with Indigenous ceremony is undertaken by settlers only by invitation, with an understanding of how it may be rightfully perceived as hurtful by some and with respect for potential Indigenous refusal (Flowers 2015). Settler entitlement is not an appropriate approach here, and a critical examination of one's motives and related action is important. Settlers who engage by invitation should do so within the context of Indigenous Protocols and communities, avoiding material benefit from the knowledge and experience they gain, and being careful not to misrepresent or claim credit for any teachings they receive. In my perspective it is important, when receiving from Indigenous ceremonies, to be mindful of reciprocity, to also engage in anti-colonial/decolonial activism, and to support ceremonial communities with our labour and material contributions. With this being said, through this type of engagement there may be significant experiential learning that contributes to the deepening of understanding of Indigenous law and lifeways that may result in growth toward living in Indigenous sovereignty, as has been the case for me. Among those whose narratives are offered in this book, there is divergence in perspectives on, experience with, and ways of engaging with Indigenous Protocols, practices, and ceremonies. For example, John, in Chapter 15, has assisted with ceremonies by cutting wood, keeping the fire, cooking, and cleaning up. In Chapter 12, Kathi Avery Kinew says she takes part in some ceremonies, but generally sees herself as a supporter who helps keep the camp and prepare feasts. There are certain ceremonies in which she won't dance as a way to show respect for something that is "theirs." Initially cautious about appropriation, Franklin (Chapter 7) was later drawn in to ceremonies through relationships and has found balance and healing by participating in and supporting Indigenous ceremonies. Silvia describes, in Chapter 16, the healing and connection she has experienced through Indigenous ceremonies. She keeps in mind that she is a guest attending sacred practices that are not her own and limits what she shares afterwards.

ENGAGING WITH INDIGENOUS NATIONHOOD, GOVERNANCE, SOVEREIGNTY, RESURGENCE, AND DECOLONIZATION

How do settlers learn to live respecting, supporting, and orienting to true Indigenous stories of nationhood, governance, sovereignty, resurgence, and decolonization? Perhaps these questions signal the most obvious connections to anti-colonial and solidarity work. As Corntassel (2006: 36) notes, settlers "will have to decide how they can relate to Indigenous struggles." Alfred writes of the necessity that movements for resurgence and the defeat of the colonial system have "the support and cooperation of allies in the Settler society" (2005: 64), and Simpson (2013a: 56) calls upon Canadians to "lend their support to various expressions of Indigenous nationhood." Ignoring these calls is not an option for us. And yet we need to know these stories so that our efforts don't interfere with or undermine Indigenous perspectives and practices around them.

Nationhood, Governance, and Sovereignty

Mills (2019) asserts that Indigenous nationhood and sovereignty are among the most important concepts of Indigenous mobilization and resistance in our times. They enable "Indigenous lives [to be] lived on their own terms, freed from colonialism" (2019: 219). One way of supporting Indigenous nationhood is to relate with Indigenous Peoples through nation-to-nation partnerships reflective of original Treaties of peace and friendship (Alfred 2005). This means Indigenous nations are treated as sovereign and self-determining, with their own governments. In fact, as Manuel and Derrickson (2017: 265) explain, "Our political and legal status as Indigenous peoples obviously long predates contact with Europeans. It supersedes any assertion or assumption of sovereignty by states such as Britain or Canada." Sylvia McAdam notes that international law defines nationhood and self-determination as "based on the laws, cultures, lands, and languages of nations" (2015: 84). European superiority narratives and claims to Indigenous Lands as well as the Indian Act place Indigenous nationhood under siege (McAdam 2015), whereas Anishinaabe stories of nationhood and governance are embodied in the Anishinaabe Clan

System rather than the Indian Act (Daabaasonaquwat, Peter Atkinson 2016). Daabaasonaquwat (Peter Atkinson) says,

> We had our own system, our own governance system, and that's the Clans. We didn't have no Indian Act. We knew who we were.... In our Clan System, we had a lot of power, and the power was carried by the Clan Mothers. Women don't realize how much power you have. I'm not talking about women's rights, men's rights. In the Clan System we don't talk about rights. We talk about responsibility.... Every part of our life was identified in the Clan System. There were societies in each one of those Clans that looked after a segment of our nationhood.... We already have a governing system. We already are a nation. We already have nationhood. We always have that. We just have to deprogram our people, and reprogram them with the truth of who we really are.... We're a sovereign people.... This is our home. White people just live here. (2016: 1:52:38–2:01:42)

Simpson, also Nishnaabeg, says, "Our nationhood is based on the idea that our Earth is our first mother, that natural resources are not natural resources at all, but gifts from that mother" (2013b: 32:46–32:54). She says, "Our nationhood is built on the foundational concept that we should give up what we can to support the integrity of our homelands for the coming generations. We should give more than we take. It's nationhood based on a series of radiating responsibilities" (2013b: 32:55–33:14). Nii Gaani Aki Inini (Dave Courchene) (2016b) shared his perspective that Indigenous nationhood defines the duties, responsibilities, and gifts of Indigenous Peoples. The animals and the natural world (natural laws) provide guidance and direction to humans, establishing the framework for Indigenous governance and nationhood. Nii Gaani Aki Inini (Dave Courchene) says,

> Nationhood is not something that another Nation can give you. It is something that the Nation believes and establishes itself.... Colonial systems, structures and laws are only a distraction from living our true Nationhood. We do not have to waste any energy trying to change their system or convince them to recognize our Nationhood. All we need to do is live our Nationhood.... In living our true Nationhood, I see a day and a time that we will no

longer feed from the hand of the colonizer, but from the hand of Mide-Aki [Earth] who provides everything we need to survive.... Our Nationhood is about showing respect for Nature's authority that is based on balance and harmony. Our Nationhood is about following Nature's Laws that serve to nurture, teach and guide our lives towards survival. Our Nationhood is about returning the deep love we all receive from Mother Earth. Our Nationhood is about returning to the beginning, that holds the memory of the original instructions we were all given on how to be a human being, that reflects respect and kindness for all life. (2016b: para. 40, 46, 68, 100–104)

Consider Nii Gaani Aki Inini's (Dave Courchene's) statement that nationhood is something the nation believes for itself. Similarly, I am suggesting that settlers believe Indigenous nationhood and governance in our own processes of orienting to Indigenous sovereignty. Indigenous nations have their own systems of governance, according to "traditional rules contained within certain clans, houses, or districts," and yet they tend to all be "governed by a commitment to the collective — the Nation" (Palmater 2015: 1). Christi Belcourt (2016), Métis, believes discussions of nationhood should recall sacred alliances and agreements with the buffalo nation, the moose nation, the bear nation, the plants, and all living spiritual beings. She said, "We're alive because of them, and yet we allow the pollution of lands and waters where they live" (2016: 41:45–41:55). Indigenous governance, for Belcourt, keeps the children and the survival of all beings at the centre of decision-making. It also includes the rematriation of Indigenous Lands. Similarly, Alfred describes Onkwehonwe governance as

founded on relationships and obligations of kinship relations, on the economic view that sustainability of relationships and perpetual reproduction of material life are prime objectives, on the belief that organizations should bind family units together with their land, and on a conception of political freedom that balances a person's autonomy with accountability to one's family. (2005: 155)

Alfred (1999: 136) advocates that Indigenous governance achieves the basic goals of "rejecting electoral politics and restructuring native governments to accommodate traditional decision-making, consultation, and dispute-resolution process"; the reintegration of native languages as each community's official language; economic self-sufficiency, which is based on expanded land bases; and nation-to-nation relations with the state, including the defence of their territories. "We can rebuild our nations by living, asserting, and defending our individual and collective sovereignty every day, remembering always that our sovereignty is an *inherent* right, which is prior to our treaties, Canada, or any legislation," writes Palmater (2015: 4).

Yet many Indigenous scholars and Knowledge Holders are careful in the way they define sovereignty. For example, Mills (2019) cautions that the term itself has its origins with Western liberalism and its interpretation related to independence, authority, disconnection, hard boundaries, and autonomy. In response, a number of Indigenous scholars have sought to redefine sovereignty in keeping with Indigenous nationhood, relational, and Creation/land-based perspectives. Jolene Rickard writes,

> This notion of sovereignty as a matter confined to the legal sphere is not the kind of sovereignty that I grew up with among the Haudenosaunee, specifically the Tuscarora. Rather, my understanding of sovereignty as a form of *direct action* was shaped by my family history. (2017: 81)

In fact, Joanne Barker, Lenape, emphasizes that definitions of sovereignty belong "to the political subjects who have deployed and are deploying it to do the work of defining their relationships with one another, their political agendas, and their strategies for decolonization and social justice" (2005: 26). As those cited above have indicated, it is often linked to "concepts of self-determination and self-government, it insists on the recognition of inherent rights to the respect for political affiliations" (Barker 2005: 26). Chickadee Richard, Anishinaabe, explains that their homelands give Indigenous Peoples their sovereignty and identify them as a people:

> One of my Elders said, as long as you practice your ceremonies on the land, you're sovereign. As long as you're growing your food on the land, you're sovereign. As long as you're speaking your language, you're sovereign. We've never given that up. We've never surrendered that. It's still inside of all of us. We have natural laws that govern all of us. And it's only when we believe those natural laws that we become that sovereign people again. Because those

were the natural laws that governed us when we were placed on this land. (Richard 2016: 1:36:30–1:37:25)

Similarly, Sylvia McAdam, Nêhiyaw, says, "Once you know where your lands are, you'll know your relatives.... To speak your language is an act of sovereignty, your nationhood" (2016: 2:10:30–2:11:06). McAdam (2016) urges Indigenous Peoples to bring back their original structures of leadership in which the women had a powerful role and to learn about and follow traditional laws. Several settlers whose narratives appear in this book have engaged deeply with understanding and supporting Indigenous nationhood and governance. For example, Kathi Avery Kinew, in Chapter 12, describes learning about Indigenous nationhood and sovereignty from First Nations leaders in Treaty 3 Territory. Adam Barker's vision for decolonization, in Chapter 10, is the restoration of Indigenous nationhood and, as a settler, supporting Indigenous resurgence. This is where I turn my focus now.

Decolonization and Resurgence

"For Nishnaabeg thinkers, resistance and resurgence are not only our response to colonialism. They are our only responsibility in the face of colonialism. Resurgence is our original instruction," writes Simpson (2011: 65). As has been noted, for Hart (personal communication, January 14, 2016), Indigenous resurgence is the centre of anti-colonialism, pushing outwards from this centre and reclaiming space that had been occupied by settler colonialism. In order to support Indigenous resurgence, settlers need to learn about it and about the work Indigenous Peoples are doing in relation to decolonization. Indigenous resurgence is the antidote to colonialism, as it creates and propels life (Simpson 2011, 2014). It entails investment in and living of Indigenous ways of being, such as legal systems, intellectual and political traditions, and ceremonies (Simpson 2011). Resurgence is land-based, as connecting with lands is essential for recovery, and it should involve reoccupying sacred places and reconnecting with land-based practices (Coulthard 2014; Simpson 2013a). Although it should be non-violent, Alfred argues that resurgence should reflect "a credible threat to the colonial order" (2005: 204) and should "remake the entire landscape of power and relationship" (2005: 27).

Coulthard sees direct action as a path to Indigenous resurgence because it is a way to "physically say 'no' to the degradation of our communities and to exploitation of the lands upon which we depend … [and say 'yes' to] another modality of being, a different way of relating to and with the world" (2014: 169). He recommends blocking resource extraction from Indigenous territories while impacting Canada's economic infrastructure in order to transform its political economy, constructing Indigenous alternatives. These types of Indigenous resurgence "embody an enactment of Indigenous law and the obligations such laws place on Indigenous peoples to uphold the relations of reciprocity that shape our engagements with the human and nonhuman world — the land" (Coulthard 2014: 170). Indigenous resurgence and decolonization also mean developing relationships of solidarity, mutual aid, and mutual empowerment between urban and land-based Indigenous communities by addressing "the interrelated systems of dispossession that shape Indigenous peoples' experiences in *both* urban and land-based settings" (Coulthard 2014: 176). Decolonization and resurgence will mean designing and building a new economy based on Indigenous values and vision that also respects others who have come to live on Indigenous Lands (Nii Gaani Aki Inini 2016a).

For settlers, supporting and working in concert with Indigenous resurgence and Indigenous decolonization perspectives is essential. In this chapter, the words of Indigenous scholars, Knowledge Holders, and activists have offered a brief glimpse of these and other foundational understandings for settlers wishing to orient themselves toward Indigenous sovereignty. Pursuing such understandings should be perpetual and relational, so that we ever deepen our capacity to fit within and support Indigenous-led transformation.

CHAPTER 9

JOY EIDSE

Joy Eidse and Elizabeth Carlson-Manathara

IDENTITY AND EARLY INFLUENCES

The granddaughter of Dutch immigrants to southern Ontario, Joy Eidse is a forty-one-year-old married, heterosexual, middle-class, recovering evangelical mother, daughter, sister, artist, and social worker. Joy sees herself as someone who has gained from the dispossession of Indigenous Peoples from their lands, people she had very little contact with during her childhood. She says, "My grandparents became farmers and were able to become somewhat wealthy, and that's been passed on to me." Joy believes her social justice sensitivity has been influenced by the teachings she received through the church:

> I remember sermons from when I was a really small child, [they] were really black and white in terms of good and bad, and justice and injustice, and right and wrong. I was a pretty receptive kid to that kind of stuff and took it to heart.... I was pretty drawn to the teachings of Jesus in terms of his perspective on *the least of these*, the poor.... That resonated with me from a pretty young age.... I feel like that foundation made me continue to pursue good and to not give up on that.

Joy's Pentecostal Church upbringing also taught her that anyone outside of her specific Christian group "would [not] make it to heaven, [and] needed to be evangelized and converted," which she believed into her early twenties.

LEARNING AND EARLY ACTIVISM

Joy's process of coming to understand colonialism in Canada occurred in tandem with a re-examination of her faith tradition as she began to realize the church's harmful effects on herself and others. The first time she considered her relationship with Aboriginal people was around the age of eighteen, due to a difficult experience while touring Alberta on a church mission trip. "The Heal our Land Tour was about relationship[s] between Aboriginal and white people, coming from an evangelical Christian perspective … with the idea that the way to heal would be to pray and to evangelize," Joy says. She describes an uncomfortable moment during the trip:

> At one point I remember we drove out to some reserve area and there were fences and signs. The leader said, "I think we're just going to go *through* the fence, and stand on the land and pray." And I remember feeling pretty uncomfortable, but we went out there and stood in a circle and prayed, and a couple of people came up from the reserve and were pretty upset with us for being on the land. I was pretty uncomfortable because we had crossed the boundaries. Our leader talked to them and I didn't catch what was all going on, but then we left afterwards and I remember him specifically talking about how "one person was fairly reasonable and okay to talk to, [but] the other person," he says, "has been drinking, and was not happy with us." So it was because he was drinking, that's why he wasn't happy with us. That was my first feeling that something's not right in this relationship. I feel like we'd done something wrong in this instant, but it was obviously much bigger than that, in my mind. So that was kind of the beginning, for me, of a decolonizing process.

After Joy met her partner, a Native studies student, they became involved in a church community in Winnipeg that operated a charitable drop-in centre and soup kitchen. Their role was to serve food and talk with people, and "hopefully to evangelize them at some point, or to find out what their needs were." This work was often from the perspective of "make sure it's a genuine need and they're not just trying to get something from you." They observed that many of the people who attended the drop-in centre and soup kitchen were Aboriginal, and they wondered why this was. They also sensed "the stereotypes that we had been told about Aboriginal people were being embedded in us just by interacting in that space alone, and so we needed to broaden our connections." Thus, Joy's partner suggested they move north to relate with Aboriginal people in a different context. Because they intended that the journey also entail a process of reconsidering their identities as evangelical Christians, they decided that when they moved north, they would not "evangelize in any way." After moving to Norway House, they visited the churches in the community to see if they could find a connection, but they found the local ministers to be perpetuating messages that Aboriginal languages and cultures were evil. Thus, they decided not to attend church. They suspected that the harm caused by Christianity through colonization might be due to its entanglement with Western culture and capitalism, and they set out to untangle it and find its core. As Joy read authors such as Adam Smith, she wondered, "What's the theory here? This is just common sense." However, as time went on, Joy realized she was so blinded by her socialization into Western culture that she couldn't discern its theories or imagine alternatives. She says, "That's the point at which I was like, 'I can't be evangelical in any way because I can't separate what's my culture and what's religion.'" This was a significant shift for Joy, who had wanted to be a missionary and had trained to become a pastor.

In Norway House, Joy encountered different relationships with Aboriginal Peoples than she had experienced in Winnipeg. She says, "Everyone was related to each other and they all had homes and families and people to care for them," and thus, "nobody was needing me for anything, really, and in fact I was the lonely person that needed some community." Joy attended a group for women and found that as the only white person in the group, she was being supported and mentored by the Indigenous women.

After moving back to Winnipeg, Joy began an access-based bachelor of social work program, which had a significant effect on her decolonial learning. Being in class with mature students — most of whom were either Aboriginal or racially marginalized — and some Aboriginal instructors was life changing, as were some of the anti-colonial readings in the curriculum. Around the same time, Joy and her partner received government funding to invite people into their home who were at risk of homelessness. The combination of housing Aboriginal Peoples and newcomers at risk of homelessness and being in school taught Joy about the dangers of paternalism. She realized that her ways of supporting the folks they housed were sometimes quite disrespectful, oppressive, and colonizing. She felt responsible for them and tried to save them. She would make decisions for people, take control of things, and impose her idea of what they needed, believing "they were not capable." Joy learned the importance of remembering, as an aspiring ally, that "this is as much your process as the people that you are aligning yourself with." She learned that holding paternalistic assumptions about what will be helpful to them was harmful, whereas walking with the community and supporting in ways that are invited, while focusing on herself and her own decolonization process, is safer.

DECOLONIZATION WORK AND CONTINUED LEARNING

Joy's decolonization practice is a very personal process. She believes that change has to start with the individual, which means understanding her identity, history, roles, and attitudes and also the ways these influence her decisions and practices in order to be more conscious.

Joy began to realize that with her Dutch and English heritage, her "community has colonized the planet, basically." For Joy, decolonization also means "taking responsibility for re-educating ourselves on our own history [and] re-educating our kids on our history." Joy's re-education has involved understanding European colonizing beliefs, such as:

> They had a mandate from God to go and take over the world … because they had the truth, and there was one truth … [thus] my ancestors went out and found some land and decided that they were the only people that really mattered, so they could live there and take that land.… They probably perceived the Indigenous people and the land as less than human, and according to scripture, they were here to dominate and rule over them, so they had every right in their own minds to push them off the land, to kill them, to change them however they wanted, and so they stole this land, and then became wealthy on it and continued to do it, because "might" makes right in European mindset.

Joy's decolonization practice infuses the parenting of her young boys. She says, "This is my family and I'm responsible for how my children turn out." It is her goal to "raise kids that understand the big picture and have really good skills of empathy and open mindedness, being able to be self-critical." She has homeschooled them and has spent time deconstructing kids' novels and games. Joy has been quick to pass on books and movies from her childhood, only to find that "I sit down with my kids with a new perspective, and I'm shocked by how blatant the messages are and how clear the indoctrination is." Joy has realized that many classic novels come from Britain and perpetuate colonial perspectives. She worries about the heritage she is passing on to her kids. She wants them to be "proud of their heritage, and yet honest about it too." She says, "At some point you have to decide what parts you are going to embrace because you can't just turn around and hate yourself because you've been bad to someone else — just flipping it on yourself is not the answer."

When living in Holland, Joy discovered, "I felt really at home there, people were really blunt, nobody beat around the bush, and I just loved it." Although parenting young children has limited Joy's availability to attend some justice-related events, they sometimes attend as a family. Joy also supports her partner's anti-colonial work:

> My partner is involved in a Hydro Justice group for Northern communities, and I'm 100% supportive of that work and support him by making sure that he has freedom to go to those things. People with young kids will understand that's a piece of work, to make sure that you can help people attend those kinds of things and do the work that they want to do in that process.

With her religious background, Joy finds symbols very meaningful. Her experience in the arts has influenced a number of decolonization projects she has been involved in. Joy says,

> It's a natural way for me to express myself. I think sometimes relying too heavily on words can be dangerous [and] … the arts community is a lot more about not trying to educate or evangelize or change people.… Sometimes using symbol[s] is a way that can be really honest, and can be moving, and it can invite people to interpret beyond what your intended message may be.… It leaves room and it gives respect to others.

Joy has been involved with an artistic collaboration about water and the state of the Red River and Lake Winnipeg. The project focused on "seeing water as a life source and seeing water as fundamental to our existence."

Along with a support group of white anti-racism activists, Joy made an artistic submission to the Truth and Reconciliation Commission of Canada. She wanted to dispel the idea that the TRC is "an Indigenous thing that has little to do with those who weren't there" and emphasize the role of Euro-Canadians in reconciliation. Joy says, "That felt really right to me in terms of being able to express something in a very meaningful [way].... Having an invitation like that was a really good, clear place to respond to." Joy's contribution to the submission was fabric art involving "quilts that were maps of places [she'd] lived and the closest Aboriginal community to it." This helped her work towards understanding the land differently, and she has reconsidered her land ownership. Joy says,

> I don't know a ton about my particular little square of land on College Avenue.... The other property, out near Rose Isle, we're just learning about. We did some research recently, and of course there was very little written about who lived on the land before the Mennonites, but there was talk about conflict between the Mennonite farmers and the Aboriginal people in the area, and I know from other texts that weren't specific to that particular spot that the Aboriginal people were farming in that area at one time and were kind of legally pushed off the land by the government, who started making rules to make it impossible for them to survive as farmers there. And then that land was given to the Mennonite community, which is my husband's family, who became quite wealthy as a result, and the Aboriginal people in that area are now relegated to the reserves and the two communities don't mix.... We bought this property a year ago, and it's 40 acres and it's beautiful nature. I definitely have mixed feelings about that piece of property and the ownership that's in our hands right now, and feeling like we're really going to need to be conscientious about what we do with this piece of paper that says we own this land and what we do with this land. It feels like it's entrusted to us to some degree, and I don't know who entrusted it, because it wasn't entrusted willingly by the people that were there before. It feels very complicated, that relationship. I don't know what the clear answer is, if I was just asked to just give it up, could I do that? I don't know. Like, I can't really imagine what scenario would happen that would make it really clear to me what the right answer would be in terms of what to do with the land that

I own, other than at this point, I feel really comfortable in being
as good steward as possible with that land, in terms of the nature
that is on that land, and caring for it.

Joy has taken part in organizing educational workshops through the
Centre for Anti-Oppression Studies related to white privilege and becoming an ally. As the Idle No More movement was gaining momentum, Joy
and a group she belonged to aspired to be allies in the movement and
planned a teach-in to "look at our role in that whole process ... around
anti-racism and white colonial perspectives, and looking at how people of
non-Aboriginal descent could participate in this movement." Joy reflects
on these educational events:

> There was so much discussion generated and people just couldn't
> get enough. It was very hopeful for me to see that people from
> all walks of society and professions were engaging in this and
> taking it as a really serious thing to move forward on, from the
> non-Aboriginal community.... I participated in that as a learner
> as much as somebody helping to organize, and so that's been a
> good process because I am not an expert.

Joy also does educational work by "trying to speak out when things are
really overtly biased in work and family situations." She tries to gauge when
to speak up and when speaking up causes too much damage to relationships. Having been a radical evangelical, Joy struggles with decolonial
practices that involve intensity, because "that's exactly what my history has
been." She sees danger in putting "the mission above the people ... where
your ideology and your truth for the day become all-encompassing at the
expense of people around you, of the relationships." This means Joy has
shied away from doing some types of activist work, not wanting to "fix
somebody, or change somebody, or convert somebody to my ideology."
She also tries to balance the time she spends working for justice with her
accountability to her family and community, not wanting these relationships to suffer because of her work. She explains,

> In family contexts and in workplaces, when somebody will say
> something that I feel is pretty racist ... or just ignorant in some
> way, and I've really had to think through, okay, what is the process
> right now for me to speak up as a self-identified ally, as a person
> who is processing this herself, as a friend of this person, as a family

member who values my relationship with them? What does this look like exactly, so it doesn't come down as this hard line, like, "you've used the wrong word in this sentence therefore you are now outside of my realm of understanding in terms of what is right and just in this situation," and that can cause rifts.

Joy is realizing the need to "come with the same amount of humility" in her interactions with people of her own community as she would when interacting with Aboriginal people; seeing the work as a process they are engaged in together and her perspective as one that does not judge or measure where the other person is at.

Joy feels her privilege allows her to "work the system for good." Despite the academy being a "very colonized model of education," it fits for her, and she finds it easy to function in that world. Therefore, Joy feels that perhaps her success in school will give her "a bit of power to make some changes in it, and to be able to speak the language in a way that could be translated." Similarly, her "history in right-wing Christianity" might allow her to "bring information to that group of people in a way that they could accept it." Because "Euro-Canadians dominate the systems," Joy feels "we need to be responsible for taking charge of those systems that are oppressing and determine what it is about them that is oppressive and correct it."

A number of emotional processes have characterized Joy's work. She has felt guilt about the negative impact she likely had on the people at risk of homelessness who stayed with her, intensified because she is someone who "really, really just wants to do the right, perfect thing every time and not make any mistakes and never hurt anyone's feelings." When she thinks about the harm she has done, she doesn't know if she's "a safe person for [Indigenous people]," and she has found herself pulling away from relationships with them, "partly out of that same anxiety." She hopes this dynamic changes as she figures things out. Joy has felt anger "on a regular basis about the ignorance and continuing oppression by the European community in Canada." And yet she wants her anger to be productive. She wonders,

> How do I affect change among my people if I'm just angry at them? Because if I experience that towards me, I certainly wouldn't feel inspired to change or to learn more. How do I have some compassion for where people are coming from because I was in that place, I did things that were really awful, totally [with] good

intentions. How do I know their intentions aren't good and they're just coming from a similar place?

Joy has also faced grief. She says,

> Learning about residential schools, I feel like every month a new thing comes out about what happened in those schools that's just really, really awful and devastating, and I grieve this horrible thing, but I still feel like I'm grieving from a distance … and I'm not sure what to do with it.

Some of Joy's experiences of guilt and anger have begun to shift as she has grown to "recognize if I can be okay [with] myself as a human being that's not going to get it all right the first time, there's a chance that I'm going to be much more okay with other people and gracious with other people." Despite the emotional struggles that have characterized Joy's journey, she sees the joy and peace in her work as she discovers different ways of knowing. Having grown up in the church and been taught to view spirituality as separate from the natural world, Joy's work and the teachings she has gained through it have helped her to heal this fracture in her life. She says, "The way that I interact with nature and other people now, in a new way of understanding, is going to bring me more life, and be kind of a healing factor in my life."

Joy and her partner have limited the time they spend earning money through employment in order to "give time to other things that don't pay," such as their decolonization work, while still "trying to be responsible parents and taking care of their children." They have discussed being willing to look at giving the land they own if it were to come up in the future. As far as being willing to risk physical harm and jail time, Joy says, "It would have to be a family decision [because] … those would deeply impact my kids…. My children's mother being harmed is a traumatic thing for a child, and going to jail would mean time away from them."

Joy envisions a future in which all people are respected and able to have agency in their own lives. It is a world in which Aboriginal Peoples are seen as "human beings that are worth consulting with when making decisions that impact their lives" and Euro-Canadians are humble about our history of perpetrating oppression, take ownership for social ills rather than blaming, and learn to ask questions and listen to answers. She wants to see Euro-Canadians take responsibility for our side of the process of reconciliation with Aboriginal Peoples. Joy does her work because she wants to know that "what I've done is valuable in life [and] has not been actually awful and harming." Joy does this work for herself, for her family, for her community, for her culture, and for all of Canada, "because we're part of this process."

CHAPTER 10

ADAM BARKER

Adam Barker and Elizabeth Carlson-Manathara

IDENTITY AND EARLY INFLUENCES

There is no one lower in society than a liar and a thief, because they take something that doesn't belong to them. His father, a career police officer, shared this sentiment with Adam Barker. Adam was born and raised in the middle-class white suburb of Stoney Creek, Hamilton, Ontario; the taken-for-granted reality that he assumed to be the backdrop of everybody's life. Inspired by the strong ethical sense of his parents, as a youth Adam was a proud, patriotic, card-carrying member of the Liberal Party of Canada who aspired to fulfill his social responsibilities by becoming a lawyer and then a politician. This changed when Adam became aware of the real history of Canada and its ongoing processes of colonialism in which he is implicated. In Mr. Hall's high school Native studies class, Adam learned that his society is invasive and occupies stolen Indigenous Land. His father's words about liars and thieves took on a new meaning for Adam, who was determined to "be responsible to that important lesson he had given me, that you don't just take things from people." He says, "I didn't want to be the one who took things."

LEARNING

Indigenous scholars have had much influence on Adam's path. During his time at McMaster University, Adam enrolled in Indigenous Studies courses at the urging his professor, Dr. Sylvia Bowerbank, due to an essay he wrote for her class. Accustomed to doing well in school, Adam floundered in these courses, failing exams and being confronted by classmates. His new learnings caused his worldview to wobble, leading to struggles with anxiety and depression. In his fourth year at McMaster, Adam attended a talk by

Taiaiake Alfred, a Mohawk scholar who ran the Indigenous Governance Program at the University of Victoria. Adam had read his book and told him he was thinking about applying for the program. Later, Dr. Alfred introduced Adam as someone who is "going to come to our program." Adam says, "It was very clear to me that it wasn't a formality, that it was sort of a demand." But Adam worried that he might "tak[e] up a spot that should be going to an Indigenous student." Dawn Martin Hill, head of the Indigenous Studies program at McMaster, encouraged Adam to apply nonetheless. She said, "When I, as a Mohawk woman, engage these issues, people dismiss me ... when it comes from you, and you have nothing personally to gain from it, they can't dismiss that."

After what he had already learned, Adam thought he really knew something coming into the Indigenous Governance Program (IGOV) at the University of Victoria. He was in a classroom with a majority of Indigenous students. Confrontations occurred in class, often as a result of Adam's oppressive practices in the classroom and his arrogant assertions that he had the answers. At times he talked over classmates and dismissed experiences they shared when these contradicted his theoretical under-standings. This culminated in a crisis point when he nearly dropped out after coming back to Ontario for the holidays one year:

> I remember lying on my bed and crying, and saying, "I can't do this! They hate me because I'm white."... Emotionally I was not handling it.... I used to have nightmares of going into that room and having [my classmate] sitting there and being "No, you're wrong! No, you're wrong! No, you're wrong!"

Adam returned at his partner Emma's insistence, since they had already bought his return plane ticket. He continued, in part due to guidance he received from Paulette Regan, a white settler person working on a PhD in the program. Paulette's use of the term *settler* helped Adam to make sense of his struggle. She advised him that discomfort was an expected and appropriate experience when coming to terms with his own complic-ity with colonialism. He says, "discomfort is an indicator that I'm going the right way. So I used it as my compass. I followed the discomfort." If the first phase of Adam's learning process was characterized by the shock and discomfort of coming to an awareness of colonialism, the second phase was characterized by his effort to find grounds for his innocence. He says, "I went through a lot of years of trying to find ways to justify my behaviour, justify my way of being on the land that made me legitimate, that gave me sort of an authentic identity as a Canadian." The third phase, then, which began towards the end of his IGOV program and continues into the present, has been an acceptance of his complicity and a commitment to work toward justice. Although he still finds himself lapsing into pursuing innocence, Adam credits his turning point in the third phase to the influences and teachings of his IGOV instructors, Taiaiake Alfred and Jeff Corntassel, along with his classmates. In particular, he says his classmate Chawwinis Ogilvie (Roots), a Nuu-chah-nulth activist, "relentlessly pursued me to stay vigilant with myself." Nonetheless, when Adam entered a collaboration with Harsha Walia on a *New Socialist* publication special edition, he again approached it as someone who thought he had everything figured out and was no longer implicated in colonialism. Harsha gently and persistently called him out on this. Adam says, "Boy did I learn a lesson that day, I got schooled. And I refused to think about it for the longest time because it made me so uncomfortable to realize that I could try so hard and blow it so badly."

Adam's partner Emma has deepened his analysis by bringing nuance to his blunt political stances. Within the context of an intimately trusting relationship, they challenge one another. They lived in the U.K. during his doctoral studies, which, he says, "ultimately has brought me back and re-involved me in a very active and embodied way in the struggles here, in what is, however illegally or illegitimately, my only home."

DECOLONIZATION WORK AND CONTINUED LEARNING

Adam's vision for his decolonization work is the restoration of Indigenous nationhood, which will ensure the land is taken care of and that current processes of resource extraction and cultural homogenization are replaced with dynamic and life-supporting ones. He says,

> The process is [that] land needs to be restored to Indigenous nations, Indigenous nations need to have the chance to have full and sustainable healthy, political, and cultural lives, and settler people need to reposition themselves as fitting into those frameworks.

"Indigenous nations are already on the path to resurgence," says Adam, and this will occur in complex and multiple ways in accordance with the

will of diverse nations. Adam sees his role as making space for this process rather than imposing his ideas as to the forms it should take. Instead
of seeking to replicate Indigenous decolonization practices, as a settler
Adam sees his role as a saboteur of colonial systems, opening space for
alternatives to emerge. Adam considers his decolonization work to have
begun in 2006 when he joined the Indigenous People's Solidarity Working
Group in Victoria and became involved in education campaigns about
issues such as mining in Indigenous territories in British Columbia. Adam
used his writings to bring an understanding of settler colonialism and
settler personhood to the *New Socialist* group there. When Adam worked
for the Ministry of Education in British Columbia, his goal was to "do
everything I can to be throwing wrenches into the machinery of this big
culture-destroying machine." He took a harm-reduction approach, hoping he could slow down the destruction. There he questioned the false
dichotomy between reformist and radical work that disrupts colonialism,
realizing these roles are complementary and we can honour work in both.

Adam has done educational work within his personal relationships by
engaging in decolonizing conversations with other settlers both in Canada
and in the U.K. Adam engages the colonially oppressive things settlers say
as a matter of responsibility because people with privilege may lash out
violently or cry in order to "centre themselves as a wounded subject," and
Indigenous Peoples should not have to deal with this. Adam has "tried to
bring an understanding of both the existence and the urgency of ongoing
colonialism and struggles for decolonization in North America to people
in the United Kingdom" and has made sure "that all [his] students knew
that Canada is not that happy, peacekeeping country of people saying 'eh',
wearing toques and playing hockey." He speaks with random others in
the U.K. who may acknowledge their imperial history but don't always
see their responsibility.

Being in the U.K. when Idle No More hit Canada afforded Adam an
opportunity, through social media, to "hear really clearly what people were
doing and what they wanted." He noticed "a lot of well-meaning settler
activists who hadn't done a lot of interrogation of their own positions," and
Adam decided to get his voice out there on social media, get involved in
conversations, and create online videos. Upon returning from the U.K., at
a teach-in with the Biskaabiyaang Collective in Thunder Bay — a city with
a serious anti-Indigenous racism problem — Adam was able to translate
some of his academic expertise into something meaningful to guide public

discourse. During a community panel in "very white, fairly well-off, and fairly conservative" Burlington about missing and murdered Indigenous women, he spoke of the roles of settler colonialism and gendered violence and how settlers are complicit in everyday actions.

Adam learned the importance of educating settlers through long-term relationships of care, a willingness to "go into hard emotional places with people," and a sound analysis. Because he is a passionate and emotional person who cares deeply about doing the right thing, he is able to create an empathic connection and spark movement in others. Adam and his partner also put time into maintaining solid relationships with settlers doing decolonization work. They try to be supportive, offer encouragement, and "make sure people are aware they're valued." Adam says,

> We've built this little family of people who are always ready to sort of jump in and help each other out ... we're people who trust each other and care about each other, and we're going to fight for each other and with each other.

"Many of us go into these dark places," Adam says, "it's not something a lot of activists like to talk about ... people bottom out and there's no care there for them." When others are struggling and doubting the importance of their work, Adam tries to "be the person who can step up to somebody else and say, 'What you do matters to me.'"

Adam is a naturally talented speaker who was pushed into positions of leadership as a youth. As a white male with privilege, he can dominate conversations, being allowed to speak when "other people might be silenced." Adam tries to use this privilege to say what needs to be heard and to work towards dismantling that very privilege. At the same time, he has realized he uses his command of conversation to control social situations in which he feels uncomfortable. He is learning to listen and just exist in social relationships, and to take more of a supportive role in his activism. Now, he is rarely the person at the front making headlines and planning actions.

Adam views his academic teaching as a way to engage in transformative decolonizing struggles through personal relationships. He "allows students to see opportunity to participate in building a different world, even as [he] insists that they understand their complicity in and responsibility for settler colonial racism, dispossession, inequality, and genocide." His academic publications are essential to his activism as spaces to reflect, interrogate, and strategize around his decolonization work. Adam embraces the field of settler colonial theory:

> Even as I move into a phase of my work where my primary pre-occupation becomes working on settler colonialism, trying to dismantle it as a settler person, transforming my own identity as a settler person, transforming settler society ... nothing I do would be possible without relationships [with Indigenous Peoples].

Settler colonial studies provides a space where Adam can "start figuring out how our machinery of colonization runs, and start taking it apart ourselves" because "Indigenous thinkers have a much bigger job to do of reconstituting their own cultures, nations, and identities, undoing the damage of colonization."

For settler people, decolonization means "a fundamental reorientation of our relationship to the land we live on," Adam says. Settlers need to change the way we think about the land and build new relationships, economies, and political practices. Indigenous communities "have particular sets of relationships and responsibilities and ways of interacting with the land," practices that can be supported by settlers through our unique contributions. Knowing that he is living on Haudenosaunee Territory is Adam's "anchor and starting point," the "referent that has to be maintained above all else." Adam emphasizes that rather than taking on Indigenous views of the world, settlers can stand next to Indigenous Peoples, adding different perspectives without imposing. He says,

> That means a lot of watching and thinking, and being deeply considerate of the implications of your actions ... and then try to fit in. Not to integrate in, not to assimilate in, not to disappear and submerge in, but to fit your difference in alongside in a way that enhances all of those relationships ... [and] improves everybody's quality of life.

Settlers use many means to try to "mediate our illegitimate status on the land ... displace[ing] the Indigenous relationship to the land." Trying to go "back to the land" disrespects that "Indigenous people have been driven off the land." Rather than doing things that Indigenous Peoples are prevented from doing and trying to become Indigenous in his own way, Adam aims to "support pre-existing Indigeneity in a way that ... enhances the Indigenous relationship rather than detracting from it." We need to replace "our current processes of extracting resources, using up the land, and pushing people aside … with one that's rooted in land as a living thing." Reorienting to the land means ceasing to think of land as property, which is difficult. He says,

> I would love to have my own house one day, and that means that I'm thinking about land as property because I'm thinking about the part of it that's fenced off that makes it mine and not someone else's. And instead, to start thinking of land as how it's interconnected and what makes that fence and what makes that property line an imposition on the land.

Instead of interpreting ownership of land as a licence to do with the land what we will, we have a responsibility to ask, "What does the land want me to do with it?"

In 2013, Adam was involved in an Indigenous-led land-focused action, in which a sacred site formerly known as Mount Douglas was re-united with its traditional name, Pkols. Chief Eric Pelkey came forward with a clear vision and had the support of his community and WSÁNEĆ nations. Taiaiake Alfred and Jarrett Martineau helped with coordination, reaching out to settler solidarity groups, which took part in respectful ways without taking over and offered strategically helpful contributions. It was important to Adam to take on tasks where his privilege, and how others perceived him, would likely keep him safe in situations that might be risky to others. In this case, Adam chatted with the police — putting to use familiarity with police as the son of a policeman and his appearance as a professional white male. Eventually, at ease, they drove away. This empowering, symbolic event had a resonating effect that inspired actions across Canada.

Adam engages in relational, cognitive, and emotional processes of growth and learning that are informed by Indigenous Peoples and undergird his decolonization work. He says,

> The ability to try and displace colonialism from my life only becomes possible because of the fact that Indigenous Peoples and literatures and ways of thinking have over time become centred in my life. The understandings that I've come to through my interactions and relationships with Indigenous communities are the wrecking ball that smashes through the structures of settler

colonialism and produce for me the option of rebuilding something different. Those relationships generate possibility.

Adam has learned about pre-colonial Indigenous societies and how these
connect with vibrant present-day resistance and resurgence. He has
learned about Indigenous political systems, Treaties and agreements, and
relationships with the land. He says, "If given a choice, I would rather live
as an immigrant or a guest of that Indigenous system than as a citizen
of this one."

Adam works to continually interrogate and transform his private self,
his everyday practice, and his relationship with the land. He has learned
to unflinchingly look at himself as a colonizer, to see the things in himself that could be decolonized, and also to admit and accept the things
that are very colonial about himself. Over the years, a number of Adam's
Indigenous friends have encouraged him to reconnect with his roots:
"Everyone's got an indigenous heritage somewhere and you should go
back there and reconnect with that — you'll understand yourself better,
where you're from." A friend of his went back to seek her roots in Ireland
and said, "As soon as I set foot in Ireland, I knew this was where I belong."
Adam has spent a number of years in the United Kingdom, from where
his grandparents had emigrated. He felt nothing like what his friend
described, but did come to a realization of how strongly the forces of settler
colonialism had shaped his identity. By accepting colonial discourses that
legitimized their belonging on someone else's land, Adam's grandparents
became settlers rather than British. Adam observes that "indigenous to
somewhere" statements can be used by settlers to "claim some kind of
authenticity and Indigeneity" and to avoid one's implication in colonialism. Adam has concluded that in his entanglements with colonialism,
he is indigenous to nowhere. He sees no authentic indigenous reality in
Britain, where relationships with land are mediated through systems of
private property, capitalism, and industrialization. He is faced with the
fact that "all I've got is this, which means I have to double down on my
responsibility here. I can't claim a connection to somewhere else, all I've
got is this one, and the claim that I've got here is violent."

Adam says, "One of the things that got me into all this politics in the first
place was how pissed off I was ... at the injustice of the world." Although
"a great deal of productive energy comes out of anger" he has had to
"learn how to direct it properly." He experiences physical stress when he
is in situations in which he has no control, which is so uncomfortable

that he wants to withdraw from engaging and gives himself the excuse that he doesn't want to take space from Indigenous Peoples. He observes that both dominating and withdrawing from activism are ways he tries to maintain control, and this awareness allows him to take a breath and face his fear. Despair has been a periodic aspect of Adam's work due to crises of faith and failures. In these moments, his "own personal struggles and the larger struggle for decolonization [may] become conflated." At times, he experiences an unhealthy constant questioning of "Am I doing enough? Am I good enough? Have I failed? Have I screwed things up? Have I hurt people?" When he faces failures, Adam remembers that people doing decolonization work are up against the "fundamental basis of oppressive power over an entire continent," and thus, failure is often not about personal deficiency.

Settler privilege may isolate us from seeing the harm we cause, whereas connections with Indigenous Peoples help us to see the damage that results from our colonial ways. Adam continues to try to let go of his ego in order to listen deeply when people tell him "your assumptions are wrong, the things that you care about and value are wrong in that they hurt people." He says, "The first thing that you feel when you start to go through that is a lot of guilt," which can be transformative. However, if settlers live in it and carry it around, it drains energy that "could be put into something productive." He tries to use feelings of guilt, shame, and embarrassment to figure out where he has gone wrong, acknowledge it and work on it, and then let the feelings go. He is also helped by accountability to community:

> In my darkest times when I was looking for that way out, it was the fact that there were people who needed me who I just couldn't let down ... this individual who I loved and who loved me and made that known, needed me to do something. That was what kept the despair from completely taking over. It's that heart to heart that makes the movement function. That's ultimately what wards off despair.... Things turn around, you find things that hearten you again, you get your perspective back.

Adam has faced risks and losses by being involved in decolonization work, many of which have already been noted. When considering what he will give up for his work, he recognizes that "when you lose something ... you're [also] burning a resource" that may not then be available for future support and activism. In his academic career, Adam has wondered whether to think of tenure as "a strategic or tactical end," earning him more freedom and security. But he goes back to his understanding that

> land needs to be restored to Indigenous nations, Indigenous nations need to have the chance to have full and sustainable, healthy political and cultural lives, and settler people need to reposition themselves as fitting into those frameworks rather than the other way around. I don't care about tenure in that process.

In the present political reality of Canada, "no one who stands up for Indigenous Rights or the concept of decolonization is safe," he says, due to increased government surveillance, paranoia, and the classing of Indigenous Peoples and their associates as terrorists. The question is, for Adam, "how unsafe are you willing to be in the moment … and what's the potential return?" He is willing to take these risks when actions are well organized, produced along good lines of solidarity, and will raise awareness. Adam says,

> I've committed far too deeply into this to think that I could ever walk away now, so if I'm always going to perpetually be at risk, I can imagine scenarios in which I would be willing to give up a lot more than I have at this point. I can imagine scenarios under which I would be willing to go to prison [or] in which I would be willing to put myself at risk of violence. I can imagine a lot of scenarios where, if I had land, I would be very, very willing to give it back. I think one of the most fundamental concrete things we should do is to transform property back into a land base for Indigenous nations.

Adam's decolonization work is not done as a favour to Indigenous Peoples because confronting colonialism is the only ethical way Adam knows to exist on Indigenous Lands and to uphold his obligations and responsibilities to Indigenous Peoples:

> I would rather risk that everything I'm doing is wrong, that every-thing I'm doing won't ultimately mean a thing, rather than sit on the sidelines and watch these people that I love really struggling. That would break my heart.… I care far too much about far too

many people not to try something. And that trying something has ended up being the preoccupation of my entire life.

His work has resulted in being happier, more centred, and more certain he is doing good things with his life than ever before. He is changed by his engagement, and the work never gets old. As long as there is still work to do, Adam doesn't see an end to his involvement.

CHAPTER 11

SUSANNE MCCREA MCGOVERN

*Susanne McCrea McGovern and
Elizabeth Carlson-Manathara*

IDENTITY AND EARLY INFLUENCES

Susanne McCrea McGovern is an artist, writer, mother, grandmother, environmentalist, activist, and ally of Indigenous people of this land. She was born and raised in an upper-middle-class neighbourhood in Winnipeg by "very humanitarian-minded" parents who campaigned in the sixties against the racial bigotry of other parents who sought to influence the private school she attended as a child. Her father, a broadcaster and actor, "found some connection of value with people in almost every circumstance, encouraging [Susanne] to have a really broad social spectrum." When Susanne transitioned to public school, she would have a few Indigenous schoolmates and would see the disparities between her relatively privileged life and theirs. In grade eight, when Susanne dated an Indigenous boy who had been in fourteen foster homes, she noticed that his foster family dynamics were not right:

> He had never had a birthday party. And these people locked the boys out of the house when they weren't home, so they couldn't go home at lunch time, they couldn't go home after school until the people got home to let them in.... He doesn't ever get a new sweater.

She says, "that did have a real impact on me, that whole experience of knowing those children ... at that time I just remember being so heartbroken for that boy." As a child, Susanne's beliefs and intuitions were respected and validated, and she faced little pressure to conform to Western religion. She was able to come to her own notion of spirituality, with some understanding that her ancestors were once a tribal people who lived in harmony with the cycles of nature.

LEARNING AND EARLY ACTIVISM

A single mom at nineteen, Susanne went to journalism school and began a career in broadcasting. When her mother built a retirement home near Pine Falls and Sagkeeng First Nation, not far from a pulp mill, power dam, and Atomic Energy facility, Susanne says,

> People in Sagkeeng were complaining that their backyards were eroding.… And then a lot of our neighbours started to get cancer from eating fish, or at least that was the apparent correlation. We started getting slipped media reports of radioisotopes that were being spilled into the Winnipeg River, and pretty soon AECL [Atomic Energy Canada Limited] was talking about the proposal to bury radioactive waste under the Precambrian Shield as a way of disposing it. That started a number of meetings with neighbours and people in the communities in our house.… We started to plot and scheme what we could do to support a campaign to deal with some of this stuff, and ultimately, I ended up being involved very seriously in a campaign to stop the radioactive waste from being buried in the shield. That led to associations with people in the city, and some of them were activists. [It] also lent itself to relationships with people in Sagkeeng that had the same concerns.

She says, "Eventually there was a big environmental hearing, and a bunch of us were able to stop [Atomic Energy Canada from burying waste under the shield]." Susanne says,

> So far, they haven't been able to completely decimate the east side of Lake Winnipeg, we still have the largest intact tract of Boreal forest in the world, and I've been involved in campaigning to protect that land.… The best thing we can do right now is just hold them off until we have a way of stopping them because they're just going to keep coming. That's why we have to keep having young people come up.

At the age of thirty-five, Susanne moved on to manage the Manitoba office of Greenpeace. There, she connected with media and did outreach work and direct action. As she started getting out to the land more, she realized the importance of considering not only the land and water, but also "the fact that there are [Indigenous] people who live there, and that those people have a lot more right to say what happens on that land than we do." She was able to help create a written policy for the organization about consulting Indigenous people. However, she did not always have the freedom to support community requests in ways she would have liked.

SOLIDARITY WORK

Susanne says, "Everyone is going to have a different angle on their work with Indigenous solidarity, and mine's mostly in the environmental realm." She believes, "the main problem is taking away the land mass and moving people into prisoner of war camps and calling them the reserves." Therefore, "where the fight is really going to be fought ... [is] on the land, directly on the land." Leaving Greenpeace marked a shift, and Susanne began working with the Boreal Forest Network, now just Boreal Action, which is the North American affiliate of the Taiga Rescue Network — a European network of organizations across the circumpolar Boreal. It is "a grassroots organization that had a mandate to support Indigenous-led campaigns on the ground," through which Susanne "got more of an international exposure to Indigenous communities and Indigenous-led campaigns, how allies could interface with those campaigns, and what was in fact helpful and appropriate." This has become a key aspect of what she has to offer in her work, as she is able to link ideas and needs with those who can help. As the executive director of Boreal Action, Susanne has done support work for Grassy Narrows First Nation in their ongoing logging blockade, bringing additional international media attention to the struggle at pivotal moments. Susanne describes the early days of the blockade:

> I can remember when I first met Judy [Da Silva]. She has a big family and ... her daughter was pretty young, and I remember her saying, "I can't watch these logging trucks go back and forth by my door every day full of logs and have my children see this and not do anything about it."... The blockade was the culmination of some things that had gone on for numerous years. So the young women went and threw logs down, and they blocked the road. At that point we had this international network of people around the whole Boreal forest area.... We were able to inform people by email around the world, at 4:30 in the morning, that

there were trucks coming down the road at four in the morning and we wanted them to send faxes and emails and phone into the little local MNR office in Kenora and say, "Get these trucks off the road!" And so the actual beginning of that blockade was really exciting and significant — to be able to get the message out that the world is watching what's going on in this little place was something that we were able to help with, and that felt great … that just felt amazing to get people to email and fax and phone from Europe and Russia.

As a supporter of the blockade at Grassy Narrows First Nation, Susanne set up speaking events and media support, "getting spokespeople on the radio and television and newspapers." "It's been such a really beautiful example of how I think a lot of things should go." Susanne says the blockade at Grassy Narrows "was a great opportunity to form relationships that were really appropriate with the community." She says,

I think a lot of people over the last twelve years have learned how to be allies and how to be supporters through that experience of a community that really knew what they wanted from people. I give Judy Da Silva a huge amount of credit for helping to develop some people that have worked on other things since then. So that's been one of the most enriching experiences that I've had, and our kids have known each other since they were little, and many other families that are both from there and from the city, even people on an international basis…. In spite of how difficult the circumstances were, the joy and welcoming from community members, the feasts that we shared out there, the people that brought food, and the various people that came out to show support by staying in the blockade and doing karaoke in the temporary round house that was built out of tarps in the middle of January, singing together. This is life, right? It's not just, "Oh we're going to win this campaign and then we're going to go back home to our own families and communities." It's community building and it's chosen family.

Susanne's involvement with campaigns that address damage to the lands and survival of a number of Indigenous nations by Manitoba Hydro has occurred over a number of years:

When Wasquatim [Dam] was being posed, [I was] working with community members and getting to tour South Indian Lake, which was devastating and probably had the most impact on me of any community I've ever been to in the sense of really seeing the impact of humans on other humans and on nature, just to get power in our homes! It's pretty shocking. And the more I investigated that, the more I became convinced that they [Hydro] knew what they were doing and that it was a sacrifice of a small number to serve a larger number in somebody's idea of a justification.

Community members of South Indian Lake First Nation were

put into Hydro shacks as they're called — they're just little ply-wood buildings. [They were] told to tear down their log homes that were all up and down the banks of the area that got flooded and were told, "We'll build you homes." And then they got put in these things that you couldn't live [in] in the middle of the winter, and had wood chips in the ceilings so fireplaces catch the places on fire. And there are holes in the walls and [they are] not properly insulated. Having eighty-year-old women hauling slop pails out in the middle of the winter. I just felt sad for humanity that people could be put in this position and lied to the way they were. [Then] they slapped Hydro meters on a place and charge them $400 a month to try to keep themselves warm, and cut them off in the middle of the winter if they don't pay. And they change the direction of the water so that the places where children used to play, now the water ran in a different direction. The ice wasn't thick enough — there were drownings, and they didn't warn parents [that] this is going to be a dangerous area for your kids now.

Another community Susanne has worked with is Hollow Water First Nation. She says,

We started working with [the late] Garry Raven in Hollow Water First Nation a long, long time ago.… We hosted a lot of gatherings at his place to develop materials around what could guide the principles for the province going forward on these communities — what did they want, what did they not want?… We did family gatherings where we would invite people from the city — families with children to come out [to Hollow Water First Nation] and just spend four days hanging around at a skill-share, cross-cultural atmosphere where Garry would do a pipe ceremony and explain what he was doing and take kids out picking plants.... It was reciprocal, the community would share things with us, and we would share things with them.

Susanne shared her skills in media support, helping "voices from the community be heard in the city, nationally, and internationally." She feels that one of the greatest impacts of these gatherings was on children, including her granddaughter. She says, "You're in your classroom and somebody makes a nasty remark about 'that Indian kid' or something about a reserve, or a racist crack; the kids'll be like, 'That's not true, you don't know what you're talking about.'"

Different situations require different approaches and different types of support work. Susanne believes that one's personality and gifts go hand in hand with what they can offer. After working on a few initiatives to stop toxic industry through environmental reform, Susanne has re-evaluated the effectiveness of this type of work and her role in it. She says,

You can try and go against that and spend all your time lobbying government, and in the back room with industry officials, but that doesn't suit my personality nor does it make the best use of my gifts.... There are professors and people who can do this well, and I think they should be doing it. It's not the best use of my time because I haven't seen that working within that colonial system really makes any difference whatsoever, in the long run.... I think that the basis for a long-lasting change is on the ground supporting the Indigenous people who live here, who have a long-term vested interest in the outcome and have much more to lose than the corporations that come in and just harvest and send the money out of the country. So from a practical standpoint, as well as a spiritual and emotional and human aspect, it's going to do more good in the long run.... We aren't really getting very far with environmental reform and the Earth is in huge trouble.

Susanne sees herself as a concerned person who does support work for "people who are operating community-led Indigenous campaigns to protect their rights on the land from resource extraction." Rather than focusing on urban campaigns, Susanne says,

My relationship has always been very much about people living on the land, because I think that a lot of the problems that happen in people moving into the cities are all directly related to losing the land and losing the rights and the resources on the land. So that's where my relationship started, with a common connection to the lands and waters.

In her work, Susanne seeks ways to "disseminate information and to magnify the voices of the Indigenous people with whom [she's] aligned." She shows up with a camera crew, offers media spokesperson training, helps publicize events and information, has participated in environmental hearings, has organized petition campaigns, and sets up social media sites. Susanne has sought to bring people onside by including Indigenous artists in events:

We do believe in putting art into a lot of our events as a way to de-intellectualize some of these things and as a way to get to the people through the heart. We've had a number of Indigenous poets come and do spoken word at cafés.... I think these things are critically important in terms of getting people out of their heads and getting people to feel things.

Having been involved in her work for some time, Susanne has reflected on successes and pitfalls. She states,

I think a lot of organizations that try to interface with Indigenous communities, in my opinion, go about it the wrong way. Their intentions are good, but they don't really know what they're doing. So they make contact with Chiefs and councils rather than with people inside communities that may have concerns, assuming that the Chiefs and council represent the views of the community members — which may be true, but may also not be true, any more than we feel that our governments represent us.... It never really made sense to me that they would go directly to what is essentially a colonial patterned government to form alliances.

Susanne has learned to look for community members who have concerns about what's happening to their environment by asking around. Susanne says, "It's crazy racist to think that just because somebody is Indigenous, that somehow means that you should follow them." She says,

> I tend to be in solidarity with the people that are the grassroots people, that are on the ground, that have integrity, that I feel like I've got somewhere on the same page with.... You have a right to be discerning in who you want to work with ... not getting all wrapped up in the romanticism.

Another pitfall Susanne sees that may happen among educated white people who have read books and listened to political theories is "what we might be working toward might actually not fly on the ground or fit with how Indigenous people see their sovereignty." She says, "A theory is only as good as it can be practised ... [don't] take those theories and try to impose them."

Susanne's spirituality has affirmed her path of solidarity work. Susanne says, "I always felt my dreams were instructing me ... I used to dream about the mountains crumbling, and the fault lines going, and earthquakes, and land changes, and the earth shifting and never being the same again." Around the time she started to do "more serious support work," she had a "spiritual moment when [she] recognized that [she] was on that path irrevocably." She recalls,

> I was walking near the Forks ... somewhere near the riverbank, and I heard drumming and singing. I was drawn to go and find it, and I felt like I knew it, I'd heard it, it was extremely lucid. It was only after a few minutes that I realized it wasn't really there. I was being called down to the river.... I heard it and I felt it, and I recognized it as a call.

Susanne also reflects on the spiritual history of her European ancestors:

> It's been hundreds and hundreds of years that we've been colonized as a people. Finding out things about our own ancestry — our own spiritual practices from hundreds of years ago, that we were a tribal people initially, from our own countries.... You start to understand that this was also done to us. But it was done to us so long ago. It's sad. We've been robbed of our own ancestral spirituality of the medicines. Our women in Europe were killed for 300 years, the wise women, the midwives, the medicine people. And then the universities were started and only the men with money were allowed to go to it.... So it's way, way back there, but if you're a spiritual person you can draw on your own

ancestors.... To some extent, you're recreating what your ancestors did because not as much is historically known about that.
But the understanding that there is spirit in all living things, the
recognition of all the elements in spirit is very much the same.
What I feel in my ancestral memory is that's a universal. If you
have respect for every living thing, which includes the plants, the
animals, the aquatic life, and the people, how can these values not
be integrated into your everyday life and into everything that you
do and are?... We know that the trees and the plants are virtually
the same where my ancestors come from as they are here, and
that plants have certain properties.

Through her journey of connecting with the Earth-based spirituality of
her ancestors, Susanne has noted the affinity with traditional Indigenous
values and practices. She says,

I have certainly participated in Indigenous ceremony and teachings ... and I think it's an honour to be invited and included. The
teachings correspond with what I already strongly believe....
Even though we have our distinctions and we don't own another
person's cultural teachings; at the root of all those things, the
understandings about creation and spirit are the same.... I have
a strong sense of who I am and where I come from and so I don't
feel that I'm asking to assimilate into someone else's culture or
teachings. It adds a rich character to my understanding of spirit.
I think if someone gives me a teaching, then they think that I
can honour that teaching, and so I've certainly accepted those
things from people that I have developed love and trust and
understanding with.

Through these teachings, Susanne has "stopped thinking about the land in
terms of forestry." She has also made a stronger connection with water as
the women's responsibility. She says, "The water is obviously intrinsically
connected with the land ... we very often forget about the watersheds."
Susanne says, "None of the support or awareness campaigns that we do
in the city are as important as the Indigenous Peoples' relationship to the
land here, and until the rest of us understand our connection to the land
here, there's not going to be a big improvement."

As Susanne's solidarity work has been integrated into all areas of her life, it is also connected to her emotions. Susanne finds herself full of gratitude for "being where I am and for the people that I know and the connections that I've made." She says, "In the end, it's the most incredible, heartfelt connection that I've made with people that has given me an incredible amount of emotional energy to go on with." Over time, Susanne says she has become more confident in what she says and in how she "represents [her] position vis-à-vis Indigenous Peoples' rights." She explains,

> I feel now that people will back me up, that I don't have to be quite as careful that I'm not covering everything or offending somebody. I feel like people know me and they know where I'm coming from, and I feel trusted and I feel supported. I don't feel like it's a landmine to navigate.

Susanne says, "I've heard it said that solidarity means that you have to take the same risks [as those with whom you are doing solidarity work]." While Susanne believes that this is not fully possible because socially privileged people can never share the same vulnerabilities as those who are marginalized, she has taken significant risks. She says,

> I've been willing to give up a fair bit of income, I've been willing to sleep outside in the winter on a blockade, I've been willing to go to jail for things that I believe in — I've never had to do jail time, but I've been arrested and put behind bars for short periods of time waiting for hearings and things.

She says, "I could've had a very different life from the one I chose, but I chose it with full consciousness that this fit my set of values." Rather than using her privilege "to have a $300,000-a-year [job] working for a PR firm that tries to mitigate the damage done to their profile by an oil spill," she has done non-profit work for almost thirty years. Earlier in her journey, she struggled a bit with the "mistaken idea that I had to suffer in order to understand suffering." She recalls,

> I think I may have gone a little too far with feeling that in order to relate, or to not feel — I don't know if guilt is the right word — but a sense that my privilege has been a matter of just being born into the right place and at the right time as a white person. I think at times I've given up too much. I remember one particular moment, going to some event that we had organized, and I had

some beater of an old bronco that [was] ready for the wrecker and I managed to get a little bit more life out of it. And I remember offering some people a ride home.... We get outside and they're like, "Oh no, we have a vehicle." And it turns out they got this brand new, beautiful SUV.... I was like, "Wait a minute here, maybe I don't have to live in poverty to be helpful and supportive, maybe in fact I could be more supportive if I had something to offer."

Although Susanne wouldn't have chosen to do different work, she might not have chosen to simultaneously give up "a lot of [her] own personal goals." Susanne has no retirement income and is on shaky financial ground in the event that she can't work. Susanne says, "I am feeling the emotional strain of being worried about the future [as] a result of the choices I've made."

Susanne states, "If you want to decolonize, you got to get the colonization vibe out of your own [self] ... in terms of questioning *is the world really the way that you grew up thinking it is? Is your history from high school, is that really the way things happened?*" "We have an obligation," according to Susanne, "to really listen to each other and ask questions, not to expect somebody in a disadvantaged position to explain it to us necessarily, but to find the truth of it within ourselves and to not react out of a place of defensiveness." Susanne believes the majority of non-Indigenous people need to realize that

there isn't this huge divide between us and the Indigenous people that are on the land here, in terms of where the Earth is going if we don't support each other. I think the Earth people kind of have to come forward now and stick together, recogniz[ing] that this colonization is not serving them in spite of the fact that on the surface of it, they appear to have a greater privilege. But it's not serving them very well.

"If they could just find that this relationship here on the ground is actually one that could give us all hope for living on this planet together," Susanne says, "that's my vision of where the future could go." "I don't think we're really being asked to leave at this point," Susanne says,

We're being asked to understand the relationship we have with Indigenous people, and the relationship they have with the land, and if we could be compatible in that way, and if the majority us could actually *get* that, then I think we might have a more just society.

Susanne sees it as a continuing priority for the future to try to shake middle-class white people out of their complacency and to "help people find an entry point to engaging in these dialogues." She sees the importance of outreach to "help other white people navigate their own decolonization," because "critical mass is important ... it would be a lot better if they were here and they really had more understanding of what's going on in the land that they live in." Susanne says people "are going to have to step up and be really supportive on the ground." She emphasizes,

> People are going to be taking back their land, people are going to be living more and more on their land, like the Unist'ot'en land, people taking back the grounds where the Hydro–Jenpeg Dam is, and people taking back Slant Lake and Grassy Narrows. You can only push people so far onto a little reserve with so much poverty and unemployment.... I think that you can only contain a people with that kind of a spirit so long.

As Indigenous people take back their land, non-Indigenous supporters are needed to "go and be there and provide a presence, provide a safety net." With racism being rampant,

> somebody better be there to watch, because you're going to [have] some redneck get out of the car and try to hit somebody. Or police violence happens too. But if there are witnesses, and witnesses there with a camera, if there are families there with cameras of all different nationalities, it's a lot less likely to happen. I think safety has got to be one of the primary roles for anyone who's doing support.

If Indigenous people could reclaim their sovereignty of this land, she says, "I think it would be a much better system than the one that we have now, quite frankly." Susanne explains,

> The people here on the land signed Treaties under duress. Treaties can't be signed under duress by international law. Treaties have to be signed by common understanding, in times of peace without duress, without coercion. So in my opinion, the Indigenous

people that were forced to basically sign and get something, or get nothing and be subject to genocide, didn't have a choice. Consequently, I still believe they are the sovereign people of this land. Sovereignty means that resource companies can't come into your land and operate without your permission, not just consult you in some marginalized way. I have a strong relationship and understanding to what sovereignty really is, and I'm all for it!

Susanne does solidarity work because it is just part of who she is. She says, "Life is an integrated thing and if this is what you believe, and this is the way you live, the line between work and life is very, very thin." She states,

I can't separate this deep affiliation and affinity that I have for the Earth, and for life, and for ceremony, and for friendship, and real kind of Treaty building. And I'm not talking about the Numbered Treaties. A real sense of an ancestral connection, that's not something that you can say "Oh, this is this compartment of my life." It's a genetic thing, it's like in your genes, in your DNA, and it's not something that you can separate out.

Susanne says, "If we don't take a stand as we go along our lives, how have we lived it, and not only what are we doing to provide an example to generations after us, but how are we going to be accountable to them?" She continues,

You start looking at it from an ancestral standpoint and digging back ... and what they would think about what's happened here on this land. I feel that I am hearing their voices and feeling guided by that sense of responsibility to be honourable, as tribal people to another tribal people.

Doing this work, for Susanne, is "just sort of a taking back of my life, a taking back of my path ... decid[ing] that [I'm] ... going to take back [my] own tribal ancestry and pick it up ... that's who I want to be for the children that come after me." "Not just for my own children," she says, "but all the ones to come, and for the animals, and the ones that fly and the ones that swim." Susanne feels "that it's our responsibility to do what we can to support the people who were here before us. It's their land."

CHAPTER 12

KATHI AVERY KINEW

Kathi Avery Kinew and Elizabeth Carlson-Manathara

IDENTITY AND EARLY INFLUENCES

Growing up in Toronto, Kathi Avery Kinew spent her childhood summers in the bush around the lakes of Muskoka and grew to be "quite connected to the land." Kathi says, "My spiritual places are all with water ... and trees, and rocks." The phrase "here other campfires burned," carved into the fireplace her great-uncle built, was emblazoned into her heart, mind, spirit, and memory as an early signifier that this is Indigenous Land, Indigenous people were here long before us, and that they are to be respected. Kathi laughed at herself as "a total WASP" with ancestors from the British Isles. Her parents taught Kathi to do the right thing: to be respectful, to listen, and to be understanding. And her parents trusted that she would. A child of the sixties, Kathi saw that the world was changing and wanted to be part of changing it. Although her parents had great respect for people and were supportive of change, Kathi felt they didn't understand her involvement in Indigenous advocacy work. As someone who would later marry and have children with Tobasonakwut Kinew, Kathi would become assimilated into, and become a member of the Ojibways of Onigaming First Nation. She says, "I feel very Anishinaabe, but I respect that I'm not."

LEARNING AND EARLY ACTIVISM

When Kathi began university in the mid-sixties, she got involved in the U.S. civil rights movement. She "marched in Toronto for Selma," and saw Canadians begin to wake up to the need to recognize First Peoples' rights here. "Kahn-Tineta Horn [a Mohawk activist] was turning people's heads around," and in 1965, Fred Kelly, who would become Kathi's brother-in-law, "led a silent march through Kenora that really woke people up." Kathi sees this march as the beginning of civil rights in Canada: "That's when people started coming on board." Newly formed organizations such as the Indian-Eskimo Association (IEA, which later became the Canadian Association in Support of Native Peoples, or CASNP) started to change Canada. Kathi joined the IEA, attended meetings, supported actions, and built friendships with Indigenous people, including her future husband. In 1968, the summer following her first year in a master of social work program, Kathi worked a summer job with the YMCA Geneva Park Camp. She lived on what was then called the Rama Reserve, which has since reclaimed its original name of Mnjikaning First Nation. Kathi brought youth from the reserve to the camp for activities, and worked at building relationships between these youth and the young Canadian helpers.

Kathi learned much by witnessing history being made around her. Indigenous veterans had come back after the Second World War and questioned why they didn't share the same rights as the Canadians they had served alongside in the trenches. When Trudeau became prime minister, elected on his campaign for a "Just Society," Kathi states that people said, "Yeah, let's do something about this." But "what happened was way more exciting and way more self-determining," she says. In 1968, two MPs (Robert Andras, from Thunder Bay, Ontario, which is known for its racism [Galloway 2019; McNeilly 2018] and Jean Chrétien from Québec) were commissioned by Trudeau to consult across the country with the agenda of amending the Indian Act, which was known as "Choosing a Path":

> It was like a travelling commission … and I went to the two hearings in Toronto and Ottawa and watched. This was probably the first time anything got out to the public to hear Indian leaders themselves, because it was followed by radio and TV.… And what [Indian leaders] said was, "Honour the Treaties, implement the Treaties, recognize Aboriginal title, recognize Aboriginal rights, and resolve land claims."… And then [in] the spring of '69, the White Paper came out. People were astounded, shocked, that they hadn't been heard.

This prompted increased activism on the part of Indigenous Peoples. Kathi says,

> My husband was very much in the activist movement — Delia Opekokew and other people in Saskatchewan — [and] we were

travelling around the west. And they were … recognizing that they had all been through something similar in the Indian-Act-Indian-agent-residential schools, although at different places. They knew where their force of will was coming from, and they recognized this will not stand. And at the same time, Dave Courchene [Sr.] here in Manitoba, and Harold Cardinal in Alberta, and other people were all organizing.… So they were successful in burying [the White Paper], when Harold Cardinal and the Alberta Indian Brotherhood came out first with the *Red Paper*, and Dave Courchene Sr. and the Manitoba Indian Brotherhood later with *Wahbung*.

WORK AND CONTINUED LEARNING

Kathi had been taking Ojibwe language lessons, and in 1970 she "moved up to the Kenora area and started working for the reserve [Ojibways of Onigaming First Nation] and for Treaty 3." Kathi's father "didn't think it was such a good idea that I get involved with and fall in love with an Ojibwe person," but, Kathi laughs, "it was too late then, anyway." She was already very much in love with Tobasonakwut, who she found to be a brilliant man. Kathi felt at home in Lake of the Woods, surrounded by lakes, rocks, and pine trees like those she had cherished during her childhood, and she began to visit older people on the reserve and learn from them. She was made to feel welcome. Kathi fell in love with the people of the Ojibways of Onigaming First Nation as an extension of her love for her husband, and she had a great time working for Treaty 3:

> That was when it was becoming clear that there was mercury poisoning in the Wabigoon River.… My husband was the executive director and then-president of Grand Council Treaty 3. This position was later renamed Grand Chief and afterwards, Ogichitaa. So we were always responding to First Nations and what they needed to be done — bridges to be built, and highway speeds to be lessened, and a whole lot of those things. So my husband was constantly going to Queen's Park to change things, or Ottawa. I didn't go on those trips, but I helped him in the background. And then I did Treaty research. I saw first-hand those archival documents and I worked with the Anishinaabe people and some lawyers.… I wrote reports, we promoted communications, we'd

write for the Treaty 3 Council Fire magazine that Tobasonakwut founded, and I followed the lead of the people and the leaders. We recorded the Chiefs' assemblies, and the resolutions became our work plans — that's what we did for eons. We were constantly writing proposals to get money for First Nations or for new initiatives, and then writing reports to make sure we carried through, the same way that people do things now.

When Kathi worked on land claim research in the archives, she saw for herself "the dirty dealings." In the seventies and eighties, she spent time in the archives and listening to the Elders. She says, "I saw the instructions to the surveyors — when you survey the reserves make sure they're 'as far as possible from any probable line of settlement and any known minerals.' That's what the surveyors had for their mandate." This first-hand learning instilled in Kathi a sense that she "knew what had to be changed and what the truth was." Kathi was taught by many First Nation leaders, usually men, about Indigenous nationhood, "political science, philosophy, traditions of Anishinaabeg." She says, "It was all advocacy for self-determination, for Treaty Rights. Aboriginal title, Aboriginal rights, and land claims." They were fighting to be recognized as nations. Kathi learned that her

husband's father went to jail with a whole bunch of men from our reserve and from the Lake of the Woods just for living according to Treaty, for cutting down wood, for fishing commercially with nets, and also making a living in the bush for their families. For hunting, trapping, they went to jail. Well, where was the recognition of Treaty Rights? They understood their Treaty because they spoke their language, but residential school was taking that away.... So people, even though they lived under such an oppressive state, they knew what their rights were. And then it seemed like the more English the kids got, the less they understood what's a Treaty, or that we have Indigenous Rights, that we are the original people of the land — where did that go? It's still there if you sing pow-wow songs ... it's still there if you go to ceremony, but it ain't in the schools.

In the late eighties, however, they were able to start an Anishinaabe language immersion preschool program in Winnipeg. In 1981, Kathi helped organize a Treaty 3 Gathering at Animakee Wa Zhing, Northwest Angle

33, which Governor General Ed Schreyer attended with Anishinaabe artist Jackson Beardy, arriving by helicopter. During that gathering, initiated by Tobasonakwut, the oral promises of Treaty 3, which had been written down by Métis interpreters at the time of the Treaty, were read. The oral promises say, "'you are to be free as by the past,'" but these oral promises are "not even mentioned in white Queen Victoria's typed version in the archives, but are in archives as written notes of final negotiations in 1983, which later became known by Grand Council Treaty 3 as the Paypom Treaty document."

With a husband who was Grand Chief of Treaty 3, Kathi says, "We were all involved in fighting of the constitutional changes." Over the years, Kathi saw phenomenal and incremental accomplishments as well as disappointments and setbacks. A pivotal moment was when Peter Lougheed "stuck in that one word, *existing*, into Section 35 of the 1982 Constitution Act — *existing* Treaty and Aboriginal Rights. We're still winning court cases [from that]." Kathi finds it unbelievable that something they were working for since the late sixties came to be part of constitutional law in 1982 and that they were able to get rid of Indian agents as well. She says, "I don't think even the environmental movement, or labour rights, or anybody can stand up to the achievement that First Nations made from where they came from during that period."

In the nineties, when Kathi came to a point where, she "couldn't see the forest for the trees," she decided to begin an interdisciplinary PhD program. She "believed in self-determination from the baseline of [her] spirit," and decided to focus her studies on self-determination and governance. Kathi recalled the way wild rice "was the most phenomenally unique thing that I saw from living in Treaty 3 and being there, getting to know people, and how it really energized the community, leading up to the August harvest." This became the focus of her thesis, titled "Manito Gitigaan: Governing in the Great Spirit's Garden" (University of Manitoba 1995). She interviewed Elders, rice gatherers, leaders from Treaty 3, and provincial and federal bureaucrats as part of her study, describing how the Anishinaabeg of Treaty 3 protected *manomin* as a gift (and responsibility) from the Creator, and not a provincial Crown resource.

While a student, Kathi was also raising her two children, born in the eighties, who became integrated into her activist work. She says,

> Our kids grew up marching on the Leg with signs and going to land claim and other political meetings.... They've listened to

elders their whole lives … we always brought our kids on the reserve in the summers and all the holidays … it was because their dad was fighting for rights.

As a family, they attended demonstrations and were at the Manitoba Legislature when J.J. Harper was killed in the late 1980s and when Elijah Harper raised the feather to prevent the Meech Lake Accord from being signed. Tobasonakwut was also resuming his traditional path, attending Sweat Lodge ceremonies with his uncle when the ceremonies were being revived. The more Kathi "learned about residential schools, the more [she] left the church behind" and they all followed the traditional path. She says, "With the kids we did smudging, and pipe ceremonies, and sweats … and then my husband started bringing me and the kids to the Sundance, so it became more of a regular part of our life." Kathi keeps to the fringe at ceremonies, not out front. She attends Sweat Lodge ceremonies, full moon ceremonies, and smokes her pipe every full moon. At pow-wows, Kathi won't dress up and dance, other than dancing Intertribals when everyone is invited to dance. At the Sundance, she doesn't dance either. Instead, she says, "I'm a supporter, I keep the camp, I keep the grandkids," and she helps to prepare feasts. She says, "I try to show my respect that way. That's theirs." With the lodges being revived after decades of being taken down by RCMP and priests, people of all walks of life are now attending. Kathi says, "There's so much strength there, so much positivity. That's what's going to make the people whole again and get rid of the colonized mind and spirit."

Kathi has worked for the Assembly of Manitoba Chiefs since 2000 on many initiatives. Recently, they did Ka Nisi Tatowin na? (Do you understand me?) research in which they "[went] around in Manitoba asking First Nations health directors, Elders, and youth, 'What's it going to take to make our people healthy?'" They heard, "'We've got to rebuild and strengthen our languages and ties to the lands and waters, because people need to have a grounded identity [connected] with the Elders, with our traditional medicines, to be who we are born to be.'" She and her colleagues have promoted the First Nations OCAP principles (that First Nations have ownership, control, access, and possession of their information/data) for research with Indigenous communities toward collaborative and respectful research relationships that change "the power imbalance in research so we're no longer subjects, we're the real actors." They have worked to encourage more First Nations youth to become academics and have worked on initiatives around murdered and missing women, youth development, and "bringing our children home *again* from CFS."

Kathi has been an instructor in the Native Studies Department at the University of Manitoba for over nineteen years, where she teaches both Indigenous and non-Indigenous students. Her purpose in teaching is "to get students to see that there is another way of thinking, another way of seeing the world, and that the original peoples of this land have so much to offer." Kathi sees her teaching as advocacy work. She was horrified to hear that someone observed at a meeting with deputy ministers in Manitoba that "they did not know there was a Section 35," something that reinforced for her the importance of her teaching work:

> They (i.e., deputy ministers) did not know that Treaty and Aboriginal Rights are entrenched in the highest law in the land. That's scary. So you have to continually be working at this.... You've got to goddamn fight every day, to remind people, to teach people, to reach out to people, and you have to tell them. And that's what I like about teaching ... if you can tell them enough, if you can show them enough, if you can get them talking to people, they do a 180.... So I'm trying to change the world now, 35 people at a time.

Kathi teaches students to memorize by rote Section 35 of the Constitution Act:

> They have to repeat it, "The existing Treaty and aboriginal rights of the Aboriginal people of Canada are hereby recognized and affirmed," and then I go into explain[ing] that Aboriginal Peoples refers to First Nations, Inuit, and Metis, and I note that the word *implemented* is not used, and that they have not been implemented, YET!... I bring that up with academics as well, that they should know. They don't have the excuse that the general public has, or people that [are] just out of high school, or people that [are] just coming to the country have — academics don't have that excuse.

Now a grandmother, Kathi attends protests, makes financial contributions, and supports advocacy groups, organizations, and community events in Winnipeg and Onigaming. Being close to the U.S. border, border crossing rights have been an issue for her reserve, and Kathi envisions continuing to take part in walks and protests for these rights. She would be willing to go to jail for her activist work if the cause was worth it to her. She has been willing to work for lower salaries to ensure she is doing work that aligns with her values and creates social change. She says, "But I'm not a 1960s Weatherman. I don't believe in killing people for a cause. I think you're admitting failure if you have to do that." In the face of the "terrible anger and frustration that [Kathi has] felt at many tables," Kathi tries to find a way to be creative. One area Kathi wishes she would have been stronger in over the years is analyzing and disrupting the colonial socialization she inherited. She says, "I just jumped in and I didn't always know or understand some things that were culturally different, but I was just living it. So I'm sure I was very disrespectful in a lot of ways, through-out time, but I tried to learn." She says, "I just kind of lived and absorbed, but I think I should have done better."

The anger Kathi has experienced on her journey has been an impetus for her work. She says, "I don't think all anger is bad, sometimes anger makes you continue." She explains,

> The more that I learned of my husband's life — I was so in love with him, and it made me angry. He met so few non-Native people that had any respect or kindness.… And it just enveloped me. And then to have some of my relatives now so oppressed and suffering from addictions, or suffered from suicide, [it] just builds anger.

After seeing the structural barriers faced by those she loves, anger arises. She says, "Why should my son have suffered from it? His dad suffered enough, his grandparents suffered enough, why should my daughter be prevented from doing things? Because they're Anishinaabe?" She feels anger about the ignorance of many Canadians: "Why don't you people know this already? Why don't you understand?… You have to know this, this is reality, this is the truth." She is sad to see that many of the issues she worked on in the sixties, seventies, and eighties are "still with us," something that is clear when she looks at the current Treaty 3 and Assembly of Manitoba Chiefs' agendas. It's still about Treaty Rights, inherent rights, protecting the land, and compensation.

As a result of the actions she has been a part of and supported, Kathi has seen the Canadian government agree to many attempts at bilateral talks, for which Indigenous Peoples never have enough resources to "keep up with thousands of bureaucrats who can bring legal and other arguments to the table." She says, "The oppressor was willing to come to the table and cool things down and pretend that they were moving ahead, and dissipate the energy. It takes a lot of energy to keep going." Nonetheless, Kathi finds much joy in the thrill of "organizing things that work and influencing young people." She sees young Indigenous community leaders working for cultural continuity with the youth, parenting in very involved ways, and teaching the youth to respect women. Kathi says, "If you've been oppressed for so many decades, you may not have been taught or you may have forgotten that there was resistance, that there were achievements and there were Ogichidaa, Ogichidaakwe [male and female warriors]." She wants the youth to know that "our greatest warriors have not died, we are them (that was the theme and phrase used at Onigaming in their 1990s joint education partnership with Harvard University) ... you have strong resistors and leaders now, and you are part of this." She was thrilled with Idle No More, which "was brought up through the grassroots," which made it "the people's movement again ... people feel alive again." She saw round dances on her reserve on the icy bay in -40°C temperatures: "It was totally everybody saying 'this is us, this is who we are.'" She says, "The most hopeful thing I saw was that August 2014 march ... after the finding of Tina Fontaine's body. All these soccer moms and dads from all over Winnipeg came out and brought their kids ... they wanted to show solidarity."

Kathi feels that she's "in a good place, and still growing, still changing." She says, "Maybe it was easier when I was younger ... but that doesn't mean you quit now." She continues,

> You don't siphon off your life, I don't think you can. I think everybody I know that's involved is — it's just taken for granted, this is what you do — you go to ceremony, you have to get out on the street, or you have to be at the table. You have to constantly change things for the better. It's part of your life.

"Our life was committed to changing Canada and changing the situation of First Nations people, and recognition," Kathi says, and she continues to work for healing, reconciliation, and the strengthening of Indigenous families and nations. She was inspired by a concept presented by non-Indigenous Australians at a conference she attended: "'We understand, we stand under ... we're behind you and we're supporting you, we follow the lead of the Original peoples.' And Indigenous people lead the way."

This is how Kathi sees her role, as background work. She won't be at the forefront unless she has to. She says, "We have to protect Mother Earth, we have to protect the people and grow the spirit.... So the best way to do that is to get involved, and visit, and talk, and work together." "How could you not be involved in this?" Kathi asks. "It's the most Canadian thing you can do. This is the country of the original peoples." She believes that Indigenous Rights are fundamental: "Indigenous people have a special role as the original people to care for this land, and keep that land going.... Indigenous Rights are Treaty and inherent rights and they need to be respected." Kathi believes that "the only hope now is that Indigenous people continue to take on their role as caretakers of the land that we all love, and more and more people come back to who they were born to be." She says,

It's a big world, and it's not putting WASP people or any other non-Indigenous people down to build Indigenous people up again, allowing them to live what I call their legacy, and to be who they were born to be. It makes us better and it makes our country better. Because we're saying we want to learn the original teachings that belong to this land. Because what I believe is *here other campfires burned.*

CHAPTER 13

RICK WALLACE

Rick Wallace and Elizabeth Carlson-Manathara

IDENTITY AND EARLY INFLUENCES

Rick Wallace is a white, middle-class Toronto-based Canadian settler who holds a PhD in peace studies and has been involved in decolonization work for at least twenty-five years. Rick's mother grew up on a small fishing island in the Bay of Fundy, Nova Scotia. He credits his experiences as a child for rooting his decolonization work. For example, he says:

> We were living in Toronto in a nice, split-level home, we would go down to visit [relatives] on this island.… It's hard to articulate it at five, six, seven years old, but I could feel something didn't feel right here. My cousins lived in a very different house, lived in a very different world than we did … there was a lot of alcoholism and poverty and lateral violence going on in the fishing community.

Disparities were also observed by Rick when riding through Saugeen First Nation on summer trips to his family's cottage in Southampton, Ontario. Fifty-three-year-old Rick recalls,

> My father plays golf and so we would drive through the reserve once or twice a week, to go meet him at the golf course. And going through a reserve in the 1960s … it was horrific, there were literally one-room shacks. It remind[ed] me of some of the poverty that I'd seen in Nova Scotia.… We'd get into our family car, we'd drive through this poor community, and then we'd go to [my father's] golf course — which of course is filled with white people on these nice lawns … that's the kind of thing that started to make me wonder at a very young age.… There seem[ed] to be

a very discernable group of people in Canada who seem to be leading a very different existence.

In spending summers on his mother's small fishing island, Rick also grew up near Bear River First Nation (near Deep Brook, Nova Scotia), without even knowing it existed. He asks, "How could I not know that?" He says, "[colonialism] really disconnects us from realizing that that relationship is still existent, it's seemingly invisible." Around the age of twelve, Rick thought, "I want to become a human rights lawyer, and I want to work on Aboriginal law." For years, he says, "that was my goal, because I could see something was wrong." Rick was also influenced by his grandmother's faith-based social justice activism, and she instilled in him a sense of social responsibility to others: "If one person is suffering, in a sense we're all suffering.... We have a responsibility out of love and caring ... not to shut our eyes to it."

EARLY ACTIVISM AND LEARNING

Rick's journey into decolonization work was marked by an accumulation of experiences that pushed him to a point of recognizing broken relationships and a history of genocide impacting Indigenous Peoples in Canada. Working with the Ontario Public Interest Research Group (OPIRG) in the eighties, Rick did solidarity work on behalf of the Inuit of Labrador in response to NATO low-level flight testing that was impacting the ecosystems of their Traditional Territories. He also did advocacy work with the Teme-Augama Anishinaabe around their land claims when clear-cutting on their Traditional Territories threatened old-growth forests. He says, "The environment was the pivotal issue, but this land belongs to First Nations people, so I was up there because of that." Through a former partner, Rick was connected to members and events of the Canadian Alliance in Solidarity with Native Peoples (CASNP), which also taught him much. For Rick, the Oka Crisis highlighted the absurdities in the relationship between Canada and the Mohawks of Kanehsatà:ke, and it was another instance that led to his work. He was struck by the

> inability to actually hear the story of a community who had been in a four-hundred-year struggle to get back their land ,which had been illegally taken, and then to have the nearby town propose

that they'll build another nine-hole golf course on land that was sacred to them.

DECOLONIZATION WORK AND CONTINUED LEARNING

For Rick, "underlying decolonization work is the idea of rebuilding, revitalizing, [and] reconstituting trustful relationships." The work is focused on the relationship between Indigenous and non-Indigenous people here, which is different for Rick from "the pro-choice, anti-poverty, or anti-nuclear work that [he's] done." He has learned from peoples in Treaty 3 that "Treaty isn't just a partnership between First Nations and settlers. There's a third party which is actually the land itself and the spirits of the land," which carry memories. He observes,

> Because people like myself ... here are immigrants, it's very easy to lose a sense of continuity with the land. We move around so much ... our families get disconnected, our memories get disconnected, our sense of attachment ... our oral histories get forgotten, even our family memories get forgotten. So I think colonialism really leaves for me a profound disconnect with the land around me, and I'm constantly having to work on it ... the land has a history, and it has a history with the peoples, and that's not spoken about. So ... we don't really have the full relationship because we don't have the full story.

Rick believes there are many ways to be involved in solidarity or decolonization work: "emotional, spiritual involvement, friendship involvement ... within my own community, and together with First Nations communities." Also, because "the world is made up of really contextualized localities," and each community has its own dynamics, Rick believes the same recipe for change will not work everywhere. This can be challenging for Euro-Canadians, whose cultures often emphasize "mechanistic, generalized, or homogenous" processes, when what is really needed is "sensitivity, deep listening, and respect."

Much of Rick's decolonization work has focused on Indigenous solidarity, political advocacy, and education. He has supported the blockades of the Grassy Narrows First Nation Anishinaabe and the Teme-Augama Anishinaabe. He sees blockades as an effective means to protect land, bring attention to Treaty violations, and put pressure on the government by changing the negotiating position. He takes part in demonstrations and believes they have impact by bringing visibility in urban centres to issues such as the Treaty violations of clear-cutting and mercury poisoning that may occur in more remote areas. Organizing public talks serves to "create spaces for First Nations communities to directly speak to people without it being filtered by the media." Rick has provided materially to campaigns, such as the Sisters in Spirit campaign, and to public events. He has used his privilege and skills to provide financial support and to access connections and create openings that help with logistics for a number of events. He has helped First Nations activists write funding proposals, circulated petitions, and produced radio shows to raise consciousness.

In Rick's experience, the trust of First Nations communities has to be earned. History has given communities many reasons not to trust settlers, and trust is earned by doing — listening, participating, and being respectful of how the Indigenous community frames the conflict and what their priorities and processes are. He says, "If decolonizing work is about anything, it's about giving up control and inversing the power relationship; and that can be a challenge sometimes, especially when I may not fully agree with the strategy." Non-Indigenous people might have common environmental or justice interests in the work, but each Indigenous community's unique context means decision-making may happen in ways "very different from how an NGO works." Therefore, it is important that non-Indigenous people "recognize that communities have a lot of knowledge [and] not be patronizing, thinking you can come in with the answers." It is important to

> listen very carefully and realize that there might be different agendas … there's not necessarily one leadership, whether you work with the band council, whether you work with traditional [people], whether you work with the community activists. They could be at loggerheads. They could have different approaches. So you need to be very careful about how you approach that. You need to ask them what they're looking for and what they need, you need to understand that if it's on their territory, this is their struggle, and so you need to work by privileging their knowledges and understandings and realizing that it's culturally different than your own.

Decolonization work may fail, in Rick's experience, if non-Indigenous activists don't take the time to develop trust with Indigenous communities and are in and out after short periods of time. It may fail when non-Indigenous people put their own priorities above those of the community; when they adopt strategies that could be dangerous for First Nations communities; when they promise things they can't do; when they ask Indigenous communities to participate in initiatives they are directing while Indigenous communities don't have equal say over the process and strategy; and when non-Indigenous people centre themselves in media engagements.

Rick says, "Decolonization work isn't only assisting and supporting First Nations communities in the struggles that they're facing. It's also about how we change our own dialogues as non-Indigenous Euro-Canadians or settlers." This involves learning more about Treaty responsibilities. Rick says, "Treaties aren't just about First Nations communities getting something — we're all getting something. We've been allowed to share this land with [Indigenous] people, but we have reciprocal obligations." "Treaties are being violated in almost every imaginable fashion in the country," he says. He would like to see "Euro-Canadians really understand what was the spirit behind the Treaties ... [because] a just society starts off with us acknowledging, understanding, and revitalizing the Treaty relationship." For Rick, this means "we are occupying the same territories together," that "First Nations communities have a right to construct their own ways of development ... and political control based on their cultural values," and that we work alongside each other as "partners, neighbours, and relatives."

Rick uses his gifts of listening, conflict resolution, facilitation, and peacebuilding to enhance his work as an educator. This work involves "facilitating group processes, developing consensus, helping people critically inspect difficult issues ... creating spaces to have good conversations ... [and] creating space to allow voices to be heard and for others to simply be able to just listen." He uses personal stories that "make it real [and] engage people [so] it doesn't become this abstract issue." Rick notes that this focus on stories is a move away from the anti-racism work he was involved with twenty years ago, which was more about critiquing one's self rather than changing the relationship. In addition to educating students from Canada and other countries, Rick makes it a point to talk with his family, friends, and others he comes across. He once spoke with a taxi driver who held misconceptions about Indigenous Peoples getting free education and not paying taxes. Rick described colonialism in Canada, drawing on international parallels the driver might be familiar with, and described the meaning of Treaties. He says,

> It's one of those opportunities where somebody's willing to listen, and you can make a bit of an educational intervention moment and relate it to experiences where they empathize really dramatically and quickly; and you can also dispel some of the prevalent misconceptions ... that typify a lot of Canadian discourse.

In his teaching, writing, publishing, and speaking, Rick seeks to create momentum and expand the capacity of larger groups to be good allies and Treaty partners. Rick's PhD work was developed into the book *Merging Fires: Grassroots Peacebuilding between Indigenous and Non-Indigenous Peoples* (2013), which involved interviews with eighty Anishinaabe and non-Indigenous community activists about decolonization, developing alliances, and creating different relationships. Rick learned from Indigenous research scholars, such as Linda Tuhiwai Smith, about strategies that disrupt mainstream academic research and are more empowering and beneficial to those involved. He has used his book to raise awareness among readers and to speak to international audiences about some of the issues faced by the Grassy Narrows First Nation and the Chippewas of Nawash First Nation, all of which may contribute to developing solidarity support systems and greater international support. The profits from his book go to the Native Women's Association of Canada (NWAC) for the Murdered and Missing Indigenous Women campaign.

Thirty years of relationships with Indigenous Peoples has taught Rick much. Three of his friends, who are sisters from Grassy Narrows, have been particularly close with Rick, who has lived with them and taken care of their kids. Rick says, "We talk about everything, and I feel like we talk honestly, and I take risks, and they take risks, and I'm constantly confronted with different ways of seeing the world." He has been transformed by the cultural and spiritual teachings he has received by listening to First Nations community members and stories they have shared. Rick also learns from "listening to various Cree songwriters in Toronto, or Inuit singers ... [and attending the] imagineNATIVE Arts Festivals." He learns by watching films by Indigenous filmmakers, by reading books by Indigenous authors such as Thompson Highway and Thomas King and non-Indigenous writer Joseph Boyden. He says, "I don't know how many events I've [attended] at the Native Canadian Centre," sometimes as the only non-Indigenous man present, learning from Indigenous activists who share their stories. Rick also reads academic books by Indigenous scholars, such as Marie Battiste, James (Sakej) Youngblood Henderson, Taiaiake Alfred, Kim Anderson, and Bonita Lawrence, and says, "My work clearly owes a huge debt to these people." Rick says, "Participation in ceremonies is a really good pedagogy." Having been invited to attend Indigenous ceremonies such as Sweat Lodges by his then-partner, Rick found he was entering very different spaces within the context of a community of people, and understanding in a more profound way Indigenous relationships with the world, beyond the intellectual realm. He says, "They have different reference points … ontologies, and belief systems about what's real in the world, and they're all quite valid." Because these systems are different from Rick's own, he's had to listen and consider:

> What are some Anishinaabe views on how the world works, both family relationships, community relationships? What's their paradigm on how community functions? How do they see themselves in connection to the land, and how do they see their own spirit, and what does spirit mean?

He learned about Indigenous relationships with the land, which are based on

> balance, reciprocity, and guardianship; the way in which life is intimately connected to the land, and by the land they mean all that [is] around them, all their relatives. Participation in ceremonies is something that's in my body, it demands me to participate in my heart … it's an experience into something that's sacred, and that's not a terminology we typically used in the environmental movement or the social justice movement.

He says:

> Ceremony is … a call for one to be connected, respectful, and to be embraced by something much larger than just our own little selves. I think that what's imperative to decolonizing and social justice activism is a belief that keeps us going in a much wider way than just simply, "Are we going to change this policy? Are we going to resolve this Treaty issue?"… I think decolonizing work is really, in many ways, about building relationships beginning

with our heart and being connected in a spiritual way with each other, because that's the most profound relationship, and that's where we need to really anchor what we're doing.

Rick believes that a truly transformative and hopeful decolonization process goes beyond being an intellectual exercise, a policy change, or even an emotional process; it becomes a spiritual journey of increasing gratitude and connection to history, life, and interdependence.

Rick believes, "If there is one act of solidarity that would probably be the most useful here, [it] would be us as Euro-Canadians talking with other Euro-Canadians to help critique our history and our relationships" in order to create space for the creation of better relationships. He has deeply considered the history of his own culture, including major historical paradigm shifts and collective traumas that we're still grappling with that enable colonial dynamics. For example, he says, the European Enlightenment makes possible an economic theory that "believes that we can have exponential growth without there being any limitations — we think it's okay to extinguish animals, to make them extinct." We have a "materialistic, scientific way of seeing the world," in which we are lords over the natural world. Rick also reflects on historical social traumas such as emigration. He asks, "Could you imagine leaving your family in the eighteenth, nineteenth century, and you're not going to see them again? Moving to a different land that you're not connected with — you don't know the stories, you don't know traditions? I think it's all very traumatizing." We can't rely on "policies, expertise, or mechanical solutions," Rick says, when we really need to change our paradigm. For Rick, colonialism has meant "I live in an unsustainable city, I live in a neighbourhood where I don't know my other neighbours, I'm a person who barely knows his family history, and barely knows his cultural history of these territories." It is a massively disconnected and arrogant way of being. Rick says, "It's created systems which I don't enjoy, it's abolished a sense of social and familial memory, and it puts me in a very odd position of wanting to resist and fight it and yet being a participant in it at the same time." Rick's family history has alerted him to the debts he seeks to repay, in part through his decolonization work. He discovered that some of his family wills document armed conflicts with Indigenous people and involvement with slavery. He says,

One could say that we have a debt to the land.... When my family, in the 1600s, decided to be part of this continent, it doesn't sound like they necessarily had permission, and certainly not for the scale that probably happened.... Part of [my ancestors] ended up in Nova Scotia in the 1750s, 1760s, [on] Mi'kmaw Territory. Once you start to know the history ... this horrific history of how we just kept invading ... and dispossessing and impoverishing other communities; somehow the family farm has a wholly different story to it. So it's about the recovery of a different narrative about what goes on, but then it's not just an intellectual narrative — that's where my grandfather was, that's where my grandmother was, that's where relatives still live, that's in part where I'm from. So when I look at that sense of debt ... I can put it in a much larger narrative which we were a part of. And I know the ongoing consequences of it.... So when I talk about a debt within my family, it is taking a spiritual responsibility for my ancestors and looking to help them, and looking to help the present so that we right this relationship.

There have been times when Rick has been colonial in his attitudes, assumptions, and words. There were moments in which he should have taken more time to learn about the issues before organizing events, and moments when he held paternalistic attitudes about helping Indigenous communities akin to charitable international aid to developing countries. He has also underestimated the capacities and knowledge of Indigenous Peoples while overestimating his own. While talking with some Indigenous friends about writing to raise awareness about the oppressiveness of the Indian Act, one of them pointed out a community member who is a specialist that had written many articles on the topic. The friend asked Rick, "Why are you waltzing in here thinking you're going to be the great white knight to save anything, getting people writing something on this when *he's* been writing tons of stuff on it?"

Rick's decolonization journey has brought up a variety of emotions. "Sometimes it's really easy to get angry about the history," he says, "there is this sense of outrage that can come, of anger, of non-comprehension." Although he has experienced guilt, Rick has not found it useful to take on collective guilt for what his ancestors have done because it is a whole lot of weight that makes it hard to keep enthusiasm and energy in his work. Rick says,

I guess the emotional journey is to just see ourselves as actually relatives, sisters and brothers, friends who are all struggling with this stuff. This is part of an identity and structure over here, but we're all struggling with stuff. But I think that makes a much easier place to enter into an authentic relationship, so that emotionally I feel prepared to have that relationship, so that's been part of the journey.

Rick has felt apprehensive at times when doing his research: "I'm meeting Elders, I'm meeting people I've never met before, I'm not really familiar with this community. I'm walking into people's houses, asking them to talk with me, a white guy from Toronto doing his PhD." "Why should they talk with me?" Rick wonders, "Can I understand what they're saying? Am I being patronizing? Arrogant?" At the same time, Rick has grown to have confidence in his own emotions as inner guidance for his work. Rick continues to struggle with questions such as,

Should I buy a house in Toronto? Should I buy land up by Bancroft, Treaty land that really belongs to somebody else? By Cape Croker, the reserve is a thousand acres; their territory was a million and a half acres, there's cottages all around them. Should I be buying a cottage up there when really this land belongs to the people of Cape Croker?

He notes the potential of work done between the city of Kenora and Treaty 3 to "develop a working relationship on land that they both claim in common."

Rick has experienced small successes in his solidarity work, but it can become frustrating when headway is made under one set of politicians, and then the leadership changes or the stakeholders change. Among settlers, Rick says "it's hard to really know what is the catalyst.... The more I do this, the more I don't understand — why are some people engaged, while other people want nothing to do with it?" He notes that Idle No More has generated engagement, and he wonders, "How do we sustain that dialogue and move it forward?" He says, "Everybody's over-extended, we have this massive land space, we have communities all over the place, activists are involved in so many things, there's not great funding." Rick suspects part of what will sustain engagement will be a long-term, spiritually based vision of "reconnecting to a much larger sense of society, ourselves, life, [and] the Earth, than we normally think about." All of this said, the discussion is different from where it was thirty years ago, due to "the strengths of First Nations, Inuit, and Metis communities." He says, "That's where the real drive for social change is coming from, and the question is how can others like myself support that." Rick states,

> My real commitment to this comes out of a place of love, but also comes out of a place of connection to spirit.... And that gives me a certain strength, that I'm not alone and that it's not all on my shoulders — that I'm a part of this transformative change. Decolonization isn't something that just happens in structures and mentalities and policies and courts and the way things are lived. We're not separate from those things. We are experiencing decolonization. We are embracing our connection with spirit in a deeper way that opens up so many more possibilities for us to actually have an authentic, and not separate, relationship with the world around us.

Rick does decolonization work out of caring for his friends, for his family, for the land, and for himself. He says, "I do it for the seven to fifteen generations prior and subsequent to me ... I have a responsibility as part of this extended historical family to make something right." He does his work out of his own desire to have a better world: "I don't think people should experience violence ... colonialism is an ongoing form of violence." Rather, he strives to create "a more loving world that has social justice as the foundation." Rick emphasizes,

> We do have these responsibilities and these issues are not going away. In fact, they continue to fester. And when you can see an epidemic in front of your eyes, infecting your friends, affecting us, and affecting the very land ... we're not allowed really to close our eyes.... What keeps me motivated is that this is completely unfinished ... and I can directly see the impacts on people I know.... What I'm really trying to say is that I stay here because this is where my heart tells me I should I be.

CHAPTER 14

WHAT INDIGENOUS PEOPLES HAVE ASKED OF US

Elizabeth Carlson-Manathara

I begin this chapter by revisiting the words shared by Aimée Craft (personal communication, April 9, 2016), who warns us against seeing the elements shared here as a checklist or recipe for settler decolonization, anti-colonialism, and solidarity work, and who emphasizes relationships and continuing dialogue. I recall Kennedy's words about being guided by our own hearts and our own spirits in the work that we agreed to do, which is between us and spirit. Listening in Indigenous sovereignty gives us an opportunity to explore and consider potential dimensions and principles for our work that have been shared by Indigenous Peoples. However, this is not enough. Dawnis Kennedy (personal communication, April 9, 2016) shared with me a story of her adopted aunt, Marjorie Heinrichs, who, if she were to be measured by some of the settler decolonization, solidarity, and ally literature, did many things wrong — except, perhaps, for what really mattered most:

> She was amazing, and funny, she had this huge laugh. Oh, you would've loved her. She came to do one journal article about Roseau [River First Nation] at the pow wow, and she never left.... You know, after she lost her son, I told her about losing my mom, and what that grieving process was like for me. And she was always there for me after that. She came to my wedding. She came to each graduation, she flew wherever she needed to be. She was my Auntie, and she was like a mom to me in many ways. She was adopted into my family.... That's one thing I want for [settlers] to know.... You are a human being with a heart. Any relationship that's a true relationship has to also be about love. Not

just about responsibility.… Marge knew it because she isn't part of that academic stuff, she was part of the community stuff. She was family. She was a member of our family. And her family is our family. And that's the way we relate to her. And that's the way she related to us. (Kennedy, personal communication, April 9, 2016)

With this perspective in mind, I turn to the question: *What are Indigenous Peoples asking of us?* It is a difficult question to answer, as again, both Indigenous nations and Indigenous individuals are diverse. And yet there are themes that are noted repeatedly when one listens to and reads literature by Indigenous scholars, activists, and Knowledge Holders.

TRUTH TELLING, LEARNING, AND ACKNOWLEDGEMENT

Many Indigenous scholars and activists recommend that settlers focus on learning and acknowledging the truth about settler colonial history and its ongoing dynamics. Recall Ward's words: "We cannot build relationships on illusions … you have to acknowledge the history of colonialism" (2015: 22:25–23:40). Simpson (2013a: 56) believes it is important for Canadians to "take it upon themselves to learn a more faithful history of this place and to teach their children to recognize these injustices and to understand how they contribute to the colonial legacy." Waziyatawin (2008) suggests that non-Indigenous allies work with Indigenous Peoples on public education truth-telling campaigns that acknowledge the genocide and ongoing colonization occurring on Dakota lands. She says, "Our non-Dakota allies can also facilitate the truth-telling process by talking with their families, friends, and communities in support of this project" (2008: 93). Lynn Gehl emphasizes the importance of allies learning and reading more about their roles, being "aware of their privileges and openly discussing them" (n.d.: 1, used with permission), and understanding oppressive power structures that marginalize people. Similarly, Benally (2013) states that solidarity activists need to build a settler consciousness and an understanding of settler privilege. Most of the narratives in this book describe a process of consciousness-raising about settler privilege and colonialism, of coming to learn the true history of Canada. For example, Monique, in Chapter 4, describes starting to learn through Native studies electives as a university student, while Joy, in Chapter 9, began to learn through relationships with Indigenous Peoples in northern Manitoba, and then in her bachelor of social work program. Murray learned by observing the difference between his experience of Indigenous Peoples he grew up with and the racist views about Indigenous Peoples that he saw being spread in society, and by developing an analysis around why this was happening (Chapter 5). Adam, in Chapter 10, shares that he was heavily influenced in his understanding by Indigenous scholars and interactions with classmates, while Silvia describes her learning through attending Indigenous solidarity events and through a TRC national event (Chapter 16).

PRACTISING HUMILITY AND LISTENING

Earlier in this book, I noted that Ward (2015) emphasizes the limits of his status as guest and helper on Stó:lō lands, and the necessary restraints to personal power that this entails, suggesting that the role of non-Indigenous people as colonizing occupiers requires even more restraint. This humility is also reflective of practices recommended by Gehl (n.d., used with permission) who urges settlers against taking the space and resources of Indigenous Peoples and taking time at community events and meetings. Gehl (n.d., used with permission) states that the role of an ally is to constantly listen and reflect, rather than thinking that one knows better, and to understand that the needs of Indigenous Peoples come first in Indigenous solidarity struggles. Indigenous Action Media (2014) likewise urge accomplices to listen more than speaking or planning and to avoid advancing their own self-interest or imposing their own agenda. Benally (2013) suggests reaching out to the people whose lands are the site of struggle in order to have meaningful discussions and ask advice about how to be effective and supportive of the local struggle. Solidarity activists need to communicate with local Indigenous Peoples and listen to the people whose lands we are on in order to understand our role, even when that is hard to do. Nonetheless, Aimée Craft (personal communication, April 9, 2016) notes that it is not actually humble to be "coming from an apologetic place all of the time," especially when it causes non-Indigenous people to believe they have no role in the work and feel absolved of their responsibility.

In Chapter 15, John describes the way that some settlers arrive on the scene of activist work having already decided what plan and methods they will use, whereas John makes it a practice to follow the lead of Indigenous organizers, with humility. In Chapter 7, Franklin emphasizes taking direction from Indigenous Peoples about how to proceed and being humble by taking on only what we can follow through with, and by not assuming we have the answers or taking up space. Similarly, in Chapter 4, Monique describes the importance of doing an extraordinary amount of listening, not imposing our ideas, asking for direction from Indigenous Peoples, and not being afraid to ask questions rather than assuming we know best.

TAKING RESPONSIBILITY FOR OUR WORK

Part of listening, as noted above, involves reading Indigenous literatures and considering what Indigenous Peoples are saying. Many, many Indigenous scholars, activists, and Knowledge Keepers have made their words accessible in order to inspire change, often speaking directly with settler audiences. Nonetheless, a number of Indigenous activists challenge white people and settlers to take responsibility for their own work, not expecting Indigenous Peoples to give them answers, educate them, or hold their hands.

Xhopakelxhit notes that although Indigenous Peoples don't "want to be dictated to or told what we should be doing by settlers" (2014: 9), nonetheless, "if you are organizing then you need to make decisions and act on them without being guided every step of the way, this causes stress and creates bad relations" (2014: 9). Indigenous Action Media (2014: 8) say, "While there may be times folks have the capacity and patience to do so, be aware of the dynamics perpetuated by hand-holding. Understand that it is not our responsibility to hold your hand through a process to be an accomplice." Ward (2015) describes being asked by an occupier to come and teach non-Indigenous children about colonialism. A friend who was with him answered, "That's not our responsibility to have to go teach your children about what you've done. We already have 500 years of colonialism to undo. That's our responsibility" (2015: 24:10–24:20, used with permission).

Franklin, in Chapter 7, describes that he has seen Indigenous people grow weary of constantly having to tell white people what to do. Rather, he suggests finding things to do that don't require intense direction, such as working with other settlers and responding to calls from Indigenous Peoples. Silvia (Chapter 16) describes learning the importance of taking responsibility for her own healing, emotions, and actions. When she makes mistakes as she does her anti-colonial work, Silvia processes this and finds ways to recover from hurt and come back in relational and humble ways.

WORKING TO EDUCATE AND
CHALLENGE OTHER WHITE SETTLERS

Chickadee Richard challenges non-Indigenous people to "educate one another — your family, your communities, your nations" (2013: 56:50–56:55). Tasha Hubbard added,

> I'm really happy that Chickadee said that because again, it's always put on us [Indigenous Peoples] to educate everybody. And we're only individuals. We can do so much. But that's what we need is people talking about what they're learning, sharing it. And I know it's not easy. I just went home and you know, half my family make their living from either the tar sands, or the oil, or the potash.… You know, those are really difficult conversations to have. I'll say it right now, they're hard conversations because people see their livelihoods being threatened. And yet it's about exposing the injustice that comes with those livelihoods, the inequality that comes, the impact that it has. So, absolutely, that's a huge thing that can be done as far as taking responsibility for this as well. (2013: 1:03:40–1:04:47)

Following Malcolm X's words, Alfred (2005) suggests that white people who wish to engage with networks of Indigenous resurgence do so by working toward breaking down the prejudice of white communities. Manuel and Derrickson (2015: 221) write, "To avoid the worst, we need our Canadian allies — including church, union, community, and environmental groups — to help us to educate the Canadian population about our rights as they are recognized internationally and about Canada's colonial position toward us."

Educating other settlers was something mentioned by many whose narratives appear in this book. John has sought to educate others through activism, including demonstrations, banner drops, and educational blockades, through his work as a musician and artist, and by responding to racist comments in the feedback sections of news reports (Chapter 15). Joy (Chapter 9) has used art to educate other settlers, as she believes it can often be more moving and less evangelistic. Steve (Chapter 6) says that he engages with his family's education process and raises awareness within the Mennonite community. Franklin believes it shouldn't be up to Indigenous people to have to educate white people, so he tries to address racism in conversations with friends, family, and co-workers in hopes of helping to deprogram settler socialization (Chapter 7). Others, such as Silvia (Chapter 16), Victoria (Chapter 18), Adam (Chapter 10), and Kathi (Chapter 12) use their roles as university instructors to educate settlers about colonialism and decolonization.

DECOLONIZING OUR HEARTS AND MINDS

A key dimension of decolonial work involves settlers working on our own personal transformations. If we forego this work and focus only on outward action, it's likely that our support of Indigenous social movements will cause harm, as we will relate in settler-socialized ways and engage in re-colonizing dynamics. Because, as Alfred says, the enemy lies in "a certain way of thinking with an imperialist's mind" (2005: 102), it is necessary to address behaviour patterns, choices, and mentalities "that developed in serving the colonization of our lands as well as the unrestrained greed and selfishness of mainstream society" (2005: 102); the "cultural, psychological, and spiritual foundations of Euroamerican arrogance" (2005: 103); and "the delusions, greeds, and hatreds that lie at the centre of colonial culture" (2005: 35). Sakej Ward says,

> What we can provide as Indigenous people is anti-colonial critique, we can explain the problems of colonization, the experiences that we've had. We can tell you what a relationship to this land looks like. We can tell you what the proper relationship with Indigenous people should look like. But it's up to you to have this personal quest about decolonizing yourself as a colonizer. (2015: 28:33–29:15, used with permission)

Waziyatawin (2009: 154) asks settlers, "Are you willing to constantly engage in critical self-reflection and routinely have your white colonizer programming challenged?"; Mills (2019: 281) challenges settlers to "work more personally and immediately: change yourself." Virtually all of the settler occupiers included in this book describe their work of self-reflection, unlearning their settler socialization, and personal transformation.

DECONSTRUCTING, RESISTING, AND SUBVERTING COLONIAL GOVERNMENTS, SYSTEMS, AND INSTITUTIONS

Alfred (2005: 155) says, "Onkwehonwe-Settler relations cannot be obviously reconciled without deconstructing the institutions that were built on racist and colonial exploitation," including a radical rehabilitation of the state. Xhopakelxhit (2014: 7) urges settlers to "confront your peers and the racism within colonial NGOs and [organizations] that are rendering the Indigenous of the lands invisible in the struggle." Similarly, Indigenous Action Media (2014: 7) state, "The work of an accomplice in anti-colonial struggle is to attack colonial structures and ideas." Flowers writes,

> In our struggles of freedom it is essential that we maintain a treaty-like relationship wherein Indigenous peoples and settlers are linked together but neither interferes in the matters of the other. When the state interferes in our business, then it is the obligation of settler subjects to oppose the misconduct of their government. Not for *our* benefit, but because that is what it means to live lawfully in a treaty relationship. (2015: 37)

Lee Maracle says,

> Racism and colonialism and patriarchy are Canadian social formations, not Indigenous ones. We are not the only ones responsible for their undoing. If you participate in dismantling the master's house and ending all forms of oppression, you are helping yourself. The sooner Canadians realize that, the better. (2017: 49)

Similarly, Manuel and Derrickson (2015) write specifically about what changes need to happen in the way the Canadian government relates with Indigenous Peoples. They say, "When Canadians are made aware of the issues — and of the injustices that are being committed in their name — they can demand that their political representatives find honourable solutions" (2015: 219). They reiterate the joint calls of the Defenders of the Land and Idle No More, calls for the repeal of Bill C-45 and other legislation that infringes on Aboriginal and Treaty Rights, as well as environmental protections. They call for greater consultation and proportional representation with regards to any legislation related to environmental protections and collective rights; following the principles of the United

Nations Declaration on the Rights of Indigenous Peoples, particularly the right of refusal and of free, prior, and informed consent; honouring the spirit and intent of historic Treaties; stopping the extinguishment of Aboriginal Title and recognizing section 35 of the Constitution Act; and creating a comprehensive national action plan and inquiry regarding violence against Indigenous women, in which Indigenous women are involved in all aspects of the process (Manuel and Derrickson 2015). Mills writes,

> At a general level, settlers should insist that putatively 'indigenous issues' are in fact 'Canadian issues' because they're caused by settler supremacy and because they impact upon all of us. Settlers afraid of overstepping their bounds should note that this means for many kinds of anti-colonial labour, settlers have not only the capacity but also the responsibility to act and aren't being good relatives if they fail to do so. (2019: 281)

USING OUR GIFTS

Kuokkanen (2007: 7) writes, "For indigenous people, the world's stability, its social order, is established and maintained mainly through giving gifts and recognizing the gifts of others, including the land." She explains, "The gift logic articulated here is grounded in an understanding of the world that is rooted in intricate relationships that extend to everyone and everything" (2007: 7). Chickadee Richard believes

> there is a lot of things that we need to do, and not everybody can do one thing. There's all of us with many, many facets of gifts. The skills that we all have, we can use our skills. It's like that puzzle — there's a puzzle there and each and every one of you is a missing piece of that puzzle. (personal communication, December 20, 2015)

Xhopakelxhit (2014: 6) says, "Creating a culture of resistance and support requires us all to know what our strong suits and talents are and to cultivate them so they benefit the cause in a manner that is respectful and meaningful." Also recall here the words of Mills (2016), who writes that we are each sacred persons who have gifts others need. Using our gifts, recalling Kennedy's words, is related to us coming to this world for a purpose and having work to do that is our own. She says,

It's impossible to [just] say "I'll just be accountable to Indigenous people." There have to be choices made along the way because your heart and your mind have to guide you. And there has to be space to do that. And a lot of this allies stuff almost seems to me like a measure of slavery. We can't fix the relationship by reversing the roles. It just won't work. (Personal communication, April 9, 2016)

As I interviewed those whose narratives appear in this book, it was very apparent to me the ways that they had integrated their own gifts and strengths into their work. Joy and John, for example, use art as a primary way of engaging their decolonial work, while Franklin and John have used their platforms as musicians in their work. Susanne has used her media skills and connections, and Victoria uses her strengths in history and theatre in her decolonization work. Monique uses her love of information, and Adam uses his gift for public speaking, while he and several others are gifted educators.

BEING DISCERNING

A number of Indigenous scholars emphasize the importance of discernment in the way settlers understand and practise our work and also in our choices of whom we work alongside. As has been noted, Tuck and Yang contend that settlers must understand decolonization to be "accountable to Indigenous sovereignty and futurity" (2012: 35) and to bring about "the repatriation of Indigenous land and life" (2012: 1), avoiding overgeneralizing decolonial work so it does not become re-colonizing or further settler colonialism. Recall Tuck and Yang's emphasis that settler moves to innocence be avoided by the discerning decolonial activist because they represent attempts to get "off the hook from the hard, unsettling work of decolonization" (2012: 4). Tuck and Yang also describe the danger of exclusively focusing one's decolonization work on decolonizing the mind: "to allow *conscientization* to stand in for the more uncomfortable task of relinquishing stolen land" (2012: 19), thereby creating no tangible disruption of settler colonialism.

Being an ally to Indigenous struggles requires that one be discerning about whom we support and with whom we work. Gehl recommends choosing to support leaders or groups that serve the needs of the peoples, especially those most oppressed, and gauging community response to the efforts:

Do the community people find this leader's efforts useful, interesting, engaging, and thus empowering? If not, allies should consider whether the efforts are moving in a questionable or possibly an inadequate direction, or worse yet, that their efforts are being manipulated and thus undermined, possibly for economic and political reasons. (n.d.: 2, used with permission)

Gehl (n.d., used with permission) emphasizes the importance of remaining attentive to structures of power and oppression, as well as lateral violence, and supporting and seeking guidance from those who are critical thinkers and understand these dynamics. Indigenous Action Media (2014: 7) suggest evaluating organizations one is considering supporting based on questions such as how they are funded and "Who is getting paid? How are they transparent? Who's defining the terms? Who sets the agenda?" and working with organizations or campaigns in which "local grassroots Indigenous People [are] directly involved with the decision making" (2014: 7). Xhopakelxhit (2014: 3) warns, "Indigenous activists are not super human mythical indigenous beings who are all knowing and all wise." She says, "We are all inherently flawed ... It does no one any greater disservice than to put them on pedestals" (2014: 4).

A number of those whose stories appear in this book discussed their processes and practices around discernment. For example, in Chapter 18, Victoria describes that when she first started her journey, she would work with anyone. Over time, she has developed better judgment and now usually avoids working with people who aren't trustworthy, aren't respected by their communities, or who carry inner baggage that makes them difficult to be around. She too has been working through her own baggage and working on becoming more trustworthy, so that she is a better person for Indigenous people to work with. Susanne, in Chapter 11, expresses that settlers have the right to be discerning about who we will work with and follow, emphasizing that following the wrong people may result in taking a wrong path. She also notes that it is important that settlers are aware that it is a mistake to focus all of their engagement with Chiefs and councils, and she advises they also connect with grassroots community members. She chooses to work with grassroots people who have integrity and with whom she shares similar perspectives.

BEING WILLING TO RISK AND GIVE

A number of scholars and activists challenge settler occupiers to take bigger risks and give more of themselves to decolonial struggles. Chickadee Richard (personal communication, December 20, 2015) described the great respect she has for a number of allies, based in part on their willingness to risk and give. She recalls Peter Kulchyski, many years ago, during an awareness-raising action saying, "Let us [non-Indigenous people] go out there, let us be on the front lines instead of you. Instead of you, let them arrest us." She says, "That's a generous step, because we're always a target on any kind of front lines" (personal communication, December 20, 2015). Xhopakelxhit (2014: 7) says, "Like it or not, and try as you might to refute it, settlers have privilege and more protection when it comes to interactions with the authorities than we do." She explains that because settlers have more leeway in the justice system and with the police and courts,

> commitment and bravery are key to bringing this into the next level by ramping up your resistance and putting yourself in front of the indigenous. Those who want to be on the frontlines should optimize their commitment for maximum benefit to the cause, this requires trust and sacrifice. (Xhopakelxhit 2014: 7)

Waziyatawin (2009: 151) challenges dedicated colonizer allies to "stand on the front lines with us." She asks, "Are you willing to do whatever is necessary to assist in our liberation struggle, including killing, dying, or life-imprisonment? … are you willing to take on a lifetime of ambiguity, uncertainty, moral torment?" (2009: 153). Recall Benally's (2013) words that accomplices are those who are willing to stand by Indigenous Peoples and take the same risks.

Questions of how much they will risk and give in order to contribute to Indigenous sovereignty are difficult for many settlers, including some of those whose narratives appear in this book. While all of them have given significantly of their time, energy, and skills, some struggled around facing arrest and giving up land. Monique (Chapter 4) describes trying to balance her financial contributions without depleting them so that she is able to continue to contribute over the long haul. She would consider going to prison for the work if it seemed like it would significantly advance revolutionary change. Both Susanne (Chapter 11) and

Kathi (Chapter 12) note that that they have worked lower-paying jobs in order to do work that contributes to social change and aligns with their values. John, in Chapter 15, shares that he has chosen to dedicate much of his labour to his anti-colonial work such that he does not receive a salary. His family has financially supported him in this as they believe in his work. Silvia describes struggling with working to dismantle, and yet using and maintaining enough privilege to have an impact. She has taken risks to advocate and speak out when vulnerable in her workplace. She states that she'd be willing to lose her job if it was over an issue that compromised her integrity too significantly (Chapter 16). Kathi is clear that she would not kill anyone for a cause, though she would go to jail for her activist work if a cause is important to her, and Susanne, in her blockade work, has been willing to go to jail for a cause that she believes in and has indeed been arrested without doing jail time. Although it is not included in his narrative because it happened more recently, Steve Heinrichs was convicted and sentenced to seven days in jail due to his participation in a pipeline protest in B.C. (Waddell 2018).

ENGAGING IN DIRECT ACTION

Direct action is a type of social change strategy that "moves beyond state sanctioned forms of protest" and breaks "with the rules those with social power have set up to contain us" (Kinsman 2017: 1). Through direct action, activists seek to directly stop what they oppose, and use "bodies and numbers to disrupt and pressure ruling relations" (Kinsman 2017: 1; Rodgers 2018). Participating in this type of action, which includes illegal dimensions, contains risks, such as arrest and jail time, as noted above. Indigenous Action Media (2014: 9) say, "Direct action is really the best and may be the only way to learn what it is to be an accomplice. We're in a fight, so be ready for confrontation and consequence." Idle No More and Defenders of the Land (2014: 358) have called upon non-Indigenous people to engage with Indigenous communities in "coordinated non-violent direct actions," believing "alternatives will only come to life if we escalate our actions, taking bold non-violent direct action that challenges the illegitimate power of corporations who dictate government policy" (2014: 358). Similarly, as was noted in Chapter 8, Coulthard (2014: 172) emphasizes that dismantling oppressive structures "will require that we continue to assert our presence on all of our territories, coupled with an escalation of confrontations with the forces of colonization through the forms of direct action." Susanne, in Chapter 11 of this book, shares a similar perspective. She notes that Indigenous Peoples are taking back their land, and that non-Indigenous supporters should step up and support them on the ground. She notes the importance of settlers witnessing, with cameras, the settler and police violence that can occur in such situations, which will likely increase the safety of Indigenous land defenders. A number of others included in this book have engaged in direct action support. For example, Rick (Chapter 13) and John (Chapter 15), in addition to Susanne, have supported the blockade at Grassy Narrows. As has also been noted above, Steve Heinrichs, in 2018, was arrested and convicted after taking part in a pipeline protest.

WORKING THROUGH OUR EMOTIONS

Working through our own emotions and using our support systems and other white settler activists — outside of our support and solidarity work with Indigenous Peoples — is key. In Chapter 2, some of the emotions of the settler condition were noted. Indigenous Action Media (2014: 3) write, "While guilt and shame are very powerful emotions, think about what you're doing before you make another community's struggle into your therapy session." This is a dimension that white settlers can help one another process so that Indigenous and racially marginalized peoples can focus on other tasks. Working through our emotions may also include developing "understanding, forbearance, and patience in the face of Indigenous seething anger, biting resentment, scathing judgment and devastating hopelessness" (Mills 2019: 281), as these should be expected in light of colonial dynamics. Several people I interviewed for this book spoke in depth about their processes of working through emotions. In Chapter 10, Adam describes some of his process of struggling with anxiety and despair when his worldview was shaken. Adam describes struggling with doubts about whether he is doing enough and whether he has caused harm, and he has found that his feelings of guilt, shame, and embarrassment can prompt him to figure out where he has gone wrong and work on it. Adam has taken on a role of engaging with other settlers when they behave in colonizing ways. He and his partner, Emma, also work to support and care for settlers who are engaged in decolonial work when they go to dark places and have doubts about their lives. Silvia takes care not to process her difficult emotions through her relationships with Indigenous Peoples, which she describes in Chapter 16. She is also careful to keep a strong and spiritual dimension, which helps her stay balanced when processing fear, vulnerability, anxiety, sorrow, and discouragement.

USING OUR PRIVILEGE AND PROVIDING PRACTICAL/LOGISTICAL SUPPORT

Indigenous Action Media (2014: 6) urge their accomplices to "find creative ways to weaponize their privilege (or more clearly, their rewards of being part of an oppressor class) as an expression of social war," rather than "resigning their agency, or capabilities as an act of 'support'" (2014: 6). Xhopakelxhit (2014: 8) says, "It helps no one if you are destitute by choice. Prosperity helps the grass roots!" Benally (2013) suggests engaging with people of our own class and own races and not distancing ourselves from our privilege and the different access it gives us. He suggests settler activists not reject our positionings, but rather engage and fight within these in order to destabilize and bring down colonial systems so that Indigenous Peoples' struggles can be more effective. This way, settler activists "can assert themselves and take initiative rather than sitting on their hands, waiting for the word from some token person" (21:15–21:26). Xhopakelxhit (2014: 7) writes of settler privilege and our "ability to acquire certain items." She says, "Let's put that to good use" (2014: 7). Xhopakelxhit (2014: 6) recommends "doing what is necessary to ensure that those who are working hard on the front lines are being supported." She suggests supporting Indigenous Peoples in their travel to events; lending or donating vehicles, equipment, electronics, and tools; providing access to office equipment; and providing childcare to radical Indigenous parents so that they can attend events. She also recommends support with event promotion in order to make sure events are well attended, and tangible support for travelling Indigenous activists such as places to stay, food, bedding, and transportation.

In Chapter 4, Monique described helping with logistics, material support, and event promotion. She would also help with ensuring people were fed and with carrying things around. Silvia shared that she and her partner have done things like bringing coffee to share at outdoor winter events and serving food to Elders during community events. Silvia has also provided financial support and food to Indigenous students in need

(Chapter 16). Franklin, in Chapter 7, describes fundraising for the legal defence of Indigenous land defenders. Adam, as a son of a police officer, used his familiarity with police and his white privilege to put the police at ease during an action he attended (Chapter 10). All of those I interviewed have provided logistical and material support to decolonial movements and have used their privilege for anti-colonial aims, and here I have offered just a few examples.

LIVING BY INDIGENOUS LAW

The phrase *Indigenous law* has only begun to be heard by most Canadians recently. Therefore, although many of those whose narratives appear in this book describe a growing respect and support for things that may be labelled as Indigenous law, they didn't use this phrase themselves. In the last decade or so, a growing number of scholars of Indigenous law have been graduating, writing, and teaching — sharing their profound ideas with others. Aaron Mills is one of these scholars, as are Aimée Craft and Dawnis Kennedy, who have contributed to and greatly influenced this book and my thinking. Mills (2017: 19) writes, "Canada must articulate how its sovereignty can be justified against the reality of already-existing constitutional orders that exhausted all of the jurisdictional space on Turtle Island." To settlers, he says, "As long as your home is on colonized Indigenous Lands … I want you to respect — and that means live by — Indigenous legalities as they exist within Indigenous constitutional orders" (2017: 20), and "If you're a settler, you're called to live lawfully on lands that were constitutionally ordered long before you or your ancestors arrived" (2017: 281). As I grew in my understanding while engaging in the work that undergirds much of this book, concepts around Indigenous law and Indigenous sovereignty came to the forefront of my thinking. I am grateful for this, as I believe that conceptualizing ourselves in relation to Indigenous law will be a key point of growth for settlers seeking to live in Indigenous sovereignty.

REMEMBERING WHO WE ARE

Over the years, I have heard of a number of Indigenous Knowledge Holders challenging settlers to look to our own ancestors to connect with our identities rather than appropriating Indigenous identities. The public controversies regarding people with distant or tenuous Indigenous ancestry who claim and benefit from Indigenous identities that are described in Chapter 2 can serve as a cautionary tale. Settlers who do come to know about distant Indigenous ancestry in their background can proceed slowly, finding evidence of their genealogy and connecting with their Indigenous family and communities. They may opt to identify as having Indigenous ancestry rather than being Indigenous in light of the dimensions of Indigenous identity that include relationships with land and community.

As a settler, I know that engaging the challenge of learning where I come from can be very difficult. Many settlers have a profound disconnection from our ancestral languages, spiritual practices, and cultures, along with little knowledge of our ancestors themselves. When attending Ojibwe language table gatherings in Minnesota in the late nineties, I had an experience that sent me searching. In accordance with Indigenous Protocols, we were to introduce ourselves including our names, our Clans, and where we come from. As has been shared earlier in this book, Clans are an important part of Anishinaabe identity and governance. To make it easier, the language table instructors shared potential phrases we could use that might fit for us. Regarding Clans, two options were the Anishinaabemowin equivalent of *I don't have a Clan* and *I don't know my Clan*. I just assumed that white people don't have Clans, so that's what I would say. But one day, an Anishinaabe friend and mentor shared her view that everyone has a Clan. While I realize that many Indigenous nations may not have teachings or practices around Clans — and I am not suggesting they are wrong — her assertion sent me on a search for my Clan, and I scoured books about pre-Christian Europe and began doing genealogy work. This has been a meaningful process for me that has strengthened aspects of my identity.

Lynn Gehl (n.d.: 1, used with permission) says that allies to Indigenous Peoples are "fully grounded in their own ancestral history and culture." She says, "Effective allies must sit in this knowledge with confidence and pride; otherwise the 'wannabe syndrome' could merely undermine Indigenous people's efforts" (n.d.: 1, used with permission). Xhopakelxhit (2014) cautions settlers against believing that they can become Indigenous, while Sakej Ward says,

> Really, as xwelítem, you have your own indigenous identity. You
> have your own. You have to go back further than us to find it.
> You have to go back to pre-Roman imperialism, pre-Christian

imperialism, and you can find your ethnic identity, whether it be Pict, Celt, Scotty, Hun, Goth, Gaul, Nordic, Rus, Tartar. Whatever your ethnic identity is, you had an Indigenous identity prior to the conquest of Roman imperialism. It was imperialism that erased our identities — our true and authentic identities.... I know enough about the Celts and Picts to say that they had Indigenous-like teachings. They understood concepts like interconnectedness. They understood concepts like respect for the land and reverence for the land and reciprocity. It was built into their teachings. So there is something there that tells me that if xwelítem will go back to their Indigenous identity, maybe that's the basis where we can define relationships. We'll find that common ground to speak on.... For xwelítem I think it's really important to understand that identity. And that becomes your decolonization work. How do you decolonize from that Roman imperial influence that you've had for two thousand years, depending on where you were at the time? (2015: 25:26–27:50, used with permission)

Some of the people I interviewed for this book shared about their ancestral identities and their identity quests. Because her parents immigrated from Austria, Silvia has experienced being immersed in Austrian culture and language and has a love for Austrian land (Chapter 16). Adam, in Chapter 10, says that when a number of Indigenous friends urged him to reconnect with his roots, he spent time in the United Kingdom. However, he saw that systems of capitalism, private property, and industrialization in Britain had eliminated any authentic Indigenous reality there and he felt no connection. Adam worries that settlers' pursuit of Indigeneity through their ancestral homelands may lead many to try to escape their colonial complicity. Susanne, on the other hand, feels connected to her ancestral memory and to her ancestors, and has sought to both recreate and tap into her ancestral traditions, which has helped her to understand who she is and where she comes from (Chapter 11).

ENGAGING WITH RESTITUTION, REPARATION, REPATRIATION, AND LAND RETURN

"One of the loudest and most frequent demands of Indigenous people in the relationship with settlers is for the return of the land," write Pasternak and King (2019: 8). The growing #LandBack movement and hashtag attest to this. As I conducted the research for this book, I found that most of those I interviewed believed that restitution needs to take place and that land should be returned to Indigenous nations. Simpson says, "Land has never really been a part of the Canadian Reconciliation discourse. And this is a critical problem because Indigenous people will not survive as Indigenous Peoples without homelands" (2013b: 24:22–24:32). As has been noted, Manuel and Derrickson (2015: 7) have written, "It is the loss of our land that has been the precise cause of our impoverishment." Taiaiake Alfred argues that because the significant impact of colonialism is largely tied to land theft, both economically and socially, colonialism "cannot be addressed in any other way than through the return of those lands to us" (2009: 182). But how can this be done? This may be done through restitution to Indigenous Peoples, as individuals and collectively, "including land, transfers of federal and provincial funds, and other compensation" (Alfred 2009: 8).

Waziyatawin (2008) suggests land reparations as a method of justice that challenges the oppressive economic system. She suggests that one place to start would be with publicly held lands. Waziyatawin (2008: 150) says, "In addition, private land owners can individually commit themselves to Indigenous land return." Parklands may be a good place to start, as these are generally not privately or individually owned by settlers, and yet Simpson (2013b) questions whether even settler allies would support this, as they may be quite invested in being able to enjoy recreation in these areas. Still, land return is what must happen. Decolonization must have at its core a vision of the repatriation of land and life (Tuck and Yang 2012). Coulthard (2014: 168) says, "Land has been stolen, and significant amounts of it must be returned. Power and authority have been unjustly appropriated, and much of it will have to be reinstated." Many settlers have a lot of fear around this dimension of decolonial work. However, as a number of Indigenous scholars, including Alfred (2009: 182), maintain, "when I say to a settler, 'Give it back,' am I talking about them giving up the country and moving away? No. Irredentism has never been in the vision of our peoples." Rather, his vision is that settlers demonstrate respect for shared lands and resources and return "enough of our power and land for us to be self-sufficient" (2009: 182). Lee Maracle (2017: 51) emphasizes that financial restitution is not sufficient: "No matter how much money you give me, it is not the same as sovereignty and the right to caretake our lands." Indeed, Manuel and Derrickson (2017) emphasize that any discussions of reconciliation must be predicated upon the recognition of Indigenous Peoples as title holders and decision makers on their lands.

As has been noted, many of those whose stories appear in this book have supported Indigenous Land reclamation and reoccupation through direct action. In theory, they believe land must be returned to Indigenous Peoples. However, considering how this can be done in practice can bring up questions and fears. For Rick, this has come up as he wonders whether and where to buy property. What does it mean to buy land on Indigenous Lands in the form of Treaty lands or lands that were once part of a shrinking reserve (see Chapter 13)? Monique, in Chapter 4, admits she is not brave enough to give up her piece of property and home in Winnipeg, even though she feels it is the right thing to do. Monique shared that she has heard about individuals giving land back to Indigenous nations. She feels a good way to start to work for land return would be to educate non-Indigenous Canadians about the problematic nature of their being on and benefiting from Indigenous Lands. She also feels it is important to listen to what Indigenous communities and nations are asking for regarding land return, and then to place enormous pressure on key decision makers to see that larger land return happens. Steve shared an example, in Chapter 6, of someone he knows who is working with a Mi'kmaw community to return nearly fifty acres of land. He also spoke of a group of Mennonites building relationships with the Young Chippewayan Cree in Saskatchewan. Although no concrete land transaction has happened yet, the Mennonites have raised funds to support the Young Chippewayan land claim. As well, the Mennonite Church's Jubilee Fund contributes annually to support land reclamation efforts of Indigenous communities. Although Adam currently does not own land, he believes that if he did there are scenarios in which he'd willingly give it back, as he believes transforming property back into a land base for Indigenous nations is one of the most concrete things we can do. As land return efforts remain few and far between among settler occupiers, understanding, in dialogue with Indigenous Peoples, and then sharing how this can be done has become a priority for me.

BEING PERSISTENT

Indigenous Action Media (2014: 4) describe parachuter allies who "rush to the front lines seemingly from out-of-nowhere. They literally move from one hot or sexy spot to the next." They also describe the floaters, who "hop from group to group and issue to issue, never being committed enough, but always wanting their presence felt and their voices heard [and who] tend to disappear when it comes to being held accountable or taking responsibility" (2014: 5). Xhopakelxhit (2014) urges settlers to never forget and never give up. She notes that Indigenous activists do not have the luxury to "give up and join the mainstream culture" (2014: 11) because "we are by our very heritage and birth born political and into a lifetime of racism, oppression, and hard times" (2014: 11). Therefore, she says,

> If you commit to this path then ensure you are on board for the long haul. Breaks are of course good and needed for mental, physical, emotional, and spiritual well being for all of us but never forget we live in a terrorist state bent on destroying our lands and waters and the future of us all for profit. (2014: 11)

This theme of staying involved for the long haul is one discussed by John in Chapter 15. He is part of a solidarity group which, as they were getting going, engaged in conversation with Indigenous activists about what they hoped to see in solidarity work. One of the primary messages they shared was that many other white allies haven't stuck around long enough to make changes. John took this to heart and has remained involved for more than ten years. Adam describes his deep commitment to the work in Chapter 10. He could never walk away now, he says, and his work has become the fundamental preoccupation of his life. Many dimensions of what Indigenous Peoples are asking of us have been explored in this chapter, along with examples of settler occupiers taking up these themes in practice. Some of these examples are contained in the last four narratives of the book, which we turn to now.

CHAPTER 15

JOHN DOE

Elizabeth Carlson-Manathara and Anonymous

IDENTITY AND EARLY INFLUENCES

John self-identifies as a "boringly straight" white male in his late forties who is an artist, activist, anarchist, atheist, problem-with-authority, and "generally totally stubborn" person. Although he is "semi-university edu-cated," John describes himself as mostly self-taught. He grew up in a prairie province rural community, parented by "good white NDP-type folks" of working-class backgrounds, union involvement, and the mild Canadian brand of socialism. John's ancestors were helped by Native peoples when they settled on the land. In his community, intermarriage, long-term relationships, integrated families, and close working relationships between Indigenous and settler peoples were not altogether uncommon. Both John's mother's and his father's family lines had unique and deep hunt-ing and fishing connections with Native and Métis folks, and John grew up "around Indian kids." John's father picked up hunting and trapping values from his Indigenous hunting buddies, which were in turn passed on to John: hunting "wasn't for sport, where you just go out and shoot your guns off, and be a man. It was [to] love and respect the land ... [to] value anything that you took the life of and use as much of it as possible."

Nonetheless, John observed much racial inequity, division, and anti-Indigenous racism in his community. John's father was a tradesperson who was often called upon to repair the substandard work of previous white contractors in Indigenous Peoples' homes on reserves. John would accompany his father on some of these work trips, and he was struck by scenes of extreme poverty and desperation. Questions about the dispar-ity between what he saw on reserves and the way his family lived would haunt him into adulthood. John did not escape the "hard-coded colonial attitudes toward Indigenous Peoples" that impacted systems around him.

He says, "Growing up, I know I've engaged in racist assumptions, said and thought terrible things, didn't stand up when I should have, let things go too many times." He picked up the "default flatness" so prevalent in Canada, characterized by being able to witness something that is wrong and not question it: "We just sort of let it go. We're not encouraged to stand up against it."

Although he is quick to acknowledge the presence of racism in his immediate and extended family, in the case of his parents this existed alongside some unarticulated anti-racism and anti-colonial thought and action. John's mother, "essentially a kind of feminist" working mom who was sympathetic to liberal causes, worked to change the hiring and training practices of her employer such that Indigenous folks had greater opportunities for training in trades and were hired for other-than-menial jobs. His father was a proponent of social integration, and John relays that upon being newly hired in one workplace, his father

> walked into the lunchroom, and all the white guys are on one side of the room playing crib, and all the Native guys are on the other side of the room playing crib — total segregation happening. Not because it was enforced by law, but that's just socially how it was. So he put a little notice on the bulletin board — we're going to have a cribbage [card game] tournament, why doesn't everybody get together and play cribbage? And so, in his own way, he brought folks together.

John indicates that his parents approached this work in everyday ways from a general human decency perspective of care and respect rather than politicized radical perspectives of actively tearing down colonial walls.

EARLY ACTIVISM AND LEARNING

John's early activism began over a decade ago, and focused on anti-globalization and anti-poverty work. He attended various trade protests around the world that became increasingly difficult to access due to location (e.g., Davos, Switzerland, or Doha, Qatar) and heightened police security and repression. With an entry point in political hardcore, punk rock, and rave music scenes, John was also engaged with alternative living movements (e.g., forming collectives, radical sharing, back-to-the-land and do-it-yourself movements). These mostly white groups were often inspired by Indigenous understandings and ways of life and were nature-based, involving sustainable agricultural practices and reduced consumption. Members reflected "different levels of appropriation" and assumptions of the ways of Indigenous Peoples. John himself sought "the best possible thought that I could draw on from any of my own traditions … without me necessarily mimicking anything or denying the fact of where I am in society currently" — his stable, white privilege.

John emphasizes the role of art in shaping his liberation and anti-oppressive understandings. When his friends and colleagues in academia would ask about essays or books he was reading related to left/liberation politics, he would half-jokingly tease, "Well, I'm actually looking more at Rothko paintings" to arrive at similar conclusions. The critical ways of seeing John developed through art have impacted his ability to apply the same clear focus to the world itself, informing his activist engagement. He says, "Believe it or not, that's the background of my skills and so I try to bring that into activist work as well."

His transition into anti-colonial and decolonization work was a process that was influenced by a desire to apply his ideals and skills closer to home and with greater frequency than was possible with international anti-globalization events. He increasingly understood that locally, Indigenous Peoples have been "getting hit with the blunt end" of structural oppression related to racism, poverty, environmental destruction, and resource extraction and that they have been at the front lines of activism locally and across Canada. Thus, he saw anti-colonial work as work at the intersections of protection of the land, protection of Indigenous Rights and sovereignty, human rights, anti-poverty, and anti-capitalism. His transition was undergirded by a process that picked up speed in his twenties, a process of collecting knowledge that would address his childhood questions about the social inequities he observed. During the early stages of his interest in radical-left and anti-colonial thought, John attended a gathering of solidarity and support for the Mohawks of Kanehsatà:ke and Kahnawà:ke in their resistance to the plans of the town of Oka, which sought to build a golf course on Mohawk Traditional Territory. Having attended the event as a curious young person, John says, "it connected to a lot of stuff I was focusing on and reading at the time." The resistance signalled a turning point of increased awareness for him and for a number of Canadians because, being explicitly racist, Oka tore off the veil and exposed the pithy core of white settler Canadian attitudes. It became blatantly clear that work needed to be done regarding the attitudinal and institutionalized racism and colonialism of the Canadian state. John and his friends on the left fringe began to question themselves about why colonial injustice had not been a focus among them. The resistance inspired them to seek out more knowledge. They shared books, magazine articles, and the circulating self-published street press on the works of white radical-left figures such as Noam Chomsky and Howard Zinn and sought to learn more about what led up to Oka. As their work became more accessible to him, John became increasingly exposed to and inspired by Indigenous authors, filmmakers, and artists.

ANTI-COLONIAL WORK AND CONTINUED LEARNING

The anti-colonial work John has been involved with has included educating himself and others, solidarity work around Indigenous sovereignty and land defence, involvement with scientists and activists at environmental racism conferences, and memberships in an Indigenous solidarity group and a decolonization group. When John's solidarity group began, they "asked Indigenous activists to come in and speak to us on these issues of 'what does solidarity mean to you guys? What should we be doing?'" The Indigenous activists recalled that the other non-Indigenous groups with whom they had worked were no longer around. They said, "That's an issue for us: that white allies don't stick around, that you don't put in enough time to make a change." They said, "Because you're privileged you can kind of shop around for causes and leap from one to the other, and if we're not fashionable, away you go." This resonated with John because "issues involved with colonization go so deep, they can't be solved overnight."

For over a decade, John has been working with Indigenous activists on their territories on issues related to their sovereignty. His group did much work with Asubpeechoseewagong Netum Anishinabek Nation (Grassy Narrows). Grassy Narrows has a long-standing blockade against logging on their territory and a fifty-year-long fight for justice concerning historical mercury poisoning that devastated the community. John supports the grassroots activists' efforts to embody sovereignty in their territory, battling this environmental racism and carrying out their responsibility of protecting their traditional lands from being exploited and damaged by commercial resource extraction companies. In light of his childhood experiences, beginning to work with Indigenous people was a comfortable fit: "It just felt right to be back working with people who lived on the land." John wanted to help alleviate suffering like he had witnessed as a child. Indigenous activists with whom he worked expressed love, friendship, and patience toward him, and the friendships and connections created were deeper than what he had experienced in previous activist work. He says, "Folks I've been working with are sensitive to each other and try to look out for each other. If we transgress, we try to make up quick and be ok." The majority of the Indigenous people he has worked with, and who have been leaders, have been women whose perspectives have informed their approaches:

> We're bringing our children, we're bringing our aunties, we're bringing our mothers and grandmothers to these protests, right on the front line. In order to do that … we're trying to be careful and care about each other and respect each other, and so certain kinds of aggression won't be tolerated in those spaces.

John and his group have operated out of a "taking direction" model in their solidarity work. They listen to what the existing Indigenous leadership is asking of them:

> Instead of arriving at their territory on the scene where the activist work is taking place, engaged with all your plans and methods already figured out — come[ing] in say[ing] "oh, we're well familiar that this is about this issue. We know all about this because we've been working on it forever, and this is how we've always conducted it and so we're just going to kind of carry on like this."… Arriving somewhat humbler and asking the people who are facing these things right on the front line, "what help can we give you? And you tell us what you need from us, and we'll try to help you with that, as best we can in whatever way, shape, or form." *They* determine, *they* ask us to carry out whatever we can do. And we might say, "well we have people who can work on *this* issue this way or *that* issue with these skills, or work on *this* facet of it … these are the ways that we can help." A good part of it is following their lead.

John also spends time reflecting on his solidarity work. He says, "I'm going to analyze what we do. Pause, reflect, assess, and then change what we need to and go on."

John sometimes wondered whether his atheism might cause rifts between him and any of the traditionalist Indigenous activists with whom he works. Despite his own feeling that "anarchism occasionally feels like a kind of political religion" in which he puts his hope and faith in the people, he wonders how this squares with his observation that a feature of "a lot of Indigenous folks' activism, in the past few years especially, has come from their [spiritual] reconnection." He recalls a conversation he had after ten years of working with a "very good Indigenous comrade" in which she observed, "Technically, your views are probably more akin to the geologists and scientists that work for the mining or logging companies than the religious side of things, than my spiritual side." John replied,

> In one sense that may be true. Maybe I would share something closer to what they understand of what the world is or how it came to be. Having said that, what they accept of the world and what they want to do to it, I'm 180 degrees opposite their goals. I'm much more inspired about your understanding and vision of where you think the world should be. That's where I'm at. That's why I work with you and against them.

John says, "I completely respect their beliefs, I really do. I'm not an anti-religion atheist." After spending time with the Indigenous comrades with whom he is in relationship, John has received an understanding of some of the spiritual sayings and teachings they have shared. He is happy to help out at the blockade camp when events or ceremonies require support:

> Cutting wood, making tea, cleaning up, a bit of cooking, a bit of maintenance, tending fires. A fire-keeper is an honoured role, has a deep significance traditionally and a specific set of duties attached to it, I've been told. Without me claiming to fully embody what it means to be a traditional fire-keeper, I was asked to perform that function, in the most basic sense, from time to time.

John says that entering into close, caring friendships with Indigenous people has personalized his work.

> When you hear all the standard racist assumptions about Natives being spewed, now it's not just happening to some poor anonymous brown person; you know these folks, you know their hearts, you know their minds. The folks that I'm so lucky to work with,

they're so solid, beautiful, and humane. It makes you want to shatter those assumptions.

In his personal decolonization work, John has sought to overcome his "good, solid background in Canadian racism." He works to address his colonial socialization and integrate anti-colonial principles into his daily life. John notes that it is taking years to deconstruct, isolate, and flush out his colonial conditioning, which he sees as a product of being raised where colonial perspectives are "the water you swim in." Such perspectives include missionary notions of "how we can go in and make their [Indigenous Peoples'] lives better," thinking that, as Euro-Canadians, we understand Indigenous Peoples' problems and are in a position to apply instant solutions, mythologies around pulling one's self up by one's bootstraps, and British empire myths of white supremacy and Indigenous people, the primitives. His decolonization work has been aided by learning from Indigenous filmmakers, authors, artists, and theorists. He has learned from authors such as Ward Churchill, Taiaiake Alfred, and Leanne Simpson. Ground-breaking documentary work by Alanis Obomsawin has been transformational, as has the work of many Indigenous artists, including the Walking With Our Sisters Collective. John says of the Walking With Our Sisters exhibit:

> It changed me, and that's interesting because I think I'm pretty familiar with the topic, but it was so personal.... You've got a collection of people contributing to this work of over 1,700 vamps, moccasin tops, decorated by people who did it because they felt an empathy for the issue. Professional artists that contributed and then a lot of work[s] that were made by people who knew people that are directly affected, or have gone through this personally, which I couldn't even pretend to know what that's like. It's, by hand, created to share with us. The feelings are mixed and overwhelming.... You're being informed on a level that you can't even put into words.

John's educational work with others has been varied. Through the decolonization group, he has taken part in discussion groups in which he and other non-Indigenous people teach one another and gain skills to address racism and colonialism in everyday conversations. He has sought out opportunities to address colonial perspectives when educating people with little background in English or in Canadian history who have attended classes he taught.

Using an activist approach, the Indigenous solidarity organization he belongs to sought to educate the general public through demonstrations, banner drops, and through an educational road blockade in which they distributed pamphlets to the drivers of cars that passed through. A series of these actions were held to spread the message of Six Nations Peoples who were demonstrating to raise awareness regarding their rights to lands on which the city of Caledonia, Ontario, had been built and on which Henco Industries Ltd. planned to build a residential subdivision. In order to do this, the solidarity group first educated themselves about the issues involved by inviting Indigenous speakers and activists to "tell us where they're at, tell us what we can do, and make suggestions on how we can approach things better." Their intent was "getting information to people that they won't be getting from the mainstream newspapers, radio, television, providing it directly to them, using a protest to actually do that."

John jokes that he is "supplementing a no-income art career with no-income activist work." As is not uncommon for artists, John is supported by close family who believe in his art and activism. John has sought to create anti-colonial change and educate others through his work as a musician, artist, and documentary filmmaker. He understands educating other white people to be a major responsibility. When he reads the racist comments in the feedback sections of news reports on Indigenous issues and resistance to colonialism, he sees an opportunity to respond and try to change those attitudes. Such comments reflect a "massive chunk of settler Canadians" who are "completely removed from any meaningful contact" with Indigenous Peoples, so they "return to the familiar uncritical stereotypes prevalent in Canadian society, often reinforced by mainstream media." John believes that relationships between Indigenous and white settler peoples are simply not encouraged foundationally and structurally in society. Thus, John works to assist white settlers in making these connections.

Because John believes in the importance of listening to Indigenous Peoples and asking them what we can do, he stresses that one should carefully choose solid people with whom to work. After all, he says, the answers you get depend on who you are talking to. John has observed that Indigenous Peoples represent a broad spectrum of perspectives. Some may be indifferent to political issues. Others are actively engaged in "mak[ing] deals with governments and corporations," while still others are grassroots activists who avoid and decry such deals. It is the grassroots activists with whom John aligns. One such activist suggested caution in aligning oneself with the Chiefs and Indian Act systems: "Do you trust *your* politicians?" she asked. Although John's ideals may not perfectly align with the Indigenous activists with whom he works, he feels many are close enough for him to compromise and do important work together.

John is critical about the now-in-vogue phrase *free, prior, and informed consent* and some of the practices that surround it. He sees it being used as a pretense for the powers that be to continue a *taking* relationship. He says,

> When the Indigenous Peoples of a territory say *no* to the offers from federal or provincial governments or corporations, that *no* should be respected. This doesn't mean exploiting their poverty by trying to divide communities with strategic injections of cash, blatantly misinforming that populace or returning every year to put pressure on the band. Trying to grab the remaining resources on their land and leaving them with the polluted desolation that destroys their contemporary hunting and gathering ways of life is genocide, no matter the slick marketing language used by government and corporate swindlers that strain the meaning of the term *partnership*. Some Indigenous folks are asking to be left alone: "stop exploiting us, stop exploiting our lands."

John has reflected on some emotional aspects of his anti-colonial work. His dissatisfaction with how things are has motivated him. John has experienced the love and caring of those with whom he is in solidarity. He has also felt a great deal of pain and regret in rare moments when his relationships with Indigenous Peoples do not work out. During one environmental racism conference he was invited to attend, John delivered a paper that was complicated by little time for translation preparation, so that important acknowledgement of sources included in the original complete presentation were skipped due to the time necessary for simultaneous translation. An Indigenous woman took offence to his paper, contending that the stories he was sharing were not his to tell and that the communities they come from should have been more overtly acknowledged. John says, "I don't blame her. This was an Indigenous woman telling me something, that I fucked up badly, I'm going to listen. How many times has she seen white guys co-opting or taking advantage of her culture or inserting their voices over topics without permission?" Although he felt she had been wrong about him in some ways, he did not want to disregard what she was saying. Rather, he tried to understand and process where he messed up. He attempted to apologize, which did not go over well.

John has also experienced feelings of guilt for not doing more in his work and at times feels he should rearrange his life to do more. At the same time, John has himself experienced burnout in his work and has

> witnessed a lot of fellow activists who've burnt out.... Some folks, depending on the kind of issues they're dealing with, mental, emotional, what have you, have burnt out and never come back. This has usually been the folks that I've witnessed who have thrown absolutely everything they had into the cause, and I understand why they'd do that.

In the end, though, John realizes that "if you run yourself ragged, you are going to be requiring more help than you can give.... You want to be in a position to help, and you have to take care of yourself." When the quality of activists' work starts to suffer, it may be time to "step back, reflect on it, take some time, correct it, and keep moving on." He says,

> Everybody has their own capacity, and you can only work within that ... it's true for other people too who may not be living up to your standards and that you may not live up to theirs. Be considerate, help each other. It's all for good work.

John does anti-colonial and decolonization work in order to be an agent of liberation for himself and others. He believes that he has lived an immorally cushioned life at the expense of Indigenous Peoples around the globe as much as in Canada. He says, our "economy is based on ripping them off, steal[ing] their labour, their resources every chance we get in order to prop up our own comfortable life." This is gross negligence on the part of settlers and rich countries, and John feels an ethical obligation to Indigenous Peoples. He is moved to try and make life better and to address and redress the situation. Living in a society that is "rolling on the foundations of colonialism" and actively blocking Indigenous sovereignty, John feels we need to halt that momentum. In the face of "colonial state violence and oppression ... imposed on Indigenous societies of Canada," John says, "I want to be an ally on their side and put a complete stop to those destructive forces and break out of that

pretend-that-you-don't-know-what's-going-on attitude, to make changes."
"We have to make up a lot for all the shit that we've done," John says. He
plans to "hang in there as long as [he] can," knowing that the work he
does is lifelong. He still has the energy to continue and is not satisfied
with where things are at. He is motivated, occasionally, by an absolute
and total anger and by love. John wishes to see justice for the Indigenous
people with whom he has entered into close friendships of care and deep
connection.

CHAPTER 16

SILVIA STRAKA

Silvia Straka with Elizabeth Carlson-Manathara

As a white Austrian-Canadian settler, I live and work on unceded and occupied Stk'emlupsemc te Secwépemc Territory. This chapter contains my story of how I have come to understand the meanings and responsibilities inherent in living on Indigenous Land. For anything I have learned, I owe a profound debt to all my Indigenous teachers: scholars, Elders, colleagues, students, friends, land defenders, and activists. I am particularly grateful for my long-term relationships, collegial and personal, with Dr. Michael Hart, Gladys Rowe, and Lisa Kisch, through whom I have experienced my deepest and most profound learning. Writing a chapter such as this is rather excruciating, as it contradicts in much of what I have learned about being a co-conspirator. What pushed me was recognizing my responsibility to share what I have learned with other settlers. While I continue to make mistakes and do this work imperfectly, I hope that something in my story may be useful to others. Each life story has unique patterns, with many threads woven together, some more intense in colour and defining the main pattern. Learning to be an Indigenous co-conspirator has been one of my defining life threads, creating new and beautiful patterns in my life. Looking back, it has been an unlikely direction but one that has been deeply transformative in defining my life's mission. In describing my story, I will honour what Indigenous people often say, "It's not about your words, but about your actions."

I was the first child of post-WWII Austrian immigrants recently settled in Toronto. My first four years were spent immersed in Austrian culture, language, and a deep love for Austrian land. My earliest family teachings were centred around these interconnections. Navigating my dual cultural identities has been a lifelong process and accompanied by struggle, mitigated by white privilege and the middle-class status my family quickly attained. The experiential knowledge I have of oppression arising from my ethnicity intersecting with female, queer, and (dis)ability identities has helped lay my foundation for doing anti-colonial work.

Two different lands have profoundly shaped who I am today: my Austrian homeland and the northern Ontario bush, where I grew up. As a younger child, I was drawn to the bush and often went there to be alone, to think, to read. I have had some deeply mystical experiences there. This connection to the northern bush is one of the most important foundations of my Canadian identity and I have thought that if anyone were to try to remove that connection from me, it would feel as though they were violently tearing out my very roots. Today, understanding myself as a settler occupier on that land, I realize the problematic nature of grounding my identity in what is actually stolen land and not mine to claim. What, then, does it mean for me to have such love for this land and what do I do with it, knowing what I now know? As settlers, we all have to unsettle our relationship to Indigenous Land, which includes our sense of "home" and the safety and the entitlement that comes with feeling we have a place where we "belong" and where we believe we have "a right to be." I came to realize that as settler occupiers, we have done immeasurable violence and unimaginable harm to people whose connections to land go back to time immemorial and whom we have dispossessed, displaced, and disconnected from their land. Beginning to understand ourselves as living on stolen land often raises resistance for settlers. We may wonder, do I even have a home? My personal way of working this through was to de-centre my sense of "dispossession" and homelessness — never having had a right to possess any of this land or make it my home — and to re-centre myself in the principles of reconciliation. I processed my feelings of instability, rootlessness, and grief without putting these emotions into my relationships with Indigenous people. Later, I reflected on stories of how Indigenous Peoples welcomed the first Europeans, helped them survive, and were open to sharing the land with them. Although settlers have not respected this relationship, I think the invitation mostly remains, although the colonial history and genocide of our country make it remarkable that there is still any possibility for reconciliation and relationship. However, Canada's long history of broken Treaties makes it so difficult to come back into some of this earlier vision of the relationship without first righting the wrongs. Engaging in solidarity actions with land defenders, taking a respectful role guided by their voices, has been an essential responsibility for me. Along with such solidarity actions in defence of Indigenous Lands,

I believe that living on Indigenous Land also means actively conspiring to take care of the land. In northern Ontario, when I walked on trails, I offered tobacco under trees as I was taught by Elders, which raised my consciousness about my responsibility to the land. I then began bringing a bag with me to pick up garbage left by others. Through such practices I am gradually coming into a different relation with the land.

My spirituality has been an important influence in my social justice work, but I have had to unpack a lot about this background. As a queer woman, I understand this reality very well and have often experienced harm at the hands of the church. At the same time, my faith has deeply nourished my motivations and values for social justice. But just as we need to unsettle our relationship to land, those of us rooted in the Christian tradition also need to unsettle that relationship. I had to let it go entirely in order to figure out how to reclaim it. The immeasurable harms Christianity has perpetrated on residential school Survivors made me want to firmly denounce and completely reject it. But I also know some Indigenous people live the tension of maintaining their Christian faith while reclaiming traditional practices, not wanting to be forced into an either/or choice. I have come to believe that Christianity, in all its diversity, can be life-giving or oppressive and sometimes both at the same time. These internal struggles have been essential, as it is important to ground myself in my own identity and cultural and spiritual traditions to be a safer co-conspirator.

SOCIAL WORK EDUCATION AND ACTIVIST DEVELOPMENT

I grew up without knowledge or awareness of any First Nations people around me. In elementary school, I thought that they were historical beings, like the ancient Greeks. I never knew that Ojibway, Cree, and Métis people were living around me. Later, I went through three social work degrees without hearing the word "colonization" once.

Although I had done some of my own reading on this topic by then, I had not yet understood the importance of relational learning. During my PhD, I shared a sessional instructor bullpen space with Haudenosaunee activist/scholar Ruth Koleszar-Green. Ruth helped organize the Gathering of Mother Earth Protectors in support of the six imprisoned leaders of the remote KI community. There, I participated in my first Indigenous solidarity event, which had a transformative impact. In attending other events since then, I have learned more about Indigenous land defenders, broken Treaties, and colonial laws and policies from such participation than from any books. It has led to my deepest and most transformative learning.

The First National Truth and Reconciliation national event was a decisive turning point. Burdened heavily by the Holocaust on my Austrian side, I had taken refuge in my Canadian identity as exemplifying freedom, social justice, and human rights, with an idealistic view of Canada as "the good guys." This national event completely unsettled me, devastated me, and made me recognize that there was no escape for me in any of my identities. I realized that Canada has also perpetrated a holocaust and that neither of my white identities was benign. Profoundly shaken, I no longer knew who I was. After bearing witness to a women's sharing circle and leaving it extremely distressed, I determined that I needed to be part of the reconciliation process. Standing there in the cold rain, I thought about my responsibility. I realized that white Europeans are the perpetrators of most of the oppression, colonialism, and genocide around the world, which I had known intellectually but was now being directly and experientially confronted with it in a way I could no longer evade. I began to reflect more on my participation in the everyday dynamics of oppression and how I benefit from racism and colonialism. I sought to engage with Indigenous knowledges and educate myself in various ways: watching the Aboriginal People's Television Network regularly, subscribing to Indigenous blogs and news sites, attending Elders' teachings at the university, reading books by Indigenous authors, connecting and talking with people — I tried to listen to what the community around me was saying. These are ways I learned to come into a better relationship with Indigenous Peoples and work towards decolonization based on their stated agendas.

Ceremony has been an important source of transformative learning. I have often accepted open invitations to all to attend Indigenous ceremonies and Elders' teachings. These experiences have always been deeply healing, energizing, and connecting, helping to sustain my anti-colonial work. At the same time, I am a guest attending a sacred practice that is not mine. I ask beforehand what I need to know to be a respectful participant. I do not share details of such ceremonies with others. Knowing a song or a story does not entitle me to share it. These are important points of respect. Participating in such events has led me to delve even deeper into my own cultural traditional practices, as those who culturally appropriate often do so in the absence of meaningful connections of their own.

This work touches my heart a great deal. I often experience fear, vulnerability, anxiety, guilt, sorrow, disillusionment, and discouragement, as well as hope and joy. When things get difficult, I remember that this work necessarily has to start by transforming myself. Unless my own spiritual roots are deep and wide, my work in the world will have little stability or lasting value. It takes heart and courage and humility to step up in this work. When Indigenous people talk about being betrayed by allies, it is important to let my anxiety come up, as it helps me remain alert to the risk of doing harm. I believe that we are each responsible for our own individual healing work and that the more we do this work, the more we are able to be safer friends, colleagues, and co-conspirators. Healing my privilege often requires a real unpacking and breaking apart my understanding of myself and my understanding of my world. Sometimes it has to crack right apart into pieces. Sometimes, if I feel really hurt by something that has happened, I do need to pull in for a bit, but not for too long. Processing the hurt and shame is personal work and I do my best to keep it out of Indigenous spaces. Usually I need to figure out how to re-engage differently, which is the place where dialogue can be helpful, once I have taken responsibility for myself and my actions. When in a group, I try to just *be* in the work and to focus on how I can be of help. Once my emotions have been processed, I have found that if I return in a relational and humble manner, there is often room to recover from most mistakes. I try to live from my heart, as Indigenous people are usually very good at discerning one's heart. But living from the heart makes us vulnerable. Anti-colonial work thus starts with me, ensuring my foundation is healthy. From there, I can let my influence radiate outwards to my home, my family, my interactions with colleagues, my academic work, my work with students, and my scholarship, in ever-widening circles.

I have reflected a great deal about relational accountability. I often reach out to Indigenous colleagues, offering to support them in their work as well as engaging in dialogue about my work. This relational engagement has helped me know when to speak up and when to take action, as well as when to wait and listen and ask before speaking up or taking action. It is my conviction that reconciliation starts with such one-on-one relationships. When reaching out to initiate such contacts, I check my motivation and confirm that it is about the relationship itself rather than something that will benefit my career. I have learned that we settlers easily go off base with our work if it remains too intellectual. The relational and dialogical aspects are key to keeping me on track and the personal friendship connection becomes intrinsic to the work.

I have had to learn how to accept correction and guidance by Indigenous friends, colleagues, or Elders, often (but not always!) offered in gentle and subtle ways that I may not always "hear." Once, I was collaborating with an Indigenous colleague and concerned about lapsing into colonial ways of relating. I asked him to tell me if he saw me doing this. His hesitant response caused me to reflect further. I came back and instead asked how *I* would know if I was shifting into a colonial way of being during our work. He shared that Indigenous people will respond by withdrawing or doing certain types of teasing — knowledge which has been incredibly valuable to my work. I am grateful that the people that I am closest to will find a way to let me know. So, I have to learn how to hear it. This is my responsibility.

Another important way I build relationships is by showing up at community events. My practice is just to show up … and keep showing up. Then, as we march or dance or stand there together in the cold, I can slowly start to build relationships. People get to recognize my face. After the first few times, I may go up to people and introduce myself. I also volunteer in very practical ways, such as serving Elders at meals during community events. This kind of work helps me get out of my head and ego and keeps me connected to Indigenous values. It has been essential to my own anti-colonial work — making relationships and just being there without any agenda other than to show up and support.

I actively work to dismantle the white colonial structures that privilege me, which does have some contradictions. At times, I have struggled with finding the balance of maintaining enough privilege to be able to put it to use in my work. In one workplace, I was told that my advocacy with Indigenous Peoples was starting to hurt me. I understood this to mean I could lose credibility with colleagues if I went beyond a certain point as an ally, and therefore would have less capacity to influence the workplace and my colleagues' attitudes. But then another part of me said, "Oh, you're just copping out." Part of my internal struggle is, when do I speak up and when do I pull back? I would be willing to lose my job on a key issue, but it would have to be an issue that I think would compromise my integrity too much to stay.

Part of this process is allowing myself to be in uncomfortable and risky situations and face losses. Once, as a junior faculty member in a politically fraught moment with potentially serious risks and repercussions, I spoke up and challenged other faculty members to take responsibility for their roles in colonialism. In a different context, I accepted discomfort and risk as one of two white settlers attending an Indigenous methodologies workshop. At the start, I felt hostility and distrust directed at me, leaving me feeling incompetent and stressed. It was a very difficult experience, but I learned much from it about my privilege and things I take for granted about my identity. It was important to experience and come face to face with the harm that people like me have done through research. I allowed myself to get slapped down a few times, choosing to just accept it and to learn from it. Such situations are always hard, but I have learned to trust myself and the process of learning from them.

In the personal realm, my partner, Mary, and I have used some of our economic privilege to provide practical support to events. For example, an Idle No More event happened during some brutally cold days. We would bring back big containers of hot chocolate and coffee, serving it to Elders and young children who were freezing in the cold. It is Indigenous people who have modelled such practices to us and anything we have done to support Indigenous students (buying groceries, helping with rent, taking them out for a meal) is most minimal compared to what I see Indigenous colleagues doing, in a way that is mostly invisible to their settler peers. Meanwhile, colonial "values" tell us that these kinds of involvements risk crossing boundaries. It would be more helpful to engage in discussions about *how* settler educators can help support Indigenous students in such ways.

It is my responsibility to educate and connect other settlers, which can be challenging. I use my educational privilege in a way that helps support Indigenous People's goals. For example, I try to find ways to express concepts like *self-governance* in ways that make sense to white people. I also invite white people to events. My Métis friend, Lisa, and I once went to our health club of elite white women and invited them to the Walking With Our Sisters exhibit. And when my eighty-eight-year-old mother, Nelda, came to visit for the holidays, I took her for an informal tour of the Residential School Survivors' Archives, where she received a book. She read a chapter each night, which raised her consciousness. Returning home, she challenged the racist views of some of her neighbours from that point on. She had acquired facts about various issues and was able to explain things to others. Educating others is something I do in all parts of my life.

IMPLICATIONS FOR MY SOCIAL WORK EDUCATION ROLE

As a social work educator, I recognized the classroom as an important site of anti-colonial practice. I continually seek to learn about Indigenous pedagogies to help decolonize my teaching. My practice renews as I learn from my students, from ongoing critical reflection, and from feedback from Indigenous peers. Indigenous-inspired circle pedagogy is a central practice, as it helps subvert power structures, teaches students to listen to each other, builds relationships, and equalizes power dynamics. I talk about mainstream education and social work practice as colonizing tools and engage students in dialogue to find ways to minimize their damage. I teach students to see what is missing, such as the under-representation of Indigenous students. We draw on anti-oppressive/anti-colonial theory to understand and address such structural problems.

It can be difficult for settler educators to understand the impact of differences in ways of knowing. A profound learning on this issue came through an Indigenous methodologies workshop led by Lee Maracle, Sto:Loh author and scholar. I had heard that Indigenous people teach through stories. But I now came to understand it experientially, because I was unable to follow Lee's narrative much of the time. She would be talking about a point and then she would tell a story, and I had no idea about how the story was connected to her point. I kept trying to figure it out — "What is she trying to teach through this story?" — as it did not make sense to me. The whole time I thought, "I feel really stupid. I have a PhD, and I'm sitting in this room feeling really dumb. This is so stressful. I want to run away." I wondered if this is how Indigenous students feel in my classroom and how can I help bridge that gap. It was a vital moment for me that I have never forgotten, one that has guided my pedagogy since then.

The barriers to integrating such learnings into my everyday teaching practice are very high. Despite the presence of Indigenization discourses, the colonial, patriarchal, neoliberal, and often inflexible structures of universities prevent change. At a basic level, how can one teach with a circle pedagogy when assigned a classroom where tables are bolted to the floor in rows? Centralized classroom booking makes it even harder to address such issues of physical space, let alone the more complex issues of pedagogy within our educational structures. I have spent many years trying different things, critically reflecting, listening carefully to students, seeing who is doing well in my classes, who is engaged, who is excluded, and taking risks. Some changes have felt small but significant; others have been larger. This is often a lonely process. However, I know I am on a good track when I see Indigenous students engage in and be excited about their learning; when they see me talk about their realities in a more respectful way that not only focuses on harms but also speaks to Indigenous resurgence; and when they see that I am trying to model respect and humility. I also know I am on a good track when they feel safe enough to openly critique their education, including challenges to my own practices.

My relational approach to teaching and my focus on Indigenous student success are a central part of my anti-colonial practice. Reaching out, even if it is just warmly greeting a student in a hallway or briefly entering Indigenous student spaces to connect, helps build relationships based on an ethic of care. I try to meet with Indigenous students with an awareness of safety and space. With ongoing outreach practices grounded in relational caring, I have found students are more comfortable talking about issues affecting their lives and their academic work. In these ways, I have learned more about the structural barriers for Indigenous students and have worked within my faculty and with support services on campus to address some of them.

In public venues, I always acknowledge how much I have gained and learned from my relationships with Indigenous Peoples. Through them, I have become a richer, fuller, and more compassionate person, with a different understanding of the world. They make me wiser, because when we open our hearts to each other we can understand each other's lived experiences better. I have gained such profound value from being invited into a closer understanding of Indigenous ways of knowing and being, including an expanded view of who I am connected to and who are part of my human family. I know I could never go back; I can only move forward. Realizing how much racism and colonialism hurt all of us, I am committed to doing this work alongside and on behalf of all of us.

CHAPTER 17

DAVE BLEAKNEY

Dave Bleakney with Elizabeth Carlson-Manathara

A SETTLER WALKING WITH GHOSTS

I am a settler in a society haunted by ghosts of our own making. Unheard stories float all around us. For many they remain buried within our society of commodification, individualism, and endless growth. We settlers are oblivious to those stories and those truths. Operating in a different and alternate universe, we deny ourselves a positive relationship with the Earth. We operate with principles that remove us from the land and renewable interrelationships with the Earth and all life. Ours is a world of profit, judgment, competition, consumption, and accumulation. It is a world of sin, redemption, and "civility." That world raised and shaped me.

Growing up in Mi'kma'ki, I learned little about the local history. I learned that settlers were noble, brave, and kind; they were charitable and helped to "civilize" others for their own good. We learned that Columbus was a hero, a man of vision, and deserving of accolades for having brought "civilization" to the new world. Other than caricatures, there was no trace or mention of Indigenous history in my school and community. We learned (some) stories about Europe going back thousands of years but nothing of the original inhabitants. Additionally, history filtered through the falsified lens of Hollywood westerns, deliberate omissions, and created myths. Settler society lives in a sinister bubble.

As a child, I recall asking where the original inhabitants went. Why did Europe have history but not here? What was going on before the Europeans arrived? Most importantly, for a five-year-old, where did the kids play? I am now sixty years old. I still do not have full answers. Typically, in this place called Canada, I often have not a clue where I truly am and what history I pass over. The place where I grew up, Westmoreland County, New Brunswick, and neighbouring Albert County, formed my universe. It was once part of a vast Mi'kmaw Territory (Mi'kma'ki). Prior to the European settlers, this region was Siknikt.

The world of the sixties and seventies was one we believed would get better. Progress was in flow. In the movies, the good guys were always amazing and white. The bad guys had accents and darker skin. Indigenous people, presented as violent or foolish caricatures, were objects. The white settlers were confident, and they were fortunate to have descended from those brilliant and gifted leaders of civilization fed by the freedom and prosperity delivered by the British Commonwealth and Western civilization. Many Canadians retain an inflated moral sense of self with relation to our U.S. neighbours on the other side of the imposed colonial border. In fact, we both represent colonial and expansionist legacies against the Indigenous population.

Finding answers has taken many turns. Here are a few stories that spoke to me. There were people who ripped the lid off that, who taught me and erased misconceptions, ultimately bringing me full circle back to my origins, trying to answer that question: *Where did they go?*

SAVAGES IN NEED OF REDEMPTION

Not once in my schooling did we learn about the values and worldview of any Indigenous people. Literally *thousands* of years of local history and knowledge were not worth a mention. Settler ancestors, on the other hand, were portrayed as patient, kind, hard-working, charitable, and moral people, contrary to the representation of Indigenous people, none of whom neither my friends nor I had ever met. They were said to be people without God and portrayed as primitive. There were no Mi'kmaw children in my school to confirm this projection.

There were never clear answers to my questions then. Always a "don't know," "they moved on," "prefer living in the woods," and "keeping to themselves." "They drink too much" — It is with shame that I repeat this here. It highlights the myths and hatred that settlers construct about others. Some Baptists — my town was a Baptist enclave — suggested that perhaps the devil had control of their souls; others, that they were not fully human. These were not just pronouncements of the seventeenth or eighteenth century but of the 1960s and 1970s. The sin and the wretchedness of other humans you had never met was a common theme in my town.

My mother said a Mi'kmaw mother and child lived in the woods by the school in the 1940s. The child attended school. One day they vanished without a trace. It is hard to imagine that a white family could disappear like that. People of settler heritage did not just "disappear" without account or interest. How could it be that a Mi'kmaw child was attending a settler school in the 1940s? Did the Indian agent get wind of this? Did they separate the child to attend a residential school? Worse, was this yet another case of the "disappeared"?

Relocating to Calgary in the early eighties, it became apparent that there was a fairly significant and visible Indigenous population. I heard disturbing and extreme discrimination in my settler conversations at work. No one spoke about the trauma of residential schools or destruction of traditional life. It was as though the displaced Indigenous people in Calgary were responsible for their lack of opportunity and poverty. It remained convenient to deny ourselves the truth about what led us here. It is not pleasant to know that a genocide occurred, and we remain accessories by remaining in denial. Over the next few years, a chain of events started to provide answers to some of those lingering questions.

OKA

The 1990 Oka crisis brought startling contradictions to the fore. The hidden (to us) saw light. One could not help but feel tremendous solidarity with the Mohawk warriors and the role of matriarchs. They drew a line in the sand with a sacrifice that resonates to this day. It was earth shattering. They spoke of a different set of values than those by which my world ran. It placed grandmothers, forests, sacred space, and future generations ahead of a golf course. I will forever be grateful to the people of Oka and all their relatives who stood with them.

IPPERWASH

By the mid-1990s, Ontario was living under the mean-spirited Mike Harris government. When the Ipperwash Crisis occurred, peaceful people — merely trying to have sacred land returned — faced the violent wrath of the Harris regime. This land was granted temporarily to the defence department for the war effort, with the understanding it would be returned after the war. Instead, it became a provincial park. After many attempts to have sacred land returned, members of the community peacefully occupied it. The Ontario Provincial Police, ordered to clear them from the park, used live ammunition against unarmed people. One man, Dudley George, bled to death in transit to the hospital. Police would not assist. His brother drove him to the hospital on tires the police had flattened. This was merely twenty-five years ago. The man who shot Dudley George, Kenneth Deane, was suspended with pay and benefits.

I felt disgusted to live in a place where that could happen. I wrote bulletins for union members and participated in demos. I cornered Mike Harris on a golf course a few years later and said, face to face, "We all know what and who murdered Dudley George." Dudley, unarmed and shot at Ipperwash for acknowledging his ancestors, respecting the integrity of the land, and enforcing a previous agreement, deserved much better. His nation deserves better. There was no justice. The spirit of Dudley George speaks today. In the end, this is what matters. Since then, I learned about the theft and imposition on the Saugeen Nawash in the 1800s in that region. These stories seem never-ending.

SUN PEAKS/GUSTAFSON LAKE

Arthur Manuel had a tremendous impact on me. I cannot recall my first encounter with him but remember well an invitation to his home in traditional Secwépemc Territory. His community had been fighting a ski resort — Sun Peaks — imposed on their territory without community approval. We visited the camps set up on the mountain to resist the project. They faced frequent harassment by police. It reminded me again that police, since the beginning of the colonial project, worked as security and muscle for private entrepreneurial and resource extraction interests.

Arthur was a guest in my home on many occasions. Patient, wise, and funny, he carried intricate knowledge about title and rights. He would take complex concepts and make them appear remarkably simple. He revealed how Indigenous people subsidized the forestry industry and received no benefit. He worked tirelessly against big trade deals and systems that further commodified our planet and the rights, welfare, and democracy of people everywhere. His premature death at a relatively young age was a shock and a great loss. However, Arthur Manuel lives on, in his community, in the struggle, and in all those he touched and inspired. Missed, but very much alive.

In May 2002, Arthur spoke at the Canadian Union of Postal Workers National Convention. Shortly after, during a visit to his territory, Arthur introduced me to the legendary Wolverine. At Gustafson Lake, B.C., a standoff occurred in 1995 on Secwépemc Territory. Attempts to conduct a traditional Sundance resulted in a massive paramilitary operation to remove the campers. Police planted an explosive device near the camp. A firefight broke out and, fortunately and miraculously, there were no deaths, though police killed one dog.

Albert Ignace, a.k.a. Wolverine, was one of those arrested and was sentenced to eight years in prison. I met him shortly after his release. He carved out a vast garden in the forest. Noticing that there was no fence to protect it, I asked how he protected the garden from the animals. He said he "had an arrangement" with them and told me "a people that cannot feed themselves and be self-sufficient will never be free." One could not help but feel they were in the presence of powerful knowledge and humility.

SIX NATIONS OF THE GRAND RIVER

By 2006, the Six Nations of the Grand River rose up with blockades to protect their community from a new subdivision. A mere 5 percent of their territory had been "granted until the end of time" by the Crown. Developers chose to build a subdivision on their land. The community resisted. I was touring Ontario with Bolivian Indigenous trade union activists. I recall a meeting at Six Nations with the Bolivians. One Bolivian spoke of an old prophecy that was said to have predicted things would change when the "condor and the eagle" meet. The energy in the room was palpable.

The Canadian Union of Postal Workers were meeting in Hamilton. A spokesperson, invited from the community, talked about the situation. Approximately forty postal workers heard first-hand about this situation, neutralizing the filtered media reports. These workers came to the territory in a show of support, bringing supplies, some donations, and a lot of solidarity. This learning, in real time, exposed buried history and highlighted the potential for settler-Indigenous solidarity. Settlers were following the community, rather than telling them what they should do. Briefly, the colonial filter was gone. It reminds us to go to the source and hear from Knowledge Keepers. In my experience, Knowledge Keepers have been more honest and truthful about history than the news media, politicians, and police.

BARRIERE LAKE

Some years later, I learned, mainly through an Ottawa group — Indigenous Peoples Solidarity Movement Ottawa — of the Anishinaabeg of Barriere Lake who lived several hours north of Ottawa. They had entered into a trilateral agreement with the federal and provincial governments over custodianship of their lands. They had never entered into Treaty and their Traditional Territory was slowly disappearing through resource extraction and encroachment. A dam, built without authorization of the Anishinaabeg, changed ice conditions and created new dangers and even death for those following their historical trap lines. Over time, a series of new encroachments followed. There were attempts by the federal government to create undemocratic Indian Act elections to undermine and divide this community and to get the outcome they desired: a compliant, if unrepresentative, local government that would surrender. The community of Barriere Lake receives substandard and almost non-existent social support.

Being invited to witness their traditional process of selecting a Chief was moving and enlightening; it was an honour to witness such a collective and consensus-driven process. This was a community with thoughtful social depth. Ours is a settler "first-past-the-post" electoral process, a competitive system of a winner and many losers. The traditional Barriere Lake process could take hours or days for completion. It finishes when the process finishes. Witnessing the assembly, I noticed this was mostly a circular gathering, where every face was visible and every voice heard. They spoke to the people assembled of many things of interest on the land. I learned that in this traditional way, that when moved to, anyone could nominate a person by bringing them forward as a potential Chief. Other procedures needed to take place. The spouse of the nominee also had to agree before the nominated person could accept. The community discussed and approved (or not), in which case the process continued until a consensus was reached. There was no hurry or rush in this democracy and no hidden corporation lurking behind the scenes with power and money. Incidentally, one did not get the sense the Chief was the boss, but merely an administrator of the collective wishes of the community. A feast followed the process. I have felt since then that had we settlers followed those customs and processes of decision-making, rather than the imposition of the colonial one that has been so competitive and destructive to all of us, we would be better off.

IDLE NO MORE

Elders and youth assembled in the cafeteria of the new Winnipeg postal plant. The Idle No More movement had taken off and round dances were occurring all over the country. Some Winnipeg postal workers had been joining the round dances, whether in the street or in the malls. The collective power of beautiful resistance filled our streets for weeks with the sound of drumming and singing.

Local stewards had arranged for these important voices to speak directly to postal workers during lunchtime. When the buzzer sounded for the workers to return to their workstations, they remained transfixed. Workers faced discipline for being the slightest bit late. Yet, there they sat, hanging on to every word and a fresh history lesson. These situations and spontaneous spectacles emerging outside the box can go a long way, in a very short time, in building solidarity and shifting narratives. It reminded me of the Six Nations experience. Creating situations for the colonial filter to fall can open colonized minds.

CUPW (Canadian Union of Postal Workers) created a new course for the membership, delivered in all regions of the country. This presents living colonial history from the point of view of the occupied. Indigenous CUPW members facilitate. Elders and Knowledge Keepers, invited from local communities, ground the participants in the history of the area on which they gather. We begin to acknowledge Indigenous Peoples with distinct cultures, languages and histories, and as distinct nations. We build relations with the people around us. We begin to see Kanien'keha:ka, Haudenosaunee, Anishinaabe, and many more. We see distinct identities, inspired relationships with the land, and a new set of unique historical values and practices.

Settlers must face our shame and confront it. The responsibility for decolonization and reconciliation is ours. It was a structure built in our name.

SOME REFLECTIONS

Wherever I go, the story of dispossession, disrespect, and genocide repeats itself in one way or another. Colonialism remains a threat to all of us. We permit and promote detachment from our natural and sustainable world. Colonialism may adapt and change form, but is always deeply rooted in power, resource extraction, finance capitalism, and commerce. Such a predominant worldview has shaky foundations.

Settler culture has something to reconcile but frequently refuses to do so. Practised in a worldview full of sin and confession, we offer apologies for days gone by. This is the easy way out. We have been "bad" and have the liberty of saying sorry. Forgive our sins; a European ethos we learned where notions of sin and forgiveness underpin a worldview that permits us to check off a box and move on. It provides a free pass to denial. Past transgressions are resolved with a few public words. We apologize. We invite forgiveness, feeling absolved and even fulfilled. Words have much greater significance in traditional cultures. In mine, sadly, they are spun, obfuscated, or just plain made up. Indigenous values teach that it is not only what you *say* that matters, but also what you *do*.

To use a Canadian analogy, it is as if we have a skating rink. We settlers created it on someone's land and we play on it. Some have better access and opportunity than others on this rink. Some are bystanders. Now we say everyone can play on our ice too — on our rink and by our rules. The colonial game played under colonial norms, whether in colonial prisons, colonial agencies, or colonized minds, adapts. It always remains the settler's rink. Colonialism and capitalism are for those who can afford to play, not those who stand in the way.

THE ERASED VILLAGE

The mystery of the past lies buried in my town. It is everywhere around us. I know today that agreements made with the Mi'kmaq by the "Crown" — whatever that is — were repeatedly violated. The civilized rule of law has never meant much when it comes to Indigenous Title anyway.

When I drive back to Salisbury, I pass the Canaan River. I remind myself this is the river Washademoak. It is my own way to acknowledge the land around me. Before English settlement, my village was a bustling French/Mi'kmaw community. It was apparently substantial for the time, but something terrible happened there. Growing up, there was no trace or mention of this "erased" settlement. The Fort Folly First Nation, located in so-called Westmoreland County, along with a number of other First Nations reserves, represents a tiny speck on what once was a vast territory called Siknikt.

Recently, I asked an older community member to tell me about the first inhabitants of Albert County. She replied by telling me about the first immigrants from Yorkshire. These were the "first" people. This says so much. A few years ago, I found my first-grade scribbler. The first thing I learned to write as a child was "I love my queen" and "I love my country." At five, I knew little, if anything, about either. For many years, I carried the view that Western society was somehow the most superior, evolved, and most enlightened in history. Today I believe this genocidal human-centred machine must stop. We act like endless growth and an economy that revolves around stock markets is somehow sustainable. We walk on land that was never ours and we have done a poor job of caring for it as we continue to pollute the rivers and make species go extinct. We raise our children on video games and treat nature like an inconvenience. We create farces of dishonesty and competition and call it democracy.

This is not pretty. It feels abusive even to imagine it. We often hear of something called "Canadian values." We are polite and say "sorry" a lot. This self-serving propaganda assumes only Canadians care about a good and healthy life for themselves and their children. Only Canadians want decent shelter, food, peace, and dignity. If we were to have an honest conversation about Canadian values, we could see a more sinister set of outcomes including, but not limited to, criminalization, forced sterilization, exploitation, isolation, kidnapping, dishonesty, broken words, torture, sexual abuse, violence, theft, and disappearance.

Settler society places little value on our connections and more on our flaws and differences. We individualize to the extent that we become absorbed in a perverse system of commercial rituals and we build pipelines over sacred land as the Earth burns. These tragedies, done in my name, reveal something else. They point to resilience, resistance, wisdom, and dignity. I take hope from that. For generations, important knowledge survived, in spite of the attempts to eliminate and assimilate. Knowledge preserved for everyone. I am here as a result of it.

As settlers, the ghosts of colonial violence haunt our conscience and memories. They remind us of what we have done but also what we could be in these times; that we could root out cynicism, and embrace one another with values of humility, dignity, honesty, sharing, and integrity. We confront generations of settler denial and cynicism. These are exciting and historic times. Traditional Indigenous values have always stood in the way of greed and destruction. These experiences give me hope. There is a sustainable path and a future worth connecting with. That world resonates for me. It is a place of comfort and change. We owe gratitude to those that keep it alive for us. We are all relatives they say.

CHAPTER 18

VICTORIA FREEMAN

Victoria Freeman and Elizabeth Carlson-Manathara

Victoria Freeman is a Canadian writer, educator, and historian of British heritage who grew up in an economically and politically privileged family in Ottawa, unceded Algonquin Territory, not knowing any Indigenous people. She has been shaped by the many generations of experience in colonization her family carries. She absorbed

> the do-gooder, leftover missionary attitude of "how can I help you," the indifference of the general society and absolute obliviousness, and the stereotypes of alcoholic Indians living in poverty on isolated reserves or drunk Indians on the street.

Victoria's early consciousness was also influenced by growing up in the sixties during times of race riots, the civil rights movement, the women's movement, and political assassinations. Victoria's anti-colonial work has been infused with greater meaning by her experience of witnessing the way her sister, who had Down Syndrome, was treated. Victoria says,

> I was so harmed by the attitudes to her, by the decision to institutionalize her. [It] still really hurts. I knew in a really gut way what exclusion was, and what it means to be thought of as sub-human, and what it means to lose somebody into a system that does not value that person enough. And how your love for someone like that can be so buried and deep and shameful, and all that mess of emotion.... So I think there were resonances for me with Indigenous people ... that allowed me to have some kind of empathy, a certain kind of sharing. Even if I didn't always recognize it, that's where some of my stuff was coming from. So I think it makes it very meaningful for me to fight against those issues of exclusion, and attitudes of superiority. I have a terror

of experts because it was "experts" who put my sister in that institution. When it comes to residential schools, there's a lot I don't understand because that was an assault on a community, on a whole nation, on language, on culture, on everything — it's different from what happened to my sister, and yet, there's some similarity too. It's very personal in some ways.

LEARNING AND EARLY ACTIVISM

Victoria's anti-colonial learning began when she heard Métis writer and activist Maria Campbell speak in 1980. She reflects,

> She was probably the first Indigenous person who I heard speak.... She was so eloquent, just talking about her own experience.... I think she woke me up to colonialism.... I had been quite active in the feminist movement ... [but] meeting her just blew it open. I saw another kind of systemic oppression, so I would credit her with really opening my eyes.

Victoria further understood the systemic oppression of Indigenous women by researching racial and sexual discrimination in housing through the Vancouver Downtown Eastside Women's Centre in the early 1980s. Around this time, Victoria co-organized Women and Words, a major feminist literary conference that intentionally included Indigenous women writers. She says, "Hearing Indigenous women's voices talking about their own experience really deepened my awareness and made me want to work on those issues." "That was when the whole question of racism in the women's movement came out," says Victoria, "and there were Black women there, there were Native women there, and I was trying to work out my relation to them." While attempting to co-organize a second Women and Words conference (which never took place), Victoria was confronted by some of the Black organizers, who expressed pain and anger about something she had done. This, Victoria says,

> Forced me to look at racism and to try and understand my own relationship to it, and to look at it in terms of attitudes I had inherited, and the subtle ways that racism plays out and power plays out. And questions of voice, and the complicatedness of it, especially in friendships and in relationships, and how people

hear each other — how their experience shapes how they hear each other.

Victoria built friendships with several Indigenous women as she did volunteer publicity for Theytus Books, a First Nations-owned and -operated publisher of Indigenous authors. Her friendship with activist Dorothy Christian (Secwépemc-Syilx) would survive painful conflicts and become a vehicle of and impetus for aspects of Victoria's decolonization journey. An argument with Dorothy led Victoria to "the seven years of research for my book *Distant Relations: How My Ancestors Colonized North America*." Through this work, Victoria says,

> I tried to understand my own family's involvement in colonialism: from when they were back in Britain, why they came here, whose territory they came to, how they ended up with the land, what their relationships were with Indigenous people at the time they were living ... trying to understand what I had inherited. What privileges [and] benefits had I gained through that whole process? What was my responsibility towards that history?

Victoria's ancestors included missionaries, a fur trader-diplomat, a woman who had been scalped at twenty-nine years old, and a residential school administrator. She wondered what attitudes and fears had been passed down to her:

> I had been carrying this really queasy, uneasy, guilty feeling that had affected my relationships with people of colour generally, but especially with Indigenous people.... And I felt threatened, because when you start to really consider what colonialism is and has been, it affects how you look at your own family, it affects how you feel about your country, it affects how you feel about your house, where you live, whose land you're on. And I felt very conflicted about all that.

Doing the research for her book helped her understand that discomfort:

> I think that was a really critical period of both learning the history, and owning my connection to the history so that it wasn't something happening over there, but that I was implicated, I was involved with it and shaped by it, and that decolonization

wasn't something that just happened for Indigenous people, it also involved people like me.

DECOLONIZATION WORK AND CONTINUED LEARNING

"Because decolonization is a transformative process," Victoria says, "we need relationship with each other for that transition to happen." Rather than being based on short-term project work, "we are in this relationship for life, how are we going to live it?" Indigenous women have told Victoria, "You're not just an 'ally'; you're a *relative*; you have to think of yourself as a relative." Within this perspective,

> we are all connected, we are all related.... For non-Indigenous people to change the way we behave towards Indigenous people, we have to think of ourselves as relatives, not just in some structural way, as political allies. It's where we are all people trying to create a future together — a relative is someone who carries out responsibilities to others in a loving way.... In fact, that's what Treaties do: in Indigenous understandings, you're creating a kinship relationship. Obviously the British really didn't get that (or want that), but that is the Indigenous understanding as far as I know.... Your relatives can be really pissed off at you, and really angry at you, but they don't necessarily hate you and want to annihilate you, which I think a lot of non-Indigenous people fear.... Taiaiake Alfred has spoken about how one of the difficult things for Indigenous people to accept is that their ancestors *did* make Treaties with non-Indigenous newcomers, and that as a result, there *is* a way for us to be here legitimately — if we carry out our responsibilities.

For Victoria, there is no one right way to do decolonization work. She says, "colonialism affects us on every level and we can address it on every level." She says,

> What scares me the most are people who think that they know the right way, whether they're Indigenous or they're non-Indigenous.... I'm wary of people who talk like that because it's often a way to assert power over other people, or it's just a limited vision that excludes and disempowers others ... there are all kinds

of people who do really interesting things who don't have a full analysis … how do you learn, except by getting your feet wet and your hands dirty?

Personal decolonization is one level of Victoria's work, which focuses on

> trying to undo the colonial programming that I was socialized with, and trying to understand the ongoing-ness of colonialism — the structure of it, how I benefit from it, the privilege I have as a result of it, how it shapes me and affects my relationships with Indigenous people, with non-Indigenous people, with the land we live on, with the past, with the future…. How do we embody [colonialism]? How we feel it — how it comes out unconsciously in our body language, our expressions, our moments of fear. Who we feel threatened by or who we just don't like — it's paying attention to all of those reactions in ourselves, trying to understand the relations of power that I'm embedded in.

Victoria believes an important decolonization initiative would be for non-Indigenous people to rethink how we parent our children. She says, "We look at what our children learn at schools, but so much is learned in the family, and that is largely unexamined." She wonders how to teach children about their implication in colonialism in empowering rather than guilt-inducing ways.

Decolonization also involves "structural change, restitution, land … and creating the public spaces so that Indigenous people's voices are heard, their own leadership is heard, their own solutions are proffered." It means "ending Indian Act domination, federal government domination, the paternalism that is so prevalent still — building a network of people to challenge those structures." Internationally, Victoria says,

> As a global community, we're only starting to come to terms with the colonization of Indigenous Peoples. And the Declaration of the Rights of Indigenous Peoples is really important, even if it seems toothless in some ways. Even as a statement of principle, it's hugely important in shifting the terms of dialogue. There are so many ways that international pressure can shame Canada into changing the status quo…. Seeing it all in terms of this nation-state that is Canada instantiates and perpetuates a colonial state, so we have to allow ourselves to think differently about

transnational processes, and Turtle Island as opposed to Canada; we have to think about territoriality so differently.

Another realm of decolonization work involves alliances to protect the land. "Not just land as territory," Victoria says, "but land as sustenance, as the ground of our being, as who we are ultimately." She says, "Reconciliation is not just a matter of human beings. To really be able to have a relationship that's honourable and just, all those other beings have to be part of it too."

Victoria has collaborated with Indigenous people on numerous Indigenous- and alliance-focused conferences, workshops, and projects, including the Baffin Writers' Project, a project that fostered writing and publishing in Inuktitut or from an Inuit perspective; Turning Point: Native Peoples and Newcomers Online, an early website for information sharing and dialogue; and Beyond Survival, a 1993 international conference of Indigenous writers, artists, and performers. While her support for such initiatives was appreciated, author Jeannette Armstrong told her, "What we really need is for people like you to help us understand white racism, and to help address white racism so it's not just us doing it." She decided to take up this challenge.

If Victoria's first book asked, "How did my ancestors get me into this colonial situation?" her 2010 PhD studies asked, "Where am I?" and focused on the lack of historical memory of the Indigenous and colonial past of Toronto. She studied the deep history of the land, how Indigenous people had lived on it and newcomers gained control of it, and what stories both groups told about it — or had not told about it.

> I was in history and I really wanted to learn the history as much as I could, and I wanted to look not just at Canada's history, but I also looked at Australia, New Zealand, and the U.S. I needed to look comparatively. I just needed to know what is academically known about this topic. I needed to read the books and do research in that, and learn what academic research was, and also figure out my own place in academia.

Victoria struggled to work in her collaborative community-based way within an academic context that did not yet recognize the validity of that process. Nonetheless, the community connections she developed through the process of her PhD led to her involvement in First Story Toronto, a project started by Anishinaabe activist Rodney Bobiwash and his partner, Heather Howard, through the Native Canadian Centre of Toronto. The project aimed to change people's perspectives of place and the relations of Indigenous and non-Indigenous peoples through a smart phone app and walking, bike, and bus tours of the city, among other activities. Through the app, "wherever you are in the city, different sites will come up with more than 11,000 years of history from different perspectives — Haudenosaunee, Wendat, Mississauga/Anishinaabe, or Métis." While at the University of Toronto, Victoria coordinated events and conferences. She says, "That brought me into larger networks of people, and also into that whole interface between universities and communities, where I still am, in a lot of ways."

At the beginning of her teaching career, Victoria worked with Lee Maracle to develop and teach a course called The Politics and Process of Reconciliation.

> We were able to really use Indigenous methodologies and blend them.... Lee and I had a basic trust. We developed the course together, we co-taught it, we marked everything together, and we agreed about how to go about doing it. So we would lecture in the first hour of every week, and then we did a sharing circle, every single class, for 24 weeks.... And it was the most transformative experience for everybody, including Lee and myself, to be able to actualize those Indigenous values and philosophies about how people learn, how people change, what transformation is, and creating a space where people could bring all of themselves together — their heart, their spirit, their emotions, their intellect, their physical beings — where you didn't have to park some of that at the door because academia didn't allow it. I learned a lot through that experience and through working with someone who had such a strong grounding in the oral tradition. And for students to hear both perspectives — and both of us are pretty forthright people, so we could talk about our emotions and our feelings and we could cry. So could everybody else. It created an extraordinary sense of community.... While that in itself doesn't change the structure of colonialism, it sure can change the will of people to keep working at changing it, it deepens your commitment ... it's those human relationships that nourish that process.

Over the years, Victoria taught courses on the history of Indigenous Peoples in Canada and developed a fourth-year Canadian studies seminar called Decolonizing Canada at York University. In her courses, students were asked to reflect on "their own relation to colonialism and how they've been shaped by it, wherever they or their ancestors have come from in the world, or if they're Indigenous, where their people originally lived and perhaps how they've been displaced." Students shared their reflections and learned from each other, building community in the classroom.

> The most amazing connections come out, because people start to realize that we've all been shaped by colonialism.... Many of our families have both experiences of being colonized and colonizer, or being enslaved or being brought involuntarily, or immigrating because of poverty ... or benefitting, being on the colonizer's side.

Victoria's aim was to create a classroom environment where all students could examine their assumptions and inheritances, learning about colonialism and decolonization using familial, local, national, and transnational frames of reference. She brought Indigenous speakers and Indigenous-authored films and readings into her classes to ensure students had access to unmediated Indigenous perspectives. While fully supporting the preferential hiring of Indigenous professors in Indigenous history and Indigenous studies, she also sees an important role for non-Indigenous allies in academia:

> We need to make sure that the burden of educating non-Indigenous and white students about racism and colonialism does not fall solely on Indigenous shoulders. It is important to say that this is the responsibility of white academics too — this is our issue — and modelling allyship (to the best of our ability) and actively supporting decolonizing education is a crucial role that we can play.

In 2017, Victoria was approached by the Sociology Department of University of Toronto, Scarborough, to develop a course on the sociology of the Truth and Reconciliation Commission. She took on this challenge because she had previously been a member of the core group that organized The Meeting Place: Truth and Reconciliation Toronto 2012, a regional gathering of the Truth and Reconciliation Commission hosted by the Toronto Council Fire Native Cultural Centre and several other organizations. Once again, she developed a co-teaching model. Council Fire staff and Survivors from their Residential School Survivors Support Group agreed to co-develop and co-teach the twelve-week course in the fall of 2017. They centred the voices and experiences of survivors: members of the survivors group attended and contributed to every class, along with their Elder, trauma counsellor, and other Council Fire staff. The course was a profound learning for all and offered students a concrete and practical experience of allyship.

Victoria subsequently published an article on her pedagogy in a 2018 special issue of the *Canadian Journal of Native Education* on "Challenges, Possibilities, and Responsibilities: Sharing Stories and Critical Questions for Changing Classrooms and Academic Institutions."

DIMENSIONS OF THE JOURNEY

At first, Victoria felt very isolated, "not knowing another ally," and her work "originally felt very traitorous." She was afraid to take a stand, and she struggled with an "amorphous sense of guilt … that I was responsible for absolutely everything." "Learning the history of [her] own family's involvement with colonialism" is what shifted her sense of guilt to "a more connected sense of accountability." During her research, she says,

> [A relative] got irritated with me and said, "you're just wallowing in guilt!" I thought about it, and realized that was actually not my feeling. I was not responsible for my ancestors' actions — although I was accountable for their legacy. What I felt was a deep grief. That's an entirely different emotion, and it's completely appropriate to grieve the horrible damage, the incredible waste of people's lives, the wreckage of the land, and what it did to all of us.… I realized that my book was in part a process of mourning. The good thing about most grief is that you can move through it.… For me, acknowledging it let me acknowledge the truth of our history.… Sometimes it's very appropriate to sort of sit in grief with someone because a lot of the stories are really hard. Sometimes all you can do is just be present and acknowledge how bad it was, how bad it is. It's such a Euro-Canadian, Western approach to be all focused on action way before it's appropriate, without thinking things through, without feeling things through. We really need to sit with all of that, to be with that, as opposed

to making busy work about how we should fix things. There have been tons of white people running around trying to fix things, but the results have been pretty disastrous, so I think we need a different approach.

In the beginning, Victoria knew few Indigenous people, and would work with anyone.

I'd end up in relationships with people who were totally inappropriate, who did not have the skills or had not worked through their own inner baggage so that they could work with me — and I hadn't done that either.… Now, because I've been connected to this community for a while — this person, I really trust, this person I know is respected in their community, this person has other things going on, and I don't really want to be around them, and I think it takes time to develop that kind of judgment, and for them to make those same judgments about you.

When there is a solid foundation of trust, it is possible to talk through issues that arise. She says,

To me it's been important to find people who want my genuine reactions, and appreciate my directness, or my candor.… Some people just want me to support what they're doing no matter what, and then I have to make a choice — is that what I want to do? And sometimes it is, and sometimes it isn't.… Sometimes it's very challenging, because as a woman and queer person — and just as a wounded person — I've needed to find my own voice and I've really struggled to be heard and seen, yet I need to step back and not speak in certain Indigenous contexts.

Victoria emphasizes that "emotions of colonization and decolonization are really tricky to deal with … denial and fear, rage, guilt … and shame. All those feelings play such important roles in how we relate to each other or don't relate to each other." In fact, as Lee Maracle reminded her, colonialism is also a structure of feeling among both colonizing and colonized peoples, and unless we attend to its psychological dimensions, we may not be able to alter its dynamics.

There are all kinds of things that can happen in these relationships.

Lynn Gehl's Ally Bill of Responsibilities is a wonderful resource for finding your way through these complex dynamics. For example, if white allies are feeling really guilty, you can actually be abused or manipulated because you're afraid to bring yourself to the table.... I've been very lucky in that I've had certain Indigenous friends who have really been willing to work through all the messiness of those emotions with me, and in particular Dorothy Christian, who has said, "We're in this for life and we're just going to keep working away at it and trying to figure it out." There have been times when it felt like we just can't sort out our difficulties, we trigger each other too much. And one of the difficulties is that we do trigger each other, Indigenous and non-Indigenous people, especially white people, we do that to each other. All our vulnerabilities get so triggered, and our fears get so triggered by each other and it's really a minefield, and that makes it so hard to work together. And so, if you can find people who are willing to try and go through the unpleasantness of sorting it out, you can really learn things that you wouldn't learn any other way.... I don't think, unless you've gone through some of those layers of feeling, that you really understand how deeply colonialism has shaped us on both sides. But I also don't think it's something you ever kind of master.

Victoria says she still struggles with her emotions when she is confronted, especially if she feels misjudged or misunderstood.

I definitely am angry at myself when I screw up, when I am insensitive or unthinking or haven't thought something through enough, or make an ignorant comment or behave in a way that betrays my utter unconsciousness of my privilege, or when I say something that really hurts somebody — that's awful. At the same time, you get tired of having your guilt impulse triggered, or your shame impulse triggered — who wants to feel those things? So of course you're angry when it happens."

Over time she has learned that when she is confronted, rather than denying, it is better to say, "'I need to go think about that,' just to give myself time to get through the reactions."

We all have our own particular issues. For me, sometimes I'd be reacting to something and have no idea why I was so upset, and I'd realize it had something to do with my sister and her institutionalization — not even really the situation at hand. Many of us have stuff like that, just traumatic things that happened to us, and so the deeply personal gets all mixed up with the political, and that's a real challenge to unravel.

Because Victoria has "been too well socialized as a settler person, as a white person, as a person of economic privilege," she accepts that she is going to make mistakes, even as she tries to counteract her conditioning. She says, "I've had to learn to forgive myself for making those mistakes, and not obsess about how I screw up, and what people will think of me." She says, "It can be really embarrassing and awful, and it's not always fair … because Indigenous people may also carry around reservoirs of anger and frustration." She says,

> I think I've got a little tougher over the years at surviving those sorts of situations and not hating myself for it. It's going to happen, all I can do is learn from it, and try to make amends, in whatever way I can.

Yet, such situations can be disheartening. For example, during a public talk, Victoria was called out for homogenizing settlers in terms of racialization. She says,

> Even though I know that stuff — I've read the debates, I'm very conscious of [the issue] — yet somehow it just didn't come out of my mouth in the appropriate way at the right time. So suddenly there I am, I'm the white person doing it again. Which is so humbling, and embarrassing, especially when you know better. But sometimes you do it. You're just not quite careful enough in what you say, or not conscious enough, or you're a little bit tired, or your knowledge of it is up here [points to head], it's not deep enough, and you've got to move it further into yourself to really incorporate it into how you do everything. There have been many, many times I've done things like that, and those are by far the most painful parts of the process, but also the most transformative, ultimately, because you don't make those mistakes again, or at least not in the same way. You find a new way to make them. [laughs]

Victoria's growth has involved learning about Indigenous perspectives and knowledges by listening to Indigenous Peoples — "to their stories, their interpretations, their concepts, their language," reading their works, attending ceremonies, and learning about the land she lives on from them. She says, "It was really through Indigenous people that I began to understand what spirituality might mean outside of the concept of organized, institutionalized religion." Upon having a dream that felt spiritually important, she discussed it with Jeannette Armstrong. She says,

> I remember afterwards, this feeling ... like all the breath came out of me, and I realized that we had been talking on a level that I never experienced before. And that something was touching me in a really deep way. That made me aware that there's a lot more going on here than I understand, and ... these people I'm working with seem to be much more comfortable with it and fluent. It was really through them that I began to be involved in ceremonies, began to know myself as a spiritual person. Even now I can't say exactly what I mean by that, I don't have the same understanding as Indigenous people of what spirituality is, but I know there's a way of being that you get to in your most meditative places, in just the most profound moments, and that connectedness.

She says,

> For non-Indigenous allies who have been deeply, deeply influenced by all of that, there's a funny in-between state that you're in that's very hard to articulate and to honour, because you're not Indigenous, it's not your culture, and yet you're so influenced by certain aspects of it.... I am in some way bicultural. It doesn't mean that I understand everything or have shed my privilege, but I've been so changed by what I've experienced with Indigenous people that I cannot say I only speak or think within the Euro-Canadian framework I was born into.

Victoria has been invited to ceremonies that take place on the land and has fasted. She says,

> On a purely personal level, if I don't spend some time outside of cities, in forests, by water, there's a part of me that doesn't feel healthy. And when I go to those places, I'm rejuvenated. So I know

that all of us need some kind of connection to nature. The disconnection that so many non-Indigenous people have is part of the problem and that when you think of non-Indigenous people in North America, on Turtle Island, we've all come from somewhere else and our connections to those lands have been severed. We've lost both the memory connections and the sentient connection.

However, Victoria says,

> It's a tricky balance. A whole lot of white people going camping, well how is that decolonization? Is it just taking over land and "indigenizing" ourselves? There's that tendency to want to be Indigenous. I mean we can be invited to be relatives or to *be* of this land, but I think that's a very delicate relationship to negotiate. At the same time, I'm very mindful of something Lee Maracle said, which is that in her culture, at least, everyone has a right to a home, so it's not the case that non-Indigenous people are not entitled to live here or have a home. The issue is greed, taking more than one needs personally, and obviously dispossessing Indigenous people from *their* connection to land. We get tied up in knots around land as property, thinking in terms of boundaries and ownership. And different Indigenous people will talk about that in different ways, so I can't say that I fully understand what land means for Indigenous people.

Victoria envisions a future in which Indigenous Peoples have the freedom and resources to choose their own futures that sustain and nourish them, their families, their communities, and their lands. She believes that some form of nation-to-nation negotiation or Treaty process is necessary to create the political structures that will ensure this. She says,

> There needs to be a lot of dialogue to sort this all out, and there obviously has to be resource transfer, land transfer. There have to be incredible education efforts, there has to be restitution … non-Indigenous people [will] have to give up some things…. I see all of those as elements, but exactly how that's going to play out, I don't know. I just want a world that makes room for the diversity of solutions that people are going to come up with and the creativity of all kinds of people to make it happen.

Victoria does decolonization work, she says, because

> I don't like the feel of being here illegitimately, so partly it's paying my rent in some way. I have to do my part to try and make an honourable outcome for this colonial situation. We have to find a way out of it. So, it's for Indigenous people but it's also for me, it's for my children, so that they can feel that they can be here in a way that is ethical, which I don't really feel is fully possible at the moment.

Victoria's personal relationships with Indigenous people sustain her commitment. She says,

> Sometimes before I give a talk, I flash on different people I've known — the stories they've shared with me, the incredible strength they've shown. Or the people who have not survived, the people who have been really damaged and died. I carry a lot of people's memory — and also the encouragement of those people who have really appreciated things I've done and who have wanted to work with me — so I don't want to let them down, and I want to honour what they've taught me.

Victoria is hopeful when she sees what the younger generation is doing. She says, "A young person today starts in an entirely different place than I did growing up." She says, "What is wonderful now is that no non-Indigenous ally needs to have that feeling of isolation … you can get connected so much more easily, and in so many different ways." She thinks of the amazing resources available now by Indigenous writers and filmmakers. "I think it's a really exciting time … things are actually moving more quickly than they have at any other time … no one can squelch it at this point, the cat's out of the bag."

POSTSCRIPT 2020

Since my initial interview, both political and personal situations have changed. There is both enormous change and enormous stasis in Canada at the moment, and the optimism of my final words of the interview is now more muted. It's much more evident how easily political changes can be rolled back and how large a proportion of the electorate in both Canada and the U.S. supports policies that perpetuate white supremacy or focus in an extremely limited way on taxes or personal freedom to the exclusion of all else, including justice. It's also more evident how untenable the "reconciliation" agenda of the Trudeau Liberals is in their attempt to please everyone — and how difficult it is to democratically change relations between Indigenous and non-Indigenous peoples in a country that is still largely a resource economy. All of this is enormously challenging. I think often of the patience that Indigenous Elders have — that Indigenous Peoples have had to maintain over generations — when oppression only worsened and there was little to offer hope. Again, I am learning from their resilience and realism.

Over the last few years, I have pulled back from some forms of organizing and educational work. Partly, it's time for others to do that work. There is a whole new generation of Indigenous historical scholars coming forward who combine Indigenous knowledge and community connections with the best aspects of academic scholarship — I am very happy to step aside for them when it comes to teaching. The ground has also shifted enormously from when I started working on Indigenous-settler issues. The context for activism is totally different. When I started, it was mainly white people (and not a lot of us) who were involved in alliance building and non-Indigenous activism in support of Indigenous Rights. Now there is profound alliance work being undertaken by Indigenous people, Black people, people of colour, and younger people of all heritages, addressing issues on many fronts — and new ways of organizing through social media. There has been tremendous Indigenous resurgence in some areas of Indigenous life and an explosion of Indigenous scholarship. I increasingly feel the limitations of my upbringing and perspective. I'm very aware that some activists have a better, more up-to-date analysis of current issues than I do, and they certainly have more energy. Now I'm learning as much or more from young people than they might conceivably learn from me. The weird thing about growing older is that while your decades of experience can provide valuable historical perspective on current struggles, the world has also changed so much that only some of your hard-won wisdom is still relevant.

I've also shifted my focus to artistic creation. I'm an artist at heart, and especially a writer. With Kanienkehaka artist Ange Loft, the associate artistic director of Jumblies Theatre, I co-wrote *The Talking Treaties Spectacle*, a site-specific performance about Treaty relationships in Toronto that featured an Indigenous cast and community dancers and singers. It drew on interviews with members of the Mississaugas of the Credit and Indigenous artists, community leaders, and historians, as well as archival texts, words, and images generated by participants at workshops held all over the city. It was performed at Fort York at the Indigenous Arts Festival in 2017 and remounted in 2018. Subsequently, Ange, filmmaker Martha Stiegman, and I created an installation and film called *By These Presents: "Purchasing" Toronto* for the 2019 Toronto Biennial of Art. For the 2021 Biennial, we are creating *A Treaty Guide for Torontonians*, an illustrated adult book in the style of a children's pop-up book — because we should have learned about Treaties as children! Ange and I are also collaborating with Jennifer Bonnell of York University's Public History program, Anishinaabe historian Al Corbiere, local First Nations, and Black Creek Pioneer Village on a project to artfully change the narrative, exhibits, and public programming of this heritage site to include Indigenous perspectives and history. Given that Black Creek Pioneer Village receives about 160,000 visitors a year, such an intervention can potentially change the thinking of a lot of people.

I like the way the arts can remind people that creation is an ongoing process, that the world is always full of possibility, and that we can dream alternate futures. We need to be reminded of these things in dark times. Art nourishes the heart and spirit; imagination invites people to open their minds, be touched by others, laugh or cry or feel wonder — all of which is healing. Sometimes art reaches people who are simply turned off by political rhetoric or academic language; it is always relational and as a collective experience it can help create community. We need every modality we can muster to address the state of the world and affirm our shared humanity. It's through art that I feel I can make my most effective contributions right now.

CHAPTER 19

HONOURINGS

Gladys Rowe and Elizabeth Carlson-Manathara

We, Gladys and Elizabeth, have been profoundly moved by the stories shared in the previous chapters. As we connected with these stories, we felt called to respond from a heart-centred space. This aligns with our understanding of relational ways of listening to and honouring experiences that are shared with us. Making sense of and finding personal meaning in these offerings has been a process of deep reflection. As one outcome of this deep reflection and in acknowledgement of the profound gifts shared by the contributors, we offer the following words in reply.

I hold your stories in my heart.

Simmer, temperatures rising
Veiled pristine environments
We learn to observe and follow
Mimic and trust

A rumbling …
Crystal vases and delicate teacups shake
Pirouetting through outstretched fingers
Trying to save a facade
Shatter mirrored spaces
Shatter familiar faces

Disintegration
Ground shaking
Fear and questions
Shame and questions
Grief and questions
A spark finds fuel
Momentum

Stumbles and falls
open eyes
Stumbles and falls
open hearts
Stumbles and falls
Will and determination
Transformations
Power the steps you keep taking

For All my relations, I hear you
For All my relations, I see you
For All my relations, I am with you.

— Gladys Rowe

AN HONOURING of Your Stories

I honour your strength, sensitivity, and questioning as children;
your abilities to spot the lies,
and the observations of injustice that took root in your young lives.

I honour the mentors, teachers, and experiences
that have caused you to grow in your understanding and in your work.

I honour the openness of your hearts to look
at what is not right in the world,
and your determination to work for something better.

I honour your anger about the sickness and greed you witness
around you and inside you.

I honour your grief, guilt, anxiety, confusion, shame, insecurity, and pain.

I honour your dignity, your sacredness, and your humanity.

I honour your hope, your joy, your liberation,
your learning, and your healing.

I honour the gifts and the uniqueness you bring to your work,
sometimes engaging in ways that I could not have imagined
or for which I lack the skills,
yet ways that contribute to the whole.

I honour your courage in sharing your mistakes and vulnerabilities
so that we can learn from them.

I honour the love you have for the life around you,
for the Earth, for Indigenous Peoples
and for other settler occupiers that inspires your commitment.

I honour your stories.

— Elizabeth Carlson-Manathara

CHAPTER 20

CONCLUSIONS

Elizabeth Carlson-Manathara and Gladys Rowe

In the previous chapters, you have read stories of white settler occupiers who have taken up the call to engage in anti-colonial activism and decolonization work; stories of how they have journeyed toward living in Indigenous sovereignty. You have read biographies of those who grew up segregated from Indigenous Peoples and biographies of those whose early lives were intertwined with Indigenous communities. You have read narratives of those whose observations raised questions in their young hearts; narratives of those who saw discrepancies between what was espoused and what happened in practice around them. They shared stories of things that influenced and triggered their involvement, and they shared their insights and their struggles. They shared accounts of the variety of spheres in which they do their work, the types of work they do, and the ways they conceptualize their work. You have read stories of those who have learned about colonialism and resistance to it both inside and outside of the academy, and stories of those whose activism occurs primarily within, primarily outside, or both inside and outside of the academy. Narrative authors have shared the emotional, spiritual, and intellectual aspects of their work. You have read narratives of those who grew up with little direct influence of organized religion, of those whose critical questioning would lead them away from organized religion, and of those who are strongly connected to an organized religion and work from within to transform it. They have shared the reasons why they do their work and what they have learned and gained through their involvements. You have read about their doubts, fears, and commitments. You have read stories of those who have engaged in their work with a grassroots and/ or direct action focus, and those who have deconstructed and started to rebuild their own socialization. You have read stories of those participants whose work focuses on supporting Indigenous actions and stories of those who work to educate and challenge non-Indigenous Canadians. You have read accounts of getting it wrong and accounts of getting it right. You have read narratives of recolonization despite intentions of doing otherwise, stories of learning from these errors, and commitments to do better.

Using oral and written Indigenous literatures as well as the narratives of white settlers engaged in decolonization work, this book has emphasized the importance of settlers engaging with Indigenous relations to acknowledge, learn, internalize, and act upon what it means to live ethically on Indigenous Lands, among Indigenous Peoples, and within Indigenous sovereignty. We have explored questions such as: *What are loving and accountable ways for settlers to be good relatives to Indigenous Peoples and lands?* Again, it is critical to ensure that our exploration into the stories of white settler anti-colonial and decolonial activists be situated correctly as one of many subplots of profound and long-standing Indigenous resistance, resurgence, and decolonization actions — or as characters in the stories of Indigenous Peoples. It is important to disrupt a white saviour narrative around this work. Although settlers will find their own pathways of doing this work that are reflective of their own gifts, spirits, and experiences, this should always be in dialogue with Indigenous Peoples who are the caretakers of Indigenous Lands. Thus, settlers will listen to what Indigenous Peoples are saying and find ways to support their efforts. Settlers will also focus on educating themselves and one another and will work to support, care for, and inspire one another in this work.

As we conclude these pages, we wish to return to the idea of *living in Indigenous sovereignty,* which we frame as living in an awareness that we are on Indigenous Lands containing their own stories, relationships, laws, Protocols, obligations, and opportunities, which have been understood and practised by Indigenous Peoples since time immemorial. Aaron Mills, an Anishinaabe scholar whose work focuses on Indigenous law and Indigenous constitutionalism, shares insights that are immensely important to understand and learn about if one is to live in Indigenous sovereignty. Thus, in this closing chapter, we wish to share his statements for settler occupiers. Mills (2017) emphasizes that Indigenous systems of law have been present on these lands since before Canada existed, and this means something for how settlers ought to live. Similar to our focus on settlers making a choice to live in Indigenous sovereignty, with or without the support or involvement of Canada, Mills writes, "I want to see what we can do together without giving Canada ... any role at all" (2017:

21), choosing to live on Indigenous Lands through Indigenous law. Mills (2017: 19) acknowledges that "conducting oneself in accordance with an Indigenous legal order must be overwhelming for most settlers," and yet, he says, "I don't see how we can have a good relationship until settlers understand and live within Indigenous systems of law." He asks settlers to "pursue an understanding of the law of the Indigenous peoples whose territory you now call home as if not only your legitimacy but also your life depended on it, because for many Indigenous persons, it does" (2017: 21). Mills sees this as a personal responsibility of settlers, who should have "no expectations of your government to do even a minute's worth of any of this for you" (2017: 21). In his recent dissertation, Mills focuses on relational aspects of Indigenous law, urging settlers to

> live upon this land knowing that you do so in relationship to it and to all of us, as a relative. Learn to root yourself and then help other settlers to do so too. Create rooted communities and then join your older brothers and sisters of Mikinaakominis [Turtle island] as treaty members of our shared earth community. (2019: 281)

As has been noted, one of the ideas that was shared by Leona Star and Aimée Craft, during the research behind this book, is that it really is up to each individual what they will learn from the narratives and from the book; this learning may evolve as they evolve. People will take what they need from the stories. As people who have been very close to the research and the book, we describe some of our own learning and reflections here. Elizabeth's journey with the research and the book involved incredible learnings:

> Learnings occurred during hundreds of moments and contexts. As I participated in consultations and was immersed in literature, gatherings, and relationships, and as I was present during interviews, reviewed the stories, and co-constructed the narratives, I learned that living in Indigenous sovereignty has far more to do with the Earth/land and far more to do with an embodied (not abstract) love than I could have predicted. I grew in my understanding of Treaty relationships as kinship relationships with Indigenous Peoples and as involving relationships with land, based both on responsibility and love. Despite my previous opportunities to hear and experience Indigenous knowledges and Protocols, I

came to understand my relationship with these knowledges and Protocols differently. I now know more clearly that learning about and respecting these knowledges and Protocols is an important way to relate to Indigenous Lands and sovereignty.

I, like many of those whose narratives appear in this book, have struggled with the weight and implications of my participation and the participation of my ancestors in perpetrating colonial harm. I was familiar, on some levels, with concepts and literatures around the importance of humility and following the lead of Indigenous Peoples in decolonial work. I have increasingly understood the importance of ongoing dialogue and checking in with Indigenous Peoples as we do our work. Although these represent important truths and practices of the work without which we'd be in real trouble, my learnings through this process have offered a counterpoint of balance in a focus also on our own sacredness as white settler occupiers, having spirits that have a purpose and work to do that is between us and spirit. I became intrigued with, and convinced of, the importance of honouring and integrating paradox and tensions between complementary (although sometimes seemingly opposing) perspectives and elements of anti-colonial and decolonial work for white settler occupiers. In some ways, this process has been therapy for me. It has been an appropriate venue, I believe, for continuing to work through my emotional struggles in the work. I have heard, by listening to the stories, that my struggles are not unusual, and I have learned new ways to consider and work through these emotions.

During my engagement with this research, I was exposed to oral and written Indigenous literatures emphasizing the centrality of land and land return for the healing of Indigenous Peoples and for meaningful decolonial work. I listened as those interviewed shared their struggles and fears around this, as well as their limitations. I listened as many described land return and land reparation as a critical focus and as an area with which they would like to grow into engag[ing] more deeply. A desire developed within me to have a more prominent focus on land reparation and land return in my own work.

Gladys has also reflected on her own learning throughout this work:

Working with Liz on this book has re-sparked an energy in me that had been tired for a while. An energy that holds possible a new relationship that has felt, on many days, like it had disappeared. Being a part of this book has been a gift in my own learning. It has allowed me to see new opportunities and to listen to stories that fan the sparks of my hope. The work and resistance of Indigenous Peoples past and present have helped us to come to this moment in time. And in this current time I ask myself what I can do to be present, to be humble, to authentically connect, and to make a difference. Through the stories shared in this book I see that other people are also doing the same. The narratives are evidence that this necessary self-reflection and personal commitment to Indigenous-led action is happening.

It is clear that in order to make significant change in the landscape of relations between Indigenous Peoples and settlers in Canada, so much needs to change and it must change now. And even though there is an urgency, there is also a slowness that needs to happen, as settlers unlearn and relearn what it means to live in relation. Leanne Simpson shares that colonialism is a choice that is made every single day (2013a). How do we choose, *every day* to work from an anti-colonial place? We must be willing to listen with humility, be willing to make mistakes from a place of humility, respect, and love. We must be willing to risk being wrong, be willing to sit uncomfortable in a space of curiosity, be open to take the gifts of learning to grow in relation to Indigenous Peoples, lands, and sovereignty. These stories demonstrate the choices that each author makes — they have laid open their hearts to share the learning about the possibilities of living in Indigenous sovereignty. I am hopeful in the sharing that each has offered.

Coming back to the bundle, or collection of stories and teachings that come through the many contributors to this book, it is our hope that readers look inside again from time to time, as our growth and evolution is dependent on new experiences, after which elements of these may make more sense than they did initially. We also urge settler occupiers to engage relational accountability in our processes, or, as Aimée Craft said in Chapter 3, "loop back into the circle of relationship, check in, and take responsibility." This, we believe, has the potential to set one firmly on a good path toward living in Indigenous sovereignty.

AFTERWORD

Gladys Rowe, Sherry Copenance, Yvonne Pompana, and Chickadee Richard

In the closing of this book, we invite you to reflect on the principles of accountability, and the responsibility that we each hold in relation to one another, the land, and new (old) governance systems and ways of living and relating within these systems to propel an urgently needed paradigm shift. Indigenous Peoples have never stopped resisting the violent and insidious contexts within which we live. The stories held in the book share AHA! moments where settlers began to see and then actively engage as supporters in this resistance. Living in Indigenous sovereignty requires active engagement — it is relational and requires accountability that is not supported in familiar governance structures. To move towards living in Indigenous sovereignty, we are asking settlers to do more than read and become uncomfortable. We are holding you accountable to rock the foundations of the comfortable paradigm and *unsettle*. Your everyday decisions about how to be *in relationship* with one another can contribute to connected and thriving communities. This afterword brings together voices of some of the supporters who have walked with Liz in the work that has become this book, people who decided that *how* to live in Indigenous sovereignty was a critical issue to lend our energy towards. We will share what this work has meant to us, and what we hope this will mean to others.

GLADYS ROWE

I have had the privilege of being a part of this research journey with Liz for many years, a relationship that I am grateful for, as the intent of Liz's work is connected to my own heart work. When I think about concepts such as reconciliation, decolonization, and Indigenization — all key terms being explored in this post-Truth and Reconciliation Commission era, I think about the necessary commitment that all people living in Canada must make. I think of the actions that must follow the words and intentions that are laid out. There have been plenty of recommendations made over the last two generations through the Aboriginal Justice Inquiry, the Royal Commission on Aboriginal Peoples, the Truth and Reconciliation Commission, and the National Inquiry into Missing and Murdered Indigenous Women and Girls. Each of these inquiries required significant time, energy, and resources in their completion and worked to represent experiences of Indigenous Peoples in Canada. Each has made a series of recommendations based on this work. Each has held Canadians and the Canadian government accountable for action — for significant, committed, and meaningful action.

The stories of the authors in this book are gifts. These are gifts of vulnerability that lay open experiences, struggles, and learning in the examination of their own relationship with the Canadian colonial state. These are markers that, when brought together, begin to lay out what it means to live in Indigenous sovereignty.

The Canadian colonial project began in exerting a dysfunctional relationship upon Indigenous Peoples, and it will end with reconciling and recentring a relationship with Indigenous Peoples based upon Indigenous sovereignty. This must be a relationship grounded in reciprocity, one that acknowledges a necessary and significant shift in the way we live with one another as Indigenous and non-Indigenous peoples in Canada. It may seem to some like a radical supposition — living in Indigenous sovereignty, but is it really all that radical? Sherry offers her perspective on how Liz's work can support a shift in our relationships, by recognizing one another as kin and acting accordingly.

SHERRY COPENACE

When Liz asked me to be a part of this work, I was very honoured. I said yes because I know Liz and I know she's a kind-hearted woman. Her work comes from a good place. Liz speaks about settler identity, and what really caught me was when she started speaking about land return. When she spoke about land return, I hadn't heard that from settler people before, that was way ahead of other non-Indigenous people. So many communities have been fighting for land return, but to hear someone else say it, I was impressed. I wondered, how can land return happen? I was excited to learn more.

For me the important part of Liz's work was that we started off in ceremony. She encouraged us all to bring our bundles with us and participate
in any way that we could. If we wanted to be interviewed or be recorded,
it was done in a very mindful, thoughtful, and respectful way. I like that
it started in ceremony and went forward from there. Having Indigenous
scholars involved with her was also a good thing. The more I got to know
Liz, the more I saw that she was walking her talk, if I could use that term.
It has come to a space where if she asks me to do something, if I'm able,
I'll do that for her to the best of my ability because I know that she's done
the same for me.

Liz is very open — one of the things that I said to her was "as a scholar,
I would encourage you to give academia a nudge." When things are being
published about research, if Indigenous Peoples are a part of that, then
we need to be recognized as co-authors. I know it is an uphill battle, but
if you plant the seed, it will go somewhere. For us, who hold valid and
just-as-equal knowledge, we don't write about it, but we can talk about
it. Some of us do write about it; a lot of us don't. For me it's not where
my interest is at this time. I will help people if they ask me. I'll talk, but I
don't feel like writing! If that's their skill and they are really great at that,
then we can put whatever I have to offer and whatever they have to offer
together. Liz was really open to that.

As a young woman, because of our own history as Indigenous Peoples,
I had a huge mistrust for our European relatives. For me, this work was a
further step for me to see how we can begin to have that journey together
of working together. This work outlines everyone's role and responsibility
as we remember what it means to be human beings. We must remember
the land is not a resource and the water is not a resource: they are actually our relatives. Once everyone understands this, maybe jointly at some
point, we will come to understand what Anishinaabe ownership means.
Anishinaabe ownership means we do everything we can to protect her and
to not ever sell her — that's our concept of ownership. Many people have
strayed far from that concept. This book and these stories could be one
model that people can learn from. This is a model for people to live — not
only to talk about, but to actually *do* something. We need to recognize
that everyone has a role, even in how we learn to live together. No one is
going to leave. What little I know and what I've heard is that my ancestors always welcomed everybody. We never shut the door on anybody.
We welcome people. Sometimes I have a problem with the terms *settler*

and *allies*. Maybe these need to be there for now until we remember that we are all relatives. If I keep calling you my relative, then you'll start to feel it and you'll start to act like it.

Sometimes I hear people remark about activists: "That's not how they're supposed to act." But how are we to know? We all have our role, and no one is more important than the other. Maybe for us, lifting the water is what we're supposed to do. Maybe for them, going out and speaking loudly is what they're supposed to do as long as they don't hurt anybody. We've strayed so far from recognizing peoples' gifts and abilities, we need to rethink that ourselves. I've heard the older people speak about our Creation Stories — they tell us that's where our research started from. The stories tell us who our relatives are. Our stories need to be common knowledge, so we can learn from them. The other thing they say is that we must never relinquish the leadership in telling these stories. Our other relatives will have their own stories to tell that will complement our stories.

This work can be an example. It's like when you plant a seed: maybe it won't even be watered until many years down the road, but the seed is there. Maybe it will sprout right away. We don't know. This is about the land and the return of the land. If people can see this, once they know they have a relationship with this land — it could be extended to all of us. People won't conceive ownership from a capitalistic view, it will be a much different concept. You know that ripple effect — what Liz is doing will have that ripple effect.

Yvonne shares her perspectives on this work's contribution to calling settlers to action and holding them accountable to be swayed by the ripples in these stories.

YVONNE POMPANA

I would like to express my appreciation to Liz and Gladys for allowing me to be a part of this exciting next step in the learning and teaching process about relational accountability.

When Liz was preparing for her PhD research, she spoke to me about her research and she asked if I was interested in being a member of her PhD committee. I was intrigued by her research topic and about accountability, particularly settler accountability. Initially I thought that Liz's research could be one way that those within academia and the general Canadian population could be exposed to the idea and practice of becoming accountable for the colonization of Canada and Indigenous Peoples within it. I suggested to Liz that it would be extremely valuable to create a video based on her research that could also serve as a teaching tool. Although the video was not a product of Liz's dissertation research, the video did come to fruition and when it premiered as part of the National Indigenous Social Work Conference: Social Work Activism, Advocacy and Agency in October 2016, I felt an immense sense of pride at the accomplishment of Liz, Gladys, Teddy, and others who contributed to the video. Liz also provided other opportunities to participate in community engagement, ceremony, as well as an offering of thanks to her contribu- tors. It was most interesting to not only read about but to hear from Liz's research participants about their experience as settlers on Turtle Island and how they were, or could be, accountable.

As a Dakota First Nations woman and a member of the academic community, it has been rewarding to know that I and other Indigenous Peoples have been able to retain aspects of our Indigeneity in spite of the colonization/assimilation efforts of the Canadian state. We have come to understand colonization, how we have been affected by colonization, and how to move toward decolonization. We have achieved the same levels of education and professional accomplishments as our "white" counterparts — who are also colonized (although they may not be aware of it). And yet when Indigenous Peoples reach the same success markers, I feel we are still somehow not viewed as equals. If Indigenous Peoples have accomplished the same levels of education and professionalism as their non-Indigenous counterparts, then what more needs to be done to achieve equality and equity? I believe, as Indigenous people, we have done our part to meet the academic and professional standards set by the colonizer, while at the same time retaining, maintaining, and refining our Indigenous knowledges.

I began to think of colonization as an equation: colonizers on one side of the equation and the colonized on the other side of the equation. Indigenous Peoples have worked tirelessly to reach the upper echelons of the academy. The majority of folks on the colonizer side, however, have not put in the same effort to create an equal and equitable playing field. I came to the conclusion that our non-Indigenous counterparts need to understand their role in the colonization of the Canadian state, and how that role has contributed to the disparity between the two peoples, to be relationally accountable. It is well past the time that non-Indigenous people educate themselves about how they acquired their privilege, their prosperity, their power — and to begin to give back.

I believe that through her research efforts, Liz is building on the decolonization efforts taken by those individuals who have contributed to her dissertation research and the subsequent video. It is time for the colonizers to become accountable for all that they have gained at the expense of Indigenous Peoples' losses, not only on Turtle Island but globally. This process will bring all of us closer to an equal and equitable playing field.

In the final reflection for this work, Chickadee shares about the centrality of land in actions towards equity.

CHICKADEE RICHARD

I first saw Liz at ceremonies, and I thought to myself, "Who is this white person here and what is she wanting?" Sometimes I see appropriation with people at ceremonies, but this wasn't Liz. I saw that she was living by these ways; I saw her commitment. When Liz asked me to be a part of her dissertation work, this was the first time I saw a settler wanting to do this work. I saw her wanting to be a part of decolonizing work. She was standing up to ask the question: What can be done?

I really enjoyed the testimonials that are in this book — learning about what each person is putting into action in their own lives. I want to see where they are and what they are doing now. Are they still committed to the work? It is important to stay active and engaged because this is long term. This is about Treaty relationships. I am asked to speak a lot about Treaty 1 from professors who want to know how they can acknowledge this land in the classroom. I challenge them to think and act beyond the acknowledgement. You can acknowledge the Treaty, but what are you doing to be responsible to this relationship? What actions are you doing? This action to uphold the Treaties is important: it is time to give back.

This is about land, and land return is an important action. It's not likely that I will have someone come up to me and say, "Here, Chickadee, here is a piece of land." My children and grandchildren will not likely see that, but it's what needs to happen. This land has sustained settlers, it has given so much, and now it is time to reciprocate. For me, right now, I see all of this land that is held in trust by the Crown, and I am going to claim that land — soon. It's my vision to occupy the land and create a community space. There are so many helpers in the community who do so much work and get burnt out; they need a space to recharge and reconnect.

This book challenges people to know better so you can do better. We need change. Institutions need to change. We are doing our part. People need to put into action the practices to be a good settler and to be a good ally. This looks like being with us on the land and being there on the front lines supporting this work. I have been to many front lines — they are there looking after the best interests of my children and grandchildren — and also *your* children and grandchildren. The resources need to come to the community so that they can continue to fight, with your support and your *action*. I ask you to think about: What are you doing now and what will you do tomorrow?

CLOSING

Each of us has come to be in relation with Liz, with her work, and with this book at various points in the journey. Throughout this journey we know several points to be true. First, Liz has embodied the values and actions of what it means to live in relationship with Indigenous sovereignty in the moments, choices, and interactions during the development of the research, the gathering of these narratives, and the bringing together of this work that you have just completed. Next, we witness this heart-filled process that is held with both hope and humility for the power and possibilities that can emerge from *your* sitting with and learning deeply from the stories within this book.

Finally, we believe that no matter where you are starting from, this book has offered concrete examples, strategies, and opportunities to begin to see yourself accountable to and in relation with Indigenous Peoples, Indigenous Lands, and Indigenous sovereignty. It offers you the space to learn, reflect, enact, and return again to view the stories with fresh eyes of experience. The gift of stories is to be able to sit with, listen, and interact from *where we are at,* and where we are at changes each day.

This book offers a challenge — you have heard and witnessed journeys of deep self-examination, building relations, and action. We challenge you to pick up the responsibilities that come with living in these lands that have been named Canada and to enact change within your lives, your families, your communities, and societal structures so that when the generations to come look back to learn from your stories, the pathway of living in Indigenous sovereignty will be evident.

REFERENCES

Absolon, K. 2011. *Kaandossiwin: How We Come to Know.* Fernwood Publishing.

Absolon, K., and C. Willett. 2005. "Putting Ourselves Forward: Location in Aboriginal Research." In L. Brown & S. Strega (eds.), *Research as Resistance* (pp. 97–126). Canadian Scholars' Press.

Adams, H. 1999. A *Tortured People: The Politics of Colonization.* Theytus Books, Ltd.

Alfred, T. 1999. *Peace, Power, Righteousness: An Indigenous Manifesto.* Oxford University Press.

___. 2005. *Wasáse: Indigenous Pathways of Action and Freedom.* Broadview Press.

___. 2008. "Opening Words." In L. Simpson (ed.), *Lighting the Eighth Fire: The Liberation, Resurgence, and Protection of Indigenous Nations* (pp. 9–11). Arbeiter Ring Publishing.

___. 2009. "Restitution Is the Real Pathway to Justice for Indigenous Peoples." In G. Younging, J. Dewar, and M. DeGagné (eds.), *Response, Responsibility, and Renewal: Canada's Truth and Reconciliation Journey* (pp. 179–187). Aboriginal Healing Foundation.

Alfred, T., and J. Corntassel. 2005. "Being Indigenous: Resurgences against Contemporary Colonialism." *Government and Opposition* 40, 4: 597–614. <doi: 10.1111/j.1477-7053.2005.00166.x>.

Amadahy, Z., and B. Lawrence. 2009. "Indigenous Peoples and Black People in Canada: Settlers or Allies?" In A. Kempf (ed.), *Breaching the Colonial Contract* (pp. 105–136). Springer.

Andrews, M. 2015. *Decolonizing the Colonizer* [video]. July 2. <https://vimeo.com/132494877>.

Angus, M. 1991. *And the Last Shall be First: Native Policy in an Era of Cutback.* NC Press.

Ani, M. 1994. *Yurugu: An African-Centred Critique of European Cultural Thought and Behavior.* Africa World Publisher.

Asch, M. 2014. *On Being Here to Stay: Treaties and Aboriginal Rights in Canada.* University of Toronto Press.

Ashcroft, B., G. Griffiths, and H. Tiffin. 2000. *Post-Colonial Studies: The Key Concepts.* Routledge.

Barker, A.J. 2006. "Being Colonial: Colonial Mentalities in Canadian Settler Society and Political Theory." Master's thesis, University of Victoria. <https://dspace.library.uvic.ca/handle/1828/2418>.

Barker, J. 2005. *Sovereignty Matters: Locations of Contestation and Possibility in*

Indigenous Struggles for Self-Determination. University of Nebraska Press.

Belcourt, C. 2016. *Notions of Nationhood* [video]. February 11. <https://www.youtube.com/watch?v=__CG4imy4_s>.

Benally, K. 2013. *Klee Benally on Decolonization.* [audio podcast]. Deep Green Philly, July 26. <https://unsettlingamerica.wordpress.com/2013/07/26/klee-benally-on-decolonization/>.

Biermann, S. 2011. "Knowledge, Power, and Decolonization." In G.J.S. Dei (ed.), *Indigenous Philosophies and Critical Education: A Reader* (pp. 386–398). Peter Lang.

Bilefsky, D. 2020. "In 'Lobster War,' Indigenous Canadians Face Attacks by Fishermen." *New York Times,* October 20. <https://www.nytimes.com/2020/10/20/world/canada/nova-scotia-lobster-war.html>.

Bird, J., L. Land, and M. Murray (eds.). 2002. *Nation to Nation: Aboriginal Sovereignty and the Future of Canada.* Irwin Publishing

Blackstock, C. 2009. "The Occasional Evil of Angels: Learning from the Experiences of Aboriginal Peoples and Social Work." *First Peoples Child & Family Review* 4, 1: 28–37. <http://journals.sfu.ca/fpcfr/index.php/FPCFR/article/view/74>.

Bone, H., S. Copenace, D. Courchene, et al. 2012. *The Journey of the Spirit of the Red Man: A Message from the Elders.* Trafford Publishing.

Borrows, J. 2005. "Indigenous Legal Traditions in Canada." *Washington University Journal of Law & Policy* 19: 167–223. <http://openscholarship.wustl.edu/law_journal_law_policy/vol19/iss1/13>.

Bussidor, I. 2000. *Night Spirits: The Story of the Relocation of the Sayisi Dene.* University of Manitoba Press.

Byrd, A.J. 2011. *The Transit of Empire: Indigenous Critiques of Colonialism.* University of Minnesota Press.

Cardinal, H. 1969. *The Unjust Society.* Douglas & McIntyre.

Cardinal, H., and W. Hildebrandt. 2000. *Treaty Elders of Saskatchewan: Our Dream Is That Our Peoples Will One Day Be Clearly Recognized as Nations.* University of Calgary Press.

Carey, M. 2008. "Whitefellas and Wadjulas: Anti-Colonial Constructions of the Non-Aboriginal Self." Doctoral dissertation, Murdoch University, Perth, Australia. <http://researchrepository.murdoch.edu.au/1757/2/02Whole.pdf>.

Carlson, E., G. Rowe, S. Story, and T. Zegeye-Gebrehiwot. 2017. "Decolonization through Collaborative Filmmaking: Sharing Stories from the Heart." *Journal of Indigenous Social Development* 6, 2. <https://journalhosting.ucalgary.ca/index.php/jisd/article/view/58458/43964>.

Carlson, E.C. 2016. "Living in Indigenous Sovereignty: Relational Accountability and the Stories of White Settler Anti-Colonial and Decolonial Activists." Doctoral dissertation, University of Manitoba. <https://mspace.lib.umanitoba.ca/bitstream/handle/1993/32028/carlson_elizabeth.pdf>.

___. 2017. "Anti-colonial methodologies and practices for settler colonial studies." *Settler Colonial Studies* 7(4), 496–517. DOI: 10.1080/2201473X.2016.1241213.

Christian, D., and V. Freeman. 2010. "The History of a Friendship, or Some Thoughts on Becoming Allies." In L. Davis (ed.), *Alliances: Re/envisioning Indigenous–Non*

Indigenous Relationships (pp. 376–390). University of Toronto Press.

Collins, P.H. 2000. *Black Feminist Thought: Knowledge, Consciousness, and the Politics of Empowerment*. Routledge.

Corntassel, J. 2006. "To Be Ungovernable." *New Socialist*, 58: 35–37. <http://www.corntassel.net/ToBeUngovernable.pdf>.

Coulthard, G.S. 2014. *Red Skin White Masks: Rejecting the Colonial Politics of Recognition*. University of Minnesota Press.

Craft, A. 2013. *Breathing Life into the Stone Fort Treaty: An Anishinabe Understanding of Treaty One*. Purich Publishing.

Crawford, T. 2020. "RCMP Arrest Six Protesters in Northern B.C. Gas Pipeline Blockade." *Vancouver Sun*, February 7. <https://vancouversun.com/news/local-news/protesters-arrested-in-b-c-gas-pipeline-blockade>.

Da Silva, J. 2010. "Grassy Narrows: Advocate for Mother Earth and Its Inhabitants." In L. Davis (ed.), *Alliances: Re/Envisioning Indigenous–Non-Indigenous Relationships* (pp. 69–76). University of Toronto Press.

Daabaasonaquwat. 2016. *Notions of Nationhood* [video]. February 10. <https://www.youtube.com/watch?v=RblaiSfiZXQ>.

Day, R.F. 2010. "Angry Indians, Settler Guilt, and the Challenges of Decolonization and Resurgence." In L. Simpson and K. Ladner (eds.), *This Is an Honour Song: Twenty Years Since the Blockades* (pp. 261–269). Arbeiter Ring Publishing.

Deer, K. 2020. "Algonquin Community Enforces Its Own Moratorium." CBC, September 14. <https://www.cbc.ca/news/indigenous/algonquin-barriere-lake-moose-moratorium-1.5723545>.

Dei, G.J.S. 2006. "Introduction: Mapping the Terrain: Towards a New Politics of Resistance." In G. Dei and A. Kempf (eds.), *Anti-Colonialism and Education* (pp. 1–24). Sense Publishers.

___. 2009. "Afterword." In A. Kempf (ed.), *Breaching the Colonial Contract: Anti-Colonialism in the US and Canada* (pp. 251–258). Springer Science+Business Media B.V.

Dei, G.J.S., and A. Asgharzadeh. 2001. "The Power of Social Theory: The Anticolonial Discursive Framework." *Journal of Educational Thought* 35, 3: 297–323. <http://www.jstor.org/stable/23767242>.

Dyer, R. 1997. *White*. Routledge.

Flaherty, J. 2016. *No More Heroes: Grassroots Challenges to the Savior Mentality*. AK Press.

Flowers, R. 2015. "Refusal to Forgive: Indigenous Women's Love And Rage." *Decolonization, Indigeneity, Education and Society* 4, 2: 32–49.

Forester, B. 2020a. "Six Nations Land Dispute Needs Time and Care, but Police Raid May Be Imminent." *APTN National News*, August 17. <https://www.aptnnews.ca/national-news/six-nations-land-dispute-needs-time-and-care-but-police-raid-may-be-imminent/>.

___. 2020b. "Police Arrest Journalist, Researcher in Connection with Caledonia Land Reclamation." *APTN National News*, September 3. <https://www.aptnnews.ca/national-news/police-arrest-journalist-researcher-in-connection-with-caledonia-land-reclamation/>.

Fornier, E. 2020. "All Eyes on the Wet'suwet'en: Indigenous Community Calls for UN Intervention." Human Rights Hub, January 18. Winnipeg.

Freeman, V. n.d. (Chrichton, K.) *Q & A: Victoria Freeman. 8th Fire. Aboriginal Peoples, Canada, and the Way Forward* [video]. Canadian Broadcasting Corporation.

___. 2000. *Distant Relations: How My Ancestors Colonized North America.* Steerforth Press.

Galloway, G. 2019. "Hate and Hope in Thunder Bay: A City Grapples with Racism Against Indigenous People." *Globe and Mail*, March 23. <https://www.theglobeandmail.com/canada/article-hate-and-hope-in-thunder-bay-a-city-grapples-with-racism-against/>.

Gehl, L. n.d. "Ally Bill of Responsibilities." <http://www.lynngehl.com/uploads/5/0/0/4/5004954/ally_bill_of_responsibilities_poster.pdf>.

Good Tracks, J.G. 1973. "Native American Non-Interference." *Social Work* 18: 30–35.

Googoo, M. 2020. "Angry Mob Trap Mi'kmaw Fishermen at a Lobster Pound in Southwestern Nova Scotia." *Ku'ku'kwes News*, October 14. <http://kukukwes.com/2020/10/14/angry-mob-trap-mikmaw-fishermen-at-a-lobster-pound-in-southwestern-nova-scotia/>.

Gosnell-Meyers, G. 2020. "White Privilege, False Claims of Indigenous Identity and Michelle Latimer: How 'Pretendians' Do Serious Damage to Indigenous People and Set Back Reconciliation Hopes." *The Tyee*, December 23. <https://thetyee.ca/Opinion/2020/12/23/White-Privilege-False-Claims-Indigenous-Michelle-Latimer/>.

Graveline, F.J. 2012. *Circle Works: Transforming Aboriginal Literacy.* Ningwakwe Learning Press.

Hart, M.A. 2002. *Seeking Mino-pimatisiwin: An Aboriginal Approach to Helping.* Fernwood Publishing.

___. 2007. "Cree Ways of Helping: An Indigenist Research Project." Unpublished doctoral dissertation, University of Manitoba, Winnipeg, MB.

___. 2009. "Anti-Colonial Indigenous Social Work: Reflections on an Aboriginal Approach." In R. Sinclair, M.A. Hart, and G. Bruyere, (eds.), *Wicihitowin: Aboriginal Social Work in Canada* (pp. 25–41). Fernwood Publishing.

Hart, M.A., and G. Rowe. 2014. "Legally Entrenched Oppressions: The Undercurrent of First Nations Peoples' Experiences with Canada's Social Policies." In H.N. Weaver (ed.), *Social Issues in Contemporary Native America* (pp. 23–41). Ashgate.

Hart, M.A., S. Straka, and G. Rowe. 2016. "Working Across Contexts: Practical Considerations of Doing Indigenist/Anti-Colonial Research." *Qualitative Inquiry* 11, 1: 1–6. <DOI: 10.1177/1077800416659084>.

Harvey, J. 2013. "For Whites (Like Me): White Paradox." *Formations: Living at the Intersections of Self, Social, Spirit* [blog]. <https://livingformations.wordpress.com/2013/08/12/for-whites-like-me-white-paradox/>.

Heaslip, R. 2017. "From Xwelítem Ways Toward Practices of Ethical Being in Stó:Lō Téméxw: A Narrative Approach to Transforming Intergenerational White Settler Subjectivities." Unpublished doctoral dissertation, University of Victoria.

Heinrichs, S. (ed.). 2013. *Buffalo Shout, Salmon Cry: Conversations on Creation, Land Justice, and Life Together.* Menno Media.

____. 2015. *Paths for Peacemaking with Host Peoples*, 4th edition. Mennonite Church Canada. <https://www.commonword.ca/FileDownload/21590/2015_Paths_for_Peacemaking_Booklet_Ed4_Final_NOBLEEDS.pdf>.

Hubbard, T. 2013. *Idle No More Teach-In* [video]. February 26. <https://www.youtube.com/watch?v=BqYCKyFhczI>.

____. 2014. "Buffalo Genocide in Nineteenth-Century North America: 'Kill, Skin, and Sell.'" In A. Woolford, J. Benvenuto, and A.L. Hinton (eds.), *Colonial Genocide in Indigenous North America* (pp. 292–305). Duke University Press.

Idle No More. 2020. INM *National Week of Action Oct. 19th–Oct. 23rd Support Mi'kmaq Treaty Rights & Livelihood.* <https://idlenomore.ca/support-mikmaq-treaty-rights-and-livelihood/>.

Idle No More and Defenders of the Land. 2014. "Idle No More Solidarity Spring: A Call into Actions." In Kino-nda-niimi Collective (ed.), *The Winter We Danced: Voices from the Past, the Future, and the Idle No More Movement* (pp. 356–358). Arbeiter Ring Publishing.

Indigenous Action Media. 2014. "Accomplices Not Allies: Abolishing the Ally Industrial Complex, an Indigenous Perspective." <http://www.indigenousaction.org/wp-content/uploads/Accomplices-Not-Allies-print.pdf>.

Jafri, B. 2012. "Privilege vs. Complicity: People of Colour and Settler Colonialism." Equity Matters. <http://www.ideas-idees.ca/blog/privilege-vs-complicity-people-colour-and-settler-colonialism>.

Johnson, H. 2007. *Two Families: Treaties and Government.* Purich Publishing.

Keefer, T. 2010. "Contradictions of Canadian Colonialism: Non-Native Responses to the Six Nations Reclamation at Caledonia." In L. Davis (ed.), *Alliances: Re/Envisioning Indigenous–Non-Indigenous Relationships* (pp. 77–90). University of Toronto Press.

Kempf, A. 2009. "Contemporary Anticolonialism: A Transhistorical Perspective." In A. Kempf (ed.), *Breaching the Colonial Contract: Anti-Colonialism in the US and Canada* (pp. 13–34). Springer Science+Buisiness Media B.V.

Kimmerer, R.W. n.d. "The Serviceberry: An Economy of Abundance." *Emergence Magazine.* <https://emergencemagazine.org/story/the-serviceberry/>.

____. 2020. *Braiding Sweetgrass: Indigenous Wisdom, Scientific Knowledge and the Teachings of Plants,* illustrated edition. Milkweed Editions.

Kinew, K.A. 1995. "Manito Gitigaan: Governing in the Great Spirit's Garden: Wild Rice in Treaty #3." Doctoral dissertation, University of Manitoba. <https://mspace.lib.umanitoba.ca/xmlui/handle/1993/3684>.

King, H., and S. Pasternak. 2019. "The Spectrum of Consent." *Land Back: A Yellowhead Institute Red Paper*: Yellowhead Institute, 15-21. <https://redpaper.yellowheadinstitute.org/wp-content/uploads/2019/10/red-paper-report-final.pdf>.

Kino-nda-niimi Collective (ed.). 2014. *The Winter We Danced: Voices from the Past, the Future, and the Idle No More Movement.* Arbeiter Ring Publishing.

Kinsman, G. 2017. "Direct Action as Political Activist Ethnography: Activist Research in the Sudbury Coalition Against Poverty." Unpublished manuscript.

Klein, N. 2016. *An Evening with Naomi Klein: This Changes Everything* [video]. April

8. <https://www.youtube.com/watch?v=TyVymaIe9EI>.

Koleszar-Green, R. 2018. "What Is a Guest? What Is a Settler?" *Cultural and Pedagogical Inquiry* 4, 2: 166–177. <https://doi.org/10.18733/cpi29452>.

Kuokkanen, R. 2007. *Reshaping the University: Responsibility, Indigenous Epistemes, and the Logic of the Gift*. UBC Press.

Ladner K. 2010. "From Little Things…" In L. Simpson and K. Ladner (eds.), *This Is an Honour Song: Twenty Years Since the Blockades* (pp. 299–314). Arbeiter Ring Publishing.

___. 2014. "Political Genocide: Killing Nations Through Legislation and Slow-Moving Poison." In A. Woolford, J. Benvenuto, and A. L. Hinton (eds.), *Colonial Genocide in Indigenous North America* (pp. 226–245). Duke University Press.

LaRocque, E. 2010. *When the Other Is Me: Native Resistance Discourse, 1850–1990*. University of Manitoba Press.

Lawrence, B. 2020. *Indigenous Responses to Black Resistance* [video]. Scholar Strike Canada. September 10. <https://www.youtube.com/watch?v=qbSwlqMRwBY>.

Lawrence, B., and E. Dua. 2011. "Decolonizing Anti-Racism." In A. Mathur, J. Dewar, and M. DeGagné (eds.), *Cultivating Canada: Reconciliation Through the Lens of Cultural Diversity* (pp. 233–262). Aboriginal Healing Foundation. <http://www.ahf.ca/downloads/cultivating-canada-pdf.pdf>.

Leroux, D. 2019. *Distorted Descent: White Claims to Indigenous Identity*. University of Manitoba Press.

Little Bear, L. 1994. "Relationship of Aboriginal People to the Land and the Aboriginal Perspective on Aboriginal Title." In Royal Commission on Aboriginal Peoples (ed.), *The Relationship of Aboriginal People to the Land and the Aboriginal Pperspective on Aboriginal Title* (pp. 1–68).

___. 2000. "Jagged Worldviews Colliding." In M. Battiste (ed.), *Reclaiming Indigenous Voice and Vision* (pp. 77–85). UBC Press.

Logan, T. 2014. "Memory, Erasure, and National Myth." In A. Woolford, J. Benvenuto, and A.L. Hinton (eds.), *Colonial Genocide in Indigenous North America* (pp. 149–165). Duke University Press.

Lopez, A.J. 2005. *Postcolonial Whiteness: A Critical Reader on Race and Empire*. State University of New York Press.

Lowman, E.B., and A.J. Barker. 2015. *Settler: Identity and Colonialism in the 21st Century Canada*. Fernwood Publishing.

MacDonald, D.B. 2019. *The Sleeping Giant Awakens: Genocide, Indian Residential Schools, and the Challenge of Conciliation*. University of Toronto Press.

Macoun, A., and E. Strakosch. 2013. "The Ethical Demands of Settler Colonial Theory." *Settler Colonial Studies* 3, 3–4: 426–443. <DOI: 10.1080/2201473X.2013.810695>.

Manly, P. 2020. "Wet'suwet'en: Rule of Law?" *Canadian Dimension*, February 20. <https://canadiandimension.com/articles/view/wetsuweten-rule-of-law>.

Manuel, A., and M. Derrickson. 2015. *Unsettling Canada: A National Wake-Up Call*. Between the Lines.

___. 2017. *The Reconciliation Manifesto: Recovering the Land, Rebuilding the Economy*. James Lorimer and Company.

Manuel, G., and M. Posluns. 1974. *The Fourth World: An Indian Reality*.

Collier-MacMillan Canada.

Maracle, L. 2017. *My Conversations with Canadians*. Book*hug Press.

McAdam, S. 2015. *Nationhood Interrupted: Revitalizing nêhiyaw Legal Systems*. Purich Publishing.

___. 2016. *Notions of Nationhood* [video]. February 10. <https://www.youtube.com/watch?v=RblaiSfiZXQ>.

McCaslin, W.D., and D. Breton. 2008. "Justice as Healing: Going Outside the Colonizer's Cage." In N. Denzin, Y. Lincoln, and L. Smith (eds.), *Handbook of Critical and Indigenous Methodologies* (pp. 511–530). Sage Publications.

McKay, E. 1999. "Eva McKay (Dakota Sioux)." In P. Kulchyski, D. McCaskill, and D. Newhouse (eds.), *In the Words of the Elders: Aboriginal Cultures in Transition* (pp. 289–310). University of Toronto Press.

McLean, S. 2018. "'We Built a Life From Nothing': White Settler Colonialism and the Myth of Meritocracy." *OS/OS — Our Schools/Our Selves* (Winter): 32–33. <https://www.policyalternatives.ca/sites/default/files/uploads/publications/National%20Office/2017/12/McLean.pdf>.

McNeilly, G. 2018. *Broken Trust: Indigenous People and the Thunder Bay Police Service*. Office of the Independent Police Review Director. <http://oiprd.on.ca/wp-content/uploads/OIPRD-BrokenTrust-Final-Accessible-E.pdf>.

Memmi, A. 1965. *The Colonizer and the Colonized*. Beacon Press.

___. 2000. *Racism*. University of Minnesota Press.

Mills, A. 2016. "In Lieu of Justice: Thoughts on Oppression, Identity & Earth." *Waakoodiwin* [blog]. July 21. <https://waakoodiwin.wordpress.com/2016/07/21/in-lieu-of-justice-thoughts-on-oppression-identity-earth/>.

___. 2017. "Nokomis and the Law in the Gift: Living Treaty Each Day." In M.J. Tait and K.L. Ladner (eds.), *Surviving Canada: Indigenous Peoples Celebrate 150 Years of Betrayal* (pp. 17–27). Arbeiter Ring Publishing.

___. 2019. "Miinigowiziwin: All that Has Been Given for Living Well Together: One Vision of Anishinaabe Constitutionalism." Unpublished doctoral dissertation, University of Victoria.

National Inquiry into Murdered and Missing Indigenous Women and Girls. 2019. *Reclaiming Power and Place: The Final Report of the National Inquiry into Murdered and Missing Indigenous Women and Girls, volume 1a*. <https://www.mmiwg-ffada.ca/wp-content/uploads/2019/06/Final_Report_Vol_1a-1.pdf>.

Newton, M., S. Sweeny, and T. Walker. 2020. *Black and Indigenous Histories of Survival and Solidarity* [video]. Caribbean Studies and African Studies-University of Toronto. Facebook, September 10. <https://www.facebook.com/154715328894­5176/videos/806973566777746>.

Nicoll, F. 2000. "Indigenous Sovereignty and the Violence of Perspective: A White Woman's Coming Out Story." *Australian Feminist Studies* 15, 33: 369–386. <DOI: 10.1080 /08164640020009802> .

___. 2004. "Reconciliation In and Out of Perspective: White Knowing, Seeing, Curating and Being at Home in and Against Indigenous Sovereignty." *Whitening Race: Essays in Social and Cultural Criticism* 1: 17–31.

Nii Gaani Aki Inini (Dave Courchene). 2016a. "Making an Alliance with the

Earth." Keynote presentation at the Communication & Culture in a Sustainable World Conference. August 2. <http://www.turtlelodge.org/2016/08/nii-gaani-aki-inini-keynote-making-an-alliance-with-the-earth-august-2-2016-at-communication-culture-in-a-sustainable-world-conference-2016/>.

___. 2016b. "The Spirit of Nationhood." Keynote address at Notions of Nationhood: Tea & Bannock Dialogues. Assembly of Manitoba Chiefs. February 10. <http://www.turtlelodge.org/2016/02/the-spirit-of-nationhood-keynote-address-by-dave-courchene-nii-gaani-aki-inini-leading-earth-man-at-notions-of-nationhood-tea-bannock-dialogues/>.

Office of the Treaty Commissioner. 2007. "Treaty Implementation: Fulfilling the Covenant." Office of the Treaty Commissioner. <http://www.otc.ca/public/uploads/resource_photo/55757_TreatyWeb.pdf>.

Palmater, P. 2015. *Indigenous Nationhood: Empowering Grassroots Citizens.* Fernwood Publishing.

Pashagumskum, J. 2020. "Meeting Between Mohawk Leadership, Minister was 'a Good Start' but Protest Remains. *APTN National News,* February 16. <https://www.aptnnews.ca/national-news/meeting-between-mohawk-leadership-minister-was-a-good-start-but-protest-remains/>.

Pasternak, S. and King, H. 2019. "Executive Summary." *Land Back: A Yellowhead Institute Red Paper:* Yellowhead Institute, 8–12. <https://redpaper.yellowheadinstitute.org/wp-content/uploads/2019/10/red-paper-report-final.pdf>.

Patel, S. 2010. "Where Are the Settlers of Colour?" *Upping the Anti,* 10. <http://uppingtheanti.org/journal/article/10-where-are-the-settlers-of-colour/>.

Phung, M. 2011. "Are People of Colour Settlers Too?" In A. Mathur, J. Dewar, and M. DeGagné (eds.), *Cultivating Canada: Reconciliation through the Lens of Cultural Diversity* (pp. 2689–2698). Aboriginal Healing Foundation. <https://www.academia.edu/424977/Are_People_of_Colour_Settlers_Too>.

Porter, J. 2020. "Deadly Force, Neglect Kills Dozens of Indigenous People in Ontario's Justice System." CBC, August 11. <https://www.cbc.ca/news/canada/thunder-bay/headlines/deadly-force-indigenous-1.5680668#:~:text=More%20than%2040%20Indigenous%20people,in%20the%20last%2020%20years&text=All%20of%20the%20Indigenous%20people,or%20testimony%20at%20their%20inquests>.

Regan, P. 2006. "Unsettling the Settler Within: Canada's Peacemaker Myth, Reconciliation, and Transformative Pathways to Decolonization" Doctoral dissertation, University of Victoria.

___. 2010. *Unsettling the Settler Within: Indian Residential Schools, Truth Telling, and Reconciliation in Canada.* UBC Press.

Report of the Royal Commission on Aboriginal Peoples. 1996. *Volume 5, Renewal: A Twenty-Year Commitment.*

Richard, C. 2013. *Idle No More Teach-In, Part 1 of 2* [video]. February 26. <https://www.youtube.com/watch?v=BqYCKyFhczI>.

___. 2016. *Notions of Nationhood* [video]. February 10. <https://www.youtube.com/watch?v=RblaiSfiZXQ>.

Rickard, J. 2017. "Diversifying Sovereignty and the Reception of Indigenous Art."

Art Journal 76, 2: 81–84. <https://doi.org/10.1080/00043249.2017.1367194>.

Ritskes, E. 2014. "The Terms of Engagement with Indigenous Nationhood." In the Kino-nda-niimi Collective (ed.), *The Winter We Danced: Voices from the Past, the Future, and the Idle No More Movement* (pp. 258–261). Arbeiter Ring Publishing.

Rodgers, K. 2018. *Protest, Activism, & Social Movements*. Oxford University Press.

Rowe, G. 2013. "Kikiskisin ná: Do You Remember? Utilizing Indigenous Methodologies to Understand the Experiences of Mixed-Blood Indigenous Peoples in Identity Re-Membering." Unpublished thesis, University of Manitoba.

___. 2014. "Implementing Indigenous Ways of Knowing into Research: Insights into the Critical Roles of Dreams as Catalysts for Knowledge Development." *Journal of Indigenous Social Development* 3, 2: 1–17.

Sartre, J.P. 1965. "Introduction." In A. Memmi, *The Colonizer and the Colonized* (pp. xxi–xxix). Beacon Press.

Sehdev, R.K. 2011. "People of Colour in Treaty." In A. Mathur, J. Dewar, and M. DeGagné (eds.), *Cultivating Canada: Reconciliation through the Lens of Cultural Diversity* (pp. 263–274). Aboriginal Healing Foundation. <https://www.academia. edu/1134960/People_of_Colour_in_Treaty>.

Simpson, L.R. 2004. "Anticolonial Strategies for the Recovery and Maintenance of Indigenous Knowledge." *American Indian Quarterly* 28, 3/4: 373–384. <http:// www.jstor.org/stable/4138923>.

Simpson, L.B. 2008. *Lighting the Eighth Fire: The Liberation, Resurgence, and Protection of Indigenous Nations*. Winnipeg, MB: Arbeiter Ring Publishing.

___. 2011. *Dancing on Our Turtle's Back: Stories of Nishnaabeg Re-Creation, Resurgence and a New Emergence*. Arbeiter Ring Publishing.

___. 2013a. "Liberated Peoples, Liberated Lands." In S. Heinrichs (ed.), *Buffalo Shout, Salmon Cry: Conversations on Creation, Land Justice, and Life Together* (pp. 50–57). Menno Media.

___. 2013b. *Restoring Nationhood: Addressing Land Dispossession in the Canadian Reconciliation Discourse* [video]. November 13. <https://www.youtube.com/ watch?v=fH1QZQIUJIo>.

___. 2014. "Land as Pedagogy: Nishnaabeg Intelligence and Rebellious Transformation." *Decolonization: Indigeneity, Education & Society* 3, 3: 1–25.

___. 2017. *As We Have Always Done: Indigenous Freedom Through Radical Resistance*. University of Minnesota Press.

Sinclair, N.J. 2014. *The Gift of Treaties* [video]. January 31. <https://www.youtube. com/watch?v=KBp0-c0PIf4>.

___. 2015. "A Treaty Is a Gift." *Geez: Contemplative Cultural Resistance* 39: 10–11.

Sinclair, R., M.A. Hart, and G. Bruyere. 2009. *Wicihitowin: Aboriginal Social Work in Canada*. Fernwood Publishing.

Smart, A. 2020a. "What the Wet'suwet'en Case Says About How Canadian Courts Address Indigenous Law." CTV News, January 9. <https://www.ctvnews.ca/ canada/what-the-wet-suwet-en-case-says-about-how-canadian-courts-address-indigenous-law-1.4759601>.

___. 2020b. "Wet'suwet'en and B.C. Government Have Been Talking Aboriginal Title for a Year." *National Post*, February 17. <https://nationalpost.com/pmn/

news-pmn/canada-news-pmn/wetsuweten-and-b-c-government-have-been-talking-aboriginal-title-for-a-year>.

Spretnak, C. 1999. *The Resurgence of the Real: Body, Nature, and Place in a Hypermodern World*. Routledge.

Sullivan, S. 2006. *Revealing Whiteness: The Unconscious Habits of Racial Privilege*. Bloomington University Press.

Tait, K., and A. Spice. 2018. "An Injunction Against the Unist'ot'en Camp: An Embodiment of Healing Faces Eviction." Yellowhead Institute, December 12. <https://yellowheadinstitute.org/2018/12/12/an-injunction-against-the-unistoten-camp/>.

TallBear, K. 2013. "Genomic Articulations of Indigeneity." *Social Studies of Science* 43, 4: 509–533. <https://doi.org/10.1177/0306312713483893>.

Thomas, K. 2002. "Friends of the Lubicon: How a Small Group of People Can Change the World." In J. Bird, L. Land, and M. Murray (eds.), *Nation to Nation: Aboriginal Sovereignty and the Future of Canada* (pp. 213–222). Irwin Publishing.

TRC (Truth and Reconciliation Commission of Canada). 2015. *Truth and Reconciliation Commission of Canada: Calls to Action*. <http://trc.ca/assets/pdf/Calls_to_Action_English2.pdf>.

Tuck, E., and M. Fine. 2007. "Inner Angles: A Range of Responses to/with Indigenous and Decolonizing Theories." In N. Denzin and M. Giardina (eds.), *Ethical Futures in Qualitative Research: Decolonizing the Politics of Knowledge* (pp. 145–168). Left Coast Press.

Tuck, E., and K.W. Yang. 2012. "Decolonization Is Not a Metaphor." *Decolonization: Indigeneity, Education & Society* 1, 1: 1–40. <https://uwaterloo.ca/faculty-association/sites/ca.faculty-association/files/uploads/files/decolonization_is_not_a_metaphor_a.pdf>.

Unist'ot'en Camp. 2017. "Background of the Campaign." <https://unistoten.camp/no-pipelines/background-of-the-campaign/>.

____. 2020. "All Eyes on Wet'suwet'en: International Call for Solidarity." February 16. <https://unistoten.camp/alleyesonwetsuweten/>.

Vowel, C. 2016. *Indigenous Writes: A Guide to First Nations, Métis, & Inuit Issues in Canada*. Highwater Press.

Waddell, A.R. 2018. "MC Canada Staffer Sentenced to Seven Days in Jail." *Canadian Mennonite*. August 10. <https://canadianmennonite.org/stories/mc-canada-staffer-sentenced-seven-days-jail>.

Wallace, R. 2013. *Merging Fires: Grassroots Peacebuilding between Indigenous and Non-Indigenous Peoples*. Fernwood Publishing.

Ward, S. 2015. *Decolonizing the Colonizer* [video]. July 2. <https://vimeo.com/132494644>.

Waziyatawin. 2008. *What Does Justice Look Like? The Struggle for Liberation in Dakota Homeland*. Living Justice Press.

____. 2009. "Understanding Colonizer Status." In Unsettling Minnesota (ed.), *Unsettling Ourselves: Reflections and Resources for Deconstructing Colonial Mentality* (pp. 152–155). <https://unsettlingminnesota.files.wordpress.com/2009/11/um_sourcebook_jan10_revision.pdf>.

Waziyatawin, and M. Yellow Bird. 2012. *For Indigenous Minds Only: A Decolonization Handbook*. School of Advances Research Press.

Whyte, K.P. 2018. "White Allies, Let's Be Honest about Decolonization." *Yes! Magazine*, April 3.

Williams, D.C. 2008. "In Praise of Guilt: How the Yearning for Moral Purity Blocks Reparations for Native Americans." In F. Lenzerini (ed.), *Reparations for Indigenous Peoples: International and Comparative Perspectives* (pp. 220–250). Oxford University Press.

Wilmot, S. 2005. *Taking Responsibility, Taking Direction: White Anti-Racism in Canada*. Arbeiter Ring Publishing.

Wilson, S. 2008. *Research Is Ceremony: Indigenous Research Methods*. Fernwood Publishing.

Wolfe, P. 1999. *Settler Colonialism and the Transformation of Anthropology: The Politics and Poetics of an Ethnographic Event*. Cassell.

Wong, R. 2019. "We Can All Learn from Wet'suwet'en Laws." *Canada's National Observer*, January 8. <https://www.nationalobserver.com/2019/01/08/opinion/we-can-all-learn-wetsuweten-laws>.

Woolford, A., and J. Benvenuto. 2016. *Canada and Colonial Genocide*. Routledge.

Xhopakelxhit. 2014. "Everyone Calls Themselves an Ally Until it Is Time to Do Some Real Ally Shit." Ancestral Pride. <https://warriorpublications.files.wordpress.com/2014/01/ancestral_pride_zine.pdf>.

Young, R.J.C. 2001. *Postcolonialism: An Historical Introduction*. Blackwell Publishing.

INDEX